EDI DEVELOPMENT STUDIES

Enterprise Restructuring and Unemployment in Models of Transition

Edited by
Simon Commander

The World Bank
Washington, D. C.

The Economic Development Institute (EDI) was established by the World Bank in 1955 to train officials concerned with development planning, policymaking, investment analysis, and project implementation in member developing countries. At present the substance of the EDI's work emphasizes macroeconomic and sectoral economic policy analysis. Through a variety of courses, seminars, and workshops, most of which are given overseas in cooperation with local institutions, the EDI seeks to sharpen analytical skills used in policy analysis and to broaden understanding of the experience of individual countries with economic development. Although the EDI's publications are designed to support its training activities, many are of interest to a much broader audience. EDI materials, including any findings, interpretations, and conclusions, are entirely those of the authors and should not be attributed in any manner to the World Bank, to its affiliated organizations, or to members of its Board of Executive Directors or the countries they represent.

The backlist of publications by the World Bank is shown in the annual *Index of Publications*, which is available from the Office of the Publisher.

At the time of writing, Simon Commander was principal economist in the New Products and Outreach Division of the World Bank's Economic Development Institute.

Library of Congress Cataloging-in-Publication Data

Enterprise restructuring and unemployment in models of transition /
    edited by Simon Commander.
       p. cm.—(EDI Development studies, ISSN 1020–105X)
    Includes bibliographical references and index.
    ISBN 0-8213-4168-5
    1. Unemployment—Europe, Eastern.   2. Structural adjustment
(Economic policy)—Europe, Eastern.   3. Europe, Eastern—Economic
policy—1989–   I. Commander, Simon.   II. Series.
HD5764.7.A6E47   1998
331.13'7947—dc21   97–46858
                                       CIP

ISBN 0-8213-4219-3 clothbound
ISBN 0-8213-4168-5 paperback

Contents

Foreword

This volume is the result of a research program, started at the World Bank, that brought together researchers from many backgrounds, including individuals from the transition economies. The work was supported by the World Bank's Research Committee and by the Economic Development Institute. The results reported here shed light on the factors that determine the shape and pace of the transition from planned to market economies. The primary focus is on the behavior of firms and the interaction of that behavior with the labor market. While finding significant variation across countries, the chapter authors point to major adjustments within firms, both in the remaining state sector and among firms that have been privatized. The volume also spotlights the critical feedback from the labor market to the decisions made by workers and managers regarding privatization and restructuring. In addition to chapters that take a detailed look at different country experiences, the volume contains some pathbreaking attempts to use this empirical information to set up and calibrate models of transition. In their findings, the authors conclusively demonstrate how sensitive the pace and efficiency of transition will be to a range of policies, including unemployment compensation and the selected forms of privatization. The volume thus provides a deft mix of empirical and analytical insights into the complex process of transition.

Vinod Thomas, Director
Economic Development Institute
The World Bank

Abbreviations and Acronyms

cd	Coefficient of dispersion
CMEA	Council for Mutual Economic Assistance
CPI	Consumer price index
CSO	Central Statistical Office (Hungary)
cv	Coefficient of variation
DRC	Domestic resource cost
FR	Financial report
FS	Forecast survey
FSU	Former Soviet Union
GDP	Gross domestic product
iv	Instrumental variable
LFS	Labor force survey
MoF	Ministry of Finance
NLC	National Labor Centre (Hungary)
OECD	Organization for Economic Cooperation and Development
OLS	Ordinary least squares
PPI	Producer price index
PPP	Purchasing price parity
SOE	State-owned enterprises
TIP	Tax-based incomes policy
WS	Wage survey
WSFP	Wage survey firm panel

1

Firm Behavior, Restructuring, and the Labor Market in the Transition: An Overview

Simon Commander

The demise of the planned economies and the advent of transition in Eastern Europe and the former Soviet Union (FSU) have had consequences for all facets of economic life, but nowhere have these consequences been more prominent than in the environment facing firms and their decisionmaking agents. The disruption of production, trading, and other networks has had profound implications for the aggregate economy, given the weight of publicly owned enterprises before the transition. While in some countries—such as Hungary, Poland, and Russia—an unofficial private sector had already emerged, all the economies were nevertheless dominated by state enterprises. With most trade restricted to the CMEA (Council for Mutual Economic Assistance) system and with quasi–fixed relative prices, the output mix was largely divorced from comparative advantage. A systemwide preference for manufacturing reinforced the discrepancy between viability under the old system and

Thanks to all participants in this research project for generously sharing their ideas and time. Thanks also to Paul Hare for detailed and helpful suggestions.

the new requirements of the price liberalization and opening to trade characteristic of the transition.[1]

Because of these and other features of the previous system, the transition has involved not only the elimination of inefficient producers and the creation of new firms, but also attempts by existing enterprises to reform themselves, a critical element in the process. In short, part of the response to the changed environment has been expressed through restructuring—as enterprises have adapted to the new environment—while another part has been through the reallocation of resources, including the growth of a new private sector. This volume is primarily, but not exclusively, concerned with the first key component of transition: restructuring. Further, while restructuring will necessarily involve a range of responses, the concern here is mainly with decisions that determine employment and wage setting.

The initial flush of reforms—inducing large shifts in relative prices and disruption of networks and institutional ties—was abrupt, unanticipated, and had profound implications for enterprises, workers, and governments. The governments were immediately faced with the need to reduce or eliminate widespread subsidies to the firm sector, which forced firms to operate under an increasingly hard budget constraint. While this power of suasion has varied substantially across countries, the ability of state firms to continue to operate with little regard for underlying viability was quickly challenged. As a result, jobs were lost and workers were forced into unemployment. In addition, the challenge of ownership and control rose to the top of the reform agenda. This was because of the widespread perception that without large-scale privatization, state firms would not only continue to extract preferential finance, but they would also remain resistant to the changes in management and overall business strategy that were so clearly required. With the state involved in decision-making, non–value-maximizing decisions would tend to dominate. With the decentralization of effective control, agency problems would be accentuated, especially given inconsistencies or lacunae in the legal or institutional environment (Schleifer and Vishny 1994). The governance problem thus effectively embraced not only standard principal-agent issues, but also the economywide balance between the state and private sectors.

Although early assumptions regarding the pace of privatization and the associated gains from change in governance generally proved to be

---

1. As indicated, for example, by the domestic resource cost calculations made by Hare and Hughes (1991).

wildly optimistic, the bulk of the transition economies have indeed seen major shifts in the behavior of firms, and ultimately in the structure of ownership. Much of the privatization that has occurred has been dominated by insiders, either through the design of the privatization process itself or through implicit incumbency rights being parlayed into explicit control rights. Further, despite cross-country variation, there is evidence that both privatized and state firms have begun to adapt and, to some extent, restructure. But there is no robust evidence that privatization has dramatically accelerated the pace of restructuring, save in cases where outside control and external investment has been forthcoming (Carlin, Van Reenen, and Wolfe 1995; Pinto, Belka, and Krajewski 1993). It is likely that this is related to the manner in which privatization has occurred—a theme that recurs throughout the coming chapters—as well as to lags.

This volume is primarily concerned with the changing behavior of firms and their complex interaction with the labor market, most particularly with unemployment. It summarizes the work that the assembled authors have undertaken over the past few years to understand the responses of state and privatized firms to the shocks that have been synonymous with transition. While a first volume concentrated mainly on the unemployment consequences of these shocks (Commander and Corecelli 1995), here we look into the black box of firm behavior in considerably greater detail. This chapter sets out the main findings of the individual chapters and places them in context. It also provides a simple analytical framework for understanding the response of firms to shocks before summarizing the principal conclusions.

The main emphasis in this book is on the Czech and Slovak Republics, Bulgaria, Hungary, Poland, and Russia, although we believe that the empirical results can indeed be generalized across all countries in transition. In addition to taking a careful, empirical look at firm responses, the volume seeks to draw together these findings analytically, and to do so in a way that is informative about the larger shape and timing of transition. In this sense, the behavior of firms will depend not only on their governance regimes, but also on conditions outside in the labor market. For example, the relative values of a range of labor market states, including unemployment, will have a crucial effect on the restructuring decisions of firms dominated by insiders. The worse the labor market conditions are, the stronger the likely opposition to restructuring. These values will depend not only on institutional factors—the generosity of the unemployment benefits regime, for example—but also on the way in which the private sector sets wages and the rate of private job creation. These factors need to be treated endogenously when looking at their impact on the overall shape and pace of transition. Models of transition that permit calibration are developed in Chapters 6 and 7; wherever appropriate, they use the empirical findings and institutional detail and structure reported in the earlier chapters.

One obvious shortcoming of this book is that relatively little attention is paid empirically to the behavior of a key player in the transition, the de novo private sector. Although this would be an important omission in the longer run, the emphasis on the performance of established firms has clear merit in the context of the early phase of these transitions.

The Budget Constraints of Firms

To understand the pressures on the constellation of firms, governments, and workers, the appropriate starting place must be the financing nexus that has tied them together. This knot was particularly tight in the era of the planned economy. While there was certainly pressure on firms to meet production and other targets, and profits were highly taxed to facilitate subsequent redistribution; firm financing, including that for investment, was primarily channeled through the government. Shocks to profitability were effectively absorbed by compensating finance, ensuring, among other consequences, that unemployment remained hidden. In the immediate prelude to stabilization—Poland in 1989, Bulgaria in 1990, Russia in 1991—enterprise losses were customarily met with increased subsidies, a sharp deterioration in the public finances, and large infusions of inflationary finance. The reduction of subsidies to firms was obviously an urgent priority. In most countries, the subsequent contraction has indeed been substantial, if not as substantial as budgetary data generally indicate. This is because firms have alternatively been able to rely on interenterprise arrears or arrears to government, either through taxes or social security payments, as well as continuing soft finance through the banking system.

Both Russia and Bulgaria offer striking examples of the way in which the channels of soft finance have been diffused. By 1994 the stock of tax arrears in Russia alone amounted to the equivalent of 4–5 percent of gross domestic product (GDP). The substitution of arrears for subsidies has also been accompanied by an ability of firms to extract soft finance from the banking system. Failure to repay or service debt, as well as recapitalization of overdue interest and rescheduled principal, has been widespread in both economies. In Bulgaria, interest arrears to banks peaked at over 10 percent of firm sales in 1992/93, before declining to around 5 percent in 1994/95 (Nenova and Ugaz 1996). The banking system unambiguously replaced the budget as the primary source of the soft budget constraint, which resulted in a rapid acceleration of losses in the banking system and mounting bad debts. Decapitalization of the financial system led to a widespread banking crisis in 1996.

While the evidence indicates considerable heterogeneity, the broad picture that emerges is that in Central Europe there has been a clear and declining incidence of subsidies and other soft supports to firms over time, as well as significant concentration in the ability to extract such support. This picture holds—but to a lesser degree—further east. In Bulgaria, where ownership reform has been the most attenuated, state firms have managed to continue extracting large supports from both the budget and the banking system. In Russia, progress has been more substantial, although ownership status does not appear to be the primary determinant of access to soft finance. Nevertheless, soft finance seems to be quite heavily concentrated and to be declining over time.

In sum, at first approximation, the assumption that state and privatized firms have had to behave as if their budget constraints were hard appears warranted in most of the countries considered in this volume. A complementary, stylized feature has been that once hard budget constraints were imposed, most of these firms reported that their profits disappeared. The empirical chapters clearly chronicle the shift to zero reported profit. Part of this decline can, of course, be traced to deterioration in their market position, as well as to tax incentives—the shift away from punitive profit taxes has been slow in coming—but part of it can also be traced to the structure of inside control and the decisions on how to appropriate revenues. This suggests that the other major factor to be considered is ownership and governance.

Ownership and Governance

Aside from hardening the budget constraint, a complementary and major source of pressure on state firms has been that of ownership reform, including closure. Table 1-1 offers some sense of the scale and pace of privatization that has occurred across the countries of the region. There is clearly large variation among countries. The Czech Republic, Slovakia, and Russia have elected to implement varieties of mass privatization programs; others, such as Poland and Hungary, have generally chosen more piecemeal and gradual privatization.[2] And, finally, there is Bulgaria, which, despite some putative attempts, has managed little organized

---

2. In 1995 Poland mass-privatized roughly 10 percent of industrial firms.

Table 1-1. Approaches to Privatization and the Size of the Private
Sector, End-1995

Country	Dominant form of privatization	Share remaining with state (number, value)[a]	Total share of private sector in GDP (est.)
Bulgaria	Very few direct sales	90 est.	37
Czech Republic	Mass voucher	10, 40	70
Hungary	Direct sales to domestic and foreign investors	22, 42	60
Poland	Liquidation, commercialization, and share sales, mass voucher (end 1995)	54, n.a.	58
Russia	Mass voucher	34, n.a.	58
Slovak Republic	Mass voucher	n.a., 42	59

n.a. Not available.
est. Estimated.
a. As percentage.
Source: World Bank and European Bank for Reconstruction and Development.

privatization of firms. This inaction, coupled with decentralized control, has nevertheless allowed the dominant firm-level parties to exert de facto control over resources.

Yet beneath these differences a common thread can be found: the importance of incumbents or insiders in the respective privatizations.[3] Whether managers and/or workers, insiders have generally been able to structure the nature of the privatization procedures themselves and, to varying degrees, the subsequent outcomes. Among other effects, the weight of inside influence has resulted in limiting the scale and rate of outright closure or liquidation of firms, even when enabling bankruptcy legislation has been enacted.

Of course, there has been variation across countries in the relative weight of insiders, as well as the way in which insider influence has manifested itself and the internal configuration of that influence. Survey evidence suggests, for example, that outsiders have been able to exert far more control and influence in decisionmaking in Czech and Hungarian firms than in the firms of Poland or Russia (Belka and others 1994; Commander, Fan, and Schaffer 1996). The form of insider control has also var-

---

3. The importance of insider privatization is dealt with in detail in Blanchard (1997).

ied. In Polish firms, where insiders have been dominant, the weight of workers relative to managers seems to have been significantly larger than in Hungary, the Czech Republic, or Russia, a clear reflection of the pre-transition control systems (see EBRD 1995, Chapter 8). The Bulgarian experience, in which firms have remained notionally in state hands, has resulted not only in maintaining a soft budget constraint, but has also facilitated the widespread diversion of assets and revenues by managers. Incoherent or contradictory messages on ownership reform induced managers to exploit their firm-specific knowledge to raise private returns to incumbency, often at substantial social cost. While the Bulgarian case is the most egregious, resort to shell companies, transfer pricing, and tax evasion have been common throughout the region.

Calibrating the extent of insider influence has proven curiously elusive. Firm surveys have regularly reported participants' perceptions that are at odds with subsequent outcomes. For example, in Russian industry, where employment adjustments in state and privatized firms have remained small compared with those in Central Europe, a large-scale survey found that workers or their agents were supposed to exert relatively little weight in decisions over either wages or employment (Commander, Dhar, and Yemtsov 1996). Yet if this were strictly true, the outcomes—primarily continued labor hoarding—would be difficult to explain. In short, measures of formal influence generally fail to capture the problem, because workers have been found to exert significant indirect influence in critical decisionmaking procedures (as argued in Commander and McHale 1996).

It is also clear that the link between an emerging managerial labor market and decisions by managers has yet to be forged in a predictable way. There certainly appears to be little empirical support for the view that "tough" managerial decisions on restructuring would be assisted by the positive labor market signaling that would simultaneously be associated with those actions (an argument made by Aghion and Blanchard 1996; see also Carlin, Van Reenen, and Wolfe 1995). Whether this is the result of the largely absent managerial labor market or the importance of more complex behavioral or social norms that constrain choices on restructuring is not yet clear.

The importance of insiders in both state and privatized firms has obvious implications for responses—including restructuring—to a hardening of the budget constraint and changes in the external and institutional environment. Restructuring potentially embraces a multitude of actions, ranging from what has been termed *reactive restructuring*, which primarily involves adjustment to employment and wages, to *strategic restructuring*, which requires trade reorientation and establishment of new marketing channels, to *deep restructuring*, which entails new investment in plant and technology.[4] Such restructuring choices, in turn, depend on conditions both inside and outside the firm. In the first case, the control regime in the firm will determine how such choices are distributed—in employment loss or relative wage adjustments, for example. In the second case, conditions in the labor market will be crucial in determining whether decision-makers go ahead with restructuring and the timing of that restructuring.

Getting some sense of how far firms have progressed along this continuum would clearly require a significant amount of detailed, firm–specific information.[5] For the most part, the datasets that form the basis for the empirical work in this volume do not permit easy discrimination over these restructuring phases. While there is selective information on investment and trade orientation, we have little that offers insight into the manner and extent of the adoption of new technology, management practices, and the like. Given that most of the focus of this book is on the responses of firms in the initial years of the transition, a reasonable working assumption is that reactive restructuring, primarily involving changes in wages and the size of the workforce, would indeed be the dominant restructuring pattern. For example, while the Polish evidence (as indicated in the chapter by Commander and Dhar) points to a clear, positive link between profits and investment, presumably largely financed by retained earnings, it is striking that new investment in Poland only picked up some three years after the resumption of growth. Deep restructuring has been restricted primarily to firms with significant capital injections, often through foreign direct investment. Many, if not the majority, of the remaining state, as well as many privatized, firms have remained in a twilight world of partial adjustment, unable to finance new investment, develop new product lines, and grow.

Yet twilight has various hues. For example, the behaviors of state firms in Poland and Bulgaria have differed substantially. In the latter case,

---

4. These categories of restructuring—reactive, strategic, and deep—are established in EBRD 1995.

5. There are now some excellent case studies that indicate the complexity of responses and, most generally, the apparent importance of outside investors and managers in inducing and executing restructuring decisions. A common theme from the case study material is the difficulty that insider-dominated firms face in financing new investment and in generating adequate management. See, inter alia, Estrin, Gelb, and Singh (1996); Johnson and Loveman (1996).

insiders, primarily managers, have largely decapitalized the firms. To achieve such an outcome has required not only accommodating government policy but also the formation of de facto expropriating coalitions of workers and managers.[6] While the latter, in particular, have used discretion to divert resources for personal gain, the cooperation of workers has been gained principally through commitments to employment stability. Although anecdotal evidence suggests that the gains to this coalition have been asymmetrically distributed in favor of managers, the result has not only been a substantial employment bias and rent appropriation, but also, as already indicated, major continuing flows of resources from the budget and banks to state firms, in part to sustain this employment bias. This disastrous outcome is, of course, a telling indictment of incoherence and reversals in policy toward ownership reform. In contrast, although privatization has also proceeded quite gradually in Poland, comparable reversal or inconsistency in government policy toward state firms has not been present, and this has proven consistent with a credible hard budget constraint on firms (see also Grosfeld and Nivet 1997).

In sum, there is significant heterogeneity across countries in the speed of privatization and the governance outcomes associated with privatization. That ownership change has largely proceeded on terms set by insiders has had major implications for both the speed and the scope of restructuring. Infusions of new investment and deep restructuring appear to be concentrated in firms where outsiders have gained effective control and foreign direct investment has been triggered. For firms that remain in the state sector, in the worst case—Bulgaria—coalitions of insiders have formed to decapitalize firms and induce flows of new soft finance, but this has not been the general pattern. Rather, faced with the threat of privatization and the imposition of hard budget constraints, they have generally attempted to adjust their behavior, while at the same time continuing to face major limitations on the resources available for restructuring.

The findings from the literature on firm behavior in the transition impel a rigorous analysis of the insider-dominated firm and its likely response to institutional and product-market shocks. The next section provides a simple framework for understanding this type of firm, as well as the motivation for some of the major empirical work that is reported in later chapters.

---

6. For a model of employment bias based on coalitional behavior, see Commander and McHale (1996).

A Framework for Understanding the Transitional Firm

Adjustment to shocks and any associated restructuring by firms will obviously depend on a variety of factors, including the overall competitive and financing environment facing a given firm, the objectives of the decisionmaking parties, and the manner in which the relative bargaining powers of the parties are distributed. While state firms, in principle, have continued to be controlled by government or particular ministries, most firms that have remained in public ownership have had their effective control largely devolved to incumbents. In this regard, the difference between state and privatized firms, both dominated by incumbents, may actually be slight. What is likely to be more significant is the difference in state firms' abilities to maintain access to subsidies or other supports. [7]

State firms entered the transition marked by strategic differences; these differences can be found not only in their objectives and control regimes, but also in their initial factor endowments. It is particularly striking that firms were clearly not governed by profit maximization and had inherited large stocks of labor. In addition, wages were largely, but not exclusively, determined exogenously, with relative wages reflecting planners' preferences rather than relative productivities.

Chronic overemployment—at least in relation to the new environment of the firms—generally required an immediate response. The rapid increase in unemployment—two years after the start of their transitions, most Central and Eastern European economies had unemployment rates above 10 percent—was one symptom of this adaptation. The distribution of employment losses has depended on a number of factors, including the availability of severance mechanisms and, most significant, labor market conditions. Where unemployment benefits have been relatively ungenerous, to remain with a firm has naturally proven to be more attractive, and resistance to employment reductions has been more vigorous. Where compensation, as in many Russian firms, has comprised firm-specific nonmonetary components, including social benefits such as housing and health care, it has tended to promote attachment and to reduce flows out of employment. In this context, insider weight in decisionmaking has led to widespread informalization of employment.

In short, consistent evidence across a range of countries shows that firms, whether state or privatized, were forced to rapidly make an employment adjustment. In addition, there were rapid and significant

---

7. This argument has been common in justifying rapid privatization, even without clear, short-run governance gains.

changes in the wage structure, notably a clear increase in earnings inequality and rising returns to skills (Orazem and Vodopivec 1995; Rutkowski 1996). The country chapters in this volume also point to workers initially accepting substantial real wage cuts, which suggests some tradeoff between wages and employment. Nevertheless, there has continued to be a clear employment bias, a bias possibly symptomatic of the influence exerted by insiders.[8]

A familiar framework for understanding the nature of the wage-employment choice is the Nash bargain, and this provides a useful point of departure. The firm is assumed to be characterized by two parties—management and workers—that bargain with each other over both wages and employment. Profit maximization is assumed to be the objective of the manager; the workers are thought to maximize their collective utility.

There are $\bar{n}$ workers in the firm at the start of transition, and their collective utility is given by

$$U(n,w) = nu(w) + (\bar{n} - n)\, u(w_r)$$

where n ($n \leq \bar{n}$) is the level of inside employment, w is the wage and w_r the outside opportunity or reservation wage, and $u(.)$ is the utility function of the individual worker with standard properties. Because the collective's objective function is increasing in both wage and employment, this implies a willingness to trade off wages for security of employment.

The manager's utility is given by profits:

$$\pi = p\, f(n) - wn + d$$

where the production function f is differentiable and concave, and where d represents the deficit the firm is allowed to run, and hence is equivalent to subsidies. This deficit is proportional to the wage bill, so that

$$d = d(n,w) = swn$$

and

$$\pi = p\, f(n) - (1 - s)wn.$$

In the event an agreement is not reached between the parties, production will not take place; all workers will get the reservation wage and profits

8. As indicated by firm surveys; for Poland, see Belka and others (1995) and Pinto, Belka, and Krajewski (1993); for Russia, see Commander, Fan, and Schaffer (1996).

will be zero. The extended Nash solution of this bargaining problem is given by

$$\max_{(w,\,n)}\{n[u(w) - u(w_r)]\}^{1-\theta}\{pf(n) - (1-s)wn\}^{\theta}.$$

Note that θ signifies the relative bargaining power of the respective parties. The first-order conditions are

$$w^* = \theta w_c + (1-\theta)w_m$$

$$pf'(n) - w = -\frac{u(w) - u(w_r)}{u'(w)}$$

where $w^* = w/p$ is real wage, $w_c = f'(n)$ is the competitive wage, and $w_m = f(n)/n$ is the monopoly wage (assuming at this stage that government subsidies are 0). Note that $w_c = f'(n)$ corresponds to point A in figure 1-1 and $w_m = f(n)/n$ corresponds to point C. The first condition, which translates into $\theta\,\delta\pi/\delta n + (1-\theta)\pi/n = 0$, says that the "pie" will be shared according to the relative bargaining powers of the agents. Workers aim at $\pi = 0$, or the real wage equal to average product, while management aims at $\pi' = 0$, or the real wage equal to marginal product. The second condition implies that the solution will lie on the (efficient) contract curve (McDonald and Solow 1981). A reasonable assumption in the transition context is that, given the initial conditions, with employment commonly to the right of even the zero isoprofit curve, a hardening of the budget constraint would, at a minimum, induce firms to cut back employment to the zero isoprofit curve.

There are two additional assumptions: (1) workers have constant relative risk aversion

$$\frac{wu''(w)}{u'(w)} = r,$$

which implies, together with the concavity of u, that $0 < \alpha = 1 - r < 1$; and (2) that the elasticity of output to employment is constant:

$$\frac{nf'(n)}{f(n)} = \varepsilon$$

with $0 < \varepsilon < 1$, since we assume decreasing returns to scale.

Figure 1-1. Wage and Employment Bargains

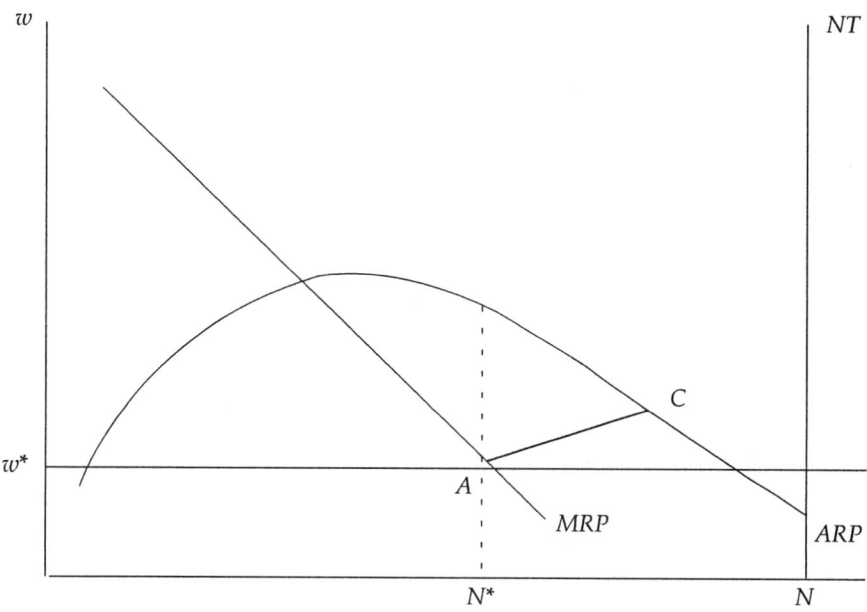

This setup yields the wage and employment pair associated with relative bargaining powers. Employment will be higher under Nash bargaining than in a competitive context, and the size of the bias will be sensitive to the position of the threat points. Thus, when workers are powerful, they will take a wage equivalent to the average product, and the point selected on the contract curve will be on the zero isoprofit curve. Any improvement in the manager's threat point would shift this inward, toward the labor demand curve, lowering employment, the wage, and utility. As represented in figure 1-1, and generally, this would yield a ray of possible wage-employment combinations running from A to C. If the workers appropriate all profit, the resulting point would be C.

To get at the effects of an exogenous change induced by changes in the external environment that favor management, and thus raise its bargaining power, some comparative statistics are in order. Factors that may account for an increase in management's bargaining power include new legislation on bankruptcy and liquidation, as well as on ownership. The principal results are as follows.

Institutional Change

(I)   – w as a function of θ is decreasing and concave
(II) – n as a function of θ is decreasing and convex
(III)– y as a function of θ is decreasing and convex.

The direction of change in wages, employment, and output arising from an increase in θ is predictable because the inefficiency is linked to overemployment and wages above competitive levels. More interesting is the sign of the second derivative. Given the slopes of employment, output, and wages with respect to θ, and hence with respect to time, if institutional changes take place at a constant rate, employment and output will tend to fall sharply at the start of transition, but then decelerate. Wages, in contrast, will decline more gently at the start, with subsequent acceleration over time.

The effects of a shock to the budget constraint can now be summarized. The change in the budget constraint is characterized as a change to subsidies.

Hard Budget Constraint

(I)   – w is independent of s
(II) – n as a function of s is increasing and convex
(III)– y as a function of s is increasing and convex
(IV)– Cross–derivatives of n and y with respect to s and θ are positive
(V) – Elasticities of n and y with respect to s are independent of θ.

In this case, the condition that net profits should be positive, $\pi \geq 0$ translates into $\pi_b / (wn \geq -s)$, where π_b denotes gross profit. This means that losses should not represent more than a given share, s, of the wage bill. This is an "efficiency" condition, as can be seen at the equilibrium where

$$s = \frac{1}{w^*}\{w^* - [\theta w_c + (1-\theta)w_m]\} .$$

In other words, the rate of subsidy equals the (relative) difference between actual and efficient or Nash wages. A soft budget constraint is an implicit subsidy to employment. Tightening the constraint (reducing s) will decrease employment and leave wages unchanged (at least if indirect effects are ignored). Convexity implies that employment will be less affected as this tightening proceeds.

These exercises give some sense of the effect of shifts in both the internal bargaining powers and the availability of external finance on key variables when both wages and employment are the objects of bargaining. The size of the employment bias—of particular relevance given the initial conditions—will clearly be extremely sensitive to the degree of worker influence in the bargain and the associated threat points of the parties. But the above setting has made a range of simplifying assumptions, including worker homogeneity. All members have been assumed to have the same preferences in wage and employment pairs. Yet such unanimity is unlikely; to the extent that it is absent, the distribution of worker influence will be important. For example, even if all workers have the same utility function and face the same outside opportunities, different treatment in the assignment of workers to jobs or layoffs can cause the orderings of wage and employment pairs to differ. Further, the manner of aggregation of the preferences for wages and job security will depend on the relative powers of the types of workers.[9]

In addition, the source of an employment bias may not be solely the raw bargaining power of workers (as measured, for example, by the degree of unionization), but may also arise from a common concern that managers and workers may ultimately need each other. Thus, granting job security to workers may be a precondition for managers to extract rents from the firms when outside control is absent or attenuated, a situation that appears to describe recent Bulgarian experience reasonably well.[10]

An associated question also arises about the dynamic behavior of firms dominated by insiders. Most of the literature on insider behavior has focused on the anti-employment bias that such dominance has generally implied.[11] The obvious question is whether, once the initially high level of

---

9. Sadly, there is little empirical evidence on the distribution of influence among workers, although employment reductions at the start of transition seemed to be concentrated more on unskilled and female labor. But this may—at least in the case of female workers—reflect a preference for nonparticipation given earlier pressures on females to work.

10. The implications of both manager-worker cooperation and worker heterogeneity are more fully addressed in Commander and McHale (1996).

11. See Lindbeck and Snower (1988) or the literature concerning the erstwhile Yugoslav labor-managed firms, for example, Spinnewyn and Svejnar (1990).

employment has been eroded—through attrition, for example—insiders might be expected to behave like classical insiders and be concerned only with their own members. In this case, a positive shock would lead to a wage increase with no effect on employment. Further, in insider-dominated firms, the weight of wages in relation to profit will be large, and this should negatively affect the equilibrium unemployment rate.

Unfortunately, because the datasets used in this volume generally do not go beyond the end of 1994, and hence cover periods characterized by generalized output declines, these hypotheses are difficult to test, and robust conclusions must await further study. Nevertheless, as we shall see below, the chapters on Hungary and Poland, while suggesting some asymmetry in the response to shocks, do not suggest that firms experiencing sales increases have generally behaved like classic insiders.

Firm Responses: Empirical Results

Although the simple bargaining framework laid out above can be helpful in setting out the basic assumptions and some of the important interactions, the empirical implementation or identification of the outcomes is problematic. Given the usual problems in jointly identifying wage and employment outcomes, the empirical chapters in this volume report a set of simple regressions that relate the change in employment and wages to the change in sales or productivity across a set of year-to-year, as well as longer multi-year, panels. This is an attempt to capture both the short- and long-run adjustments made by firms in response to shocks as measured over sales. By discretely estimating both wage and employment changes, we can get some sense of the way adjustment has been distributed over wages and employment.

Table 1-2 pulls together the main results. A number of features stand out. There is clear variation across time and, perhaps most striking, across countries. In both Hungary and Poland, although the initial speed of employment adjustment was too slow to avoid declines in productivity, the relationship between employment and sales changes has tended to strengthen over time. The long panels report roughly comparable elasticities of around 0.3. A similar estimate is derived from a panel of Bulgarian firms.[12] In the Czech and Slovak Republics, the relationship between sales and employment strengthened substantially, with elasticities on the order of 0.4–0.5 reported by 1991/93. The data also suggest that profitability has been a key factor driving the size of the employment change. Further,

---

12. The Bulgaria results are taken from Nenova and Ugaz (1996).

Table 1-2. Employment and Wage Elasticities to Sales and Productivity or Sales

Panels	Short panels			Long panels	
	1991/92	*1992/93*	*1992/94*	*1989/92*	*1990/94*
Bulgaria					
Employment			0.37		
Wage			*0.13*		
Czech Republic					
Employment	0.51	0.42			
Wage	0.05	0.01			
Hungary					
Employment		0.23		0.33	
Wage		0.07		0.14	
Poland					
Employment	0.18	0.19			0.32
Wage	0.77 (0.6)	0.84 (0.7)			0.76 (0.53)
Russia					
Employment			0.03		0.09
Wage			0.10 (0.09)		0.08 (0.05)
Slovak Republic					
Employment	0.35				
Wage	*0.30*				

Note: Figures in italics for wage equations give estimated results in a regression with the change in sales (rather than sales per worker) on the right-hand side.

Source: Chapters in this volume; Commander, Dhar, and Yemtsov (1996) for Russia; Nenova and Ugaz (1996) for Bulgaria.

when controlling for the direction of change in sales, the empirical chapters report no systematic decrease in responsiveness for firms experiencing sales growth, which might be expected if standard insider behavior dominated. Indeed, in Hungary, responsiveness of employment to sales increases for firms with sales growth. In addition, there is no evidence of a tighter association between wage changes and changes in productivity. In Hungary, these estimates suggest that increases in productivity were largely translated into profits, and less so into wages. Similarly, in the Czech Republic, the estimated elasticities of wage to sales remain negligible, a finding that suggests that government policies (aimed at restraining the ability of insiders to extract rents, such as explicit wage controls) were effective.

The picture is somewhat different in Poland and the Slovak Republic. In the latter, by 1991/92 there is a large, positive elasticity, indicating a clear and early divergence from the neighboring Czech Republic. The sample in Poland—primarily large or medium-size state and privatized firms—shows a consistently high responsiveness of wages to productivity. This clearly suggests an ability of insiders to appropriate rents, an ability that appears largely undisturbed through our reference period. But it is important to appreciate that rent appropriation seems less apparent in Polish firms that are experiencing sales growth, in both the short and the long panels, than it does in firms doing relatively badly in the product market.

This is not the case in Bulgaria. Although the estimated wage elasticity for all firms is not that large, it camouflages the negative association in the changes in wages and sales for a significant share of the panel (over one-third reported pre-tax losses). Further, the strongest real wage growth after 1992 was in loss-making firms, a clear indication of decapitalizing behavior.

The Russia results, generated from a large, representative firm survey of manufacturing firms, differ in several respects.[13] While changes in sales or productivity have mattered in setting both wages and employment and in determining the size of the wage markup over the reservation wage, the respective elasticities have remained quite small. The sensitivity of changes in employment to changes in sales is notably less than in Central and Eastern Europe. Given the initial conditions, firms have been weakly responsive to firm-specific measures of performance in both their wage and employment decisions.[14]

How much of this lack of responsiveness can be attributed to an absent hard budget constraint? It is clear that Russian firms, in comparison with their Central European counterparts, have maintained access to soft finance for a long period, but subsidy flows have also declined substantially. A detailed look at the evidence indicates that the great majority of the surveyed firms were clearly constrained in their wage settlements by the operating surplus. Few firms showed any signs of decapitalization through wage setting, a finding widely replicated in Central Europe, although not in Bulgaria. In Russia, low responsiveness of wages to changes in either sales or productivity points to a continuing willingness

---

13. These results and the ensuing discussion are drawn from Commander, Dhar, and Yemtsov (1996).

14. As given by a measure of firm profitability, while also controlling for size, location, branch, and a number of other attributes.

of insiders to sanction low levels of monetary compensation; priority is given to employment stability. This is consistent with aggregate data that have reported not only a sharp decline in the labor share, but also a surprising stability in employment, given the size of the shocks.

Pulling together the threads of the analysis, it appears that state—and subsequently privatized—firms have indeed cut deep into the excess stocks of labor that they carried into the transition. For instance, in Poland, firms doing business in 1990 had cut their employment by around 50 percent by 1994; in the Czech and Slovak Republics, mean employment in the industrial enterprises reporting in 1993 was under 40 percent of the level in 1989/90. In the wage setting, the elimination of profit points to full rent appropriation. In addition, the country chapters suggest that there is some asymmetry in the responses to the direction of change in sales or output; output expansion does not translate into employment growth. It is likely that this is an outgrowth of the continuing employment adjustment to be made and to the persistent employment bias in these firms. And while the Polish results point to the clearly powerful ability of insiders to influence the wage setting, the classical insider model does not appear to be confirmed by the data.

What of the effects of labor market conditions on firm-level decisions? The country chapters generally pick up an increasing responsiveness of wages to unemployment over time. Using region-specific data, evidence from the Czech and Slovak Republics, Hungary, Bulgaria, and Russia indicates a clear and predictably inverse relationship between unemployment and wages. This is not replicated in the case of Poland, suggesting that the larger, predominantly state firms have continued to set wages, independent of outside conditions. The relatively weak impact of outside conditions is also witnessed by the lack of substantial wage differentials between private and state firms in almost all countries; both have represented significant markups over reservation wages as set by unemployment benefits.

With these results in mind, we can now ask the question of where in the wage-employment space, characterized by figure 1-1, the state and privatized firms have come to lie. Wages clearly have remained above the reservation level given by benefits, and while employment reductions have been far from trivial, insider influence, combined with the initial conditions, has kept employment to the right of the competitive point. Thus, although there is evidence that changes conducive to an increase in management's bargaining power have occurred since the start of transition, it is striking that these firms continue to display an employment bias. The reason must ultimately be traced back to the degree of insider influence and the continuing ability of insiders to bargain over both wages and employment.

Firms and the Labor Market in Models of Transition

The response of firms has obvious, broader implications for the pace and shape of transition. The interaction of firms and their decisionmakers with the labor market appears to be particularly critical. Although there is some variation across samples, in general it appears that wages are indeed sensitive to labor market conditions. While this is not a significant departure in itself from market economies, where, for example, regional wages have been found to be consistently sensitive to regional unemployment rates (Blanchflower and Oswald 1994), it is striking that this regularity has emerged quite early in the transitions. Further, it clearly provides motivation to think more deeply about the ways in which labor market conditions outside the firm will affect key decisions in the firm, such as those relating to the scale and pace of restructuring, and the ways in which these will, in turn, depend on the structure of control within the firm.

One approach that has been used to model transition is to think of the economy in two core sectors, the state and private sectors, with an additional labor market state, unemployment. While this requires an obvious set of simplifying assumptions, it has several advantages. First, it captures the strategic involvement of the transfer of labor and capital from an initially dominant state sector to a private sector composed of new firms and firms that have been privatized. The behavior of private firms over time will tend to be different in a crucial area—they will act as profit maximizers, and hence will be constrained by their labor demand curves. The transfer of resources to the private sector yields productivity improvements that lead to growth in output and welfare.

By contrast, state firms will not only tend to be less productive, but also can best be characterized as pursuing more complex objectives. Given our empirical findings—the move toward a hard budget constraint and the dominance of insiders in decisionmaking—the simplest way to capture this complexity is to assume that state firms make their wage and employment decisions off the labor demand curve, with wages set equal to average product. In terms of figure 1-1, this implies a wage-employment combination on the zero isoprofit curve.

Yet in a rapidly changing world where firms are likely to be subject to significant shifts in relative prices; to changes in the institutional setting, including the probability of being in public or private ownership; and to changes in the fiscal regime, understanding the dynamics of the state and private sectors is crucial. For example, in a world of insider-dominated state firms, decisions about restructuring will depend on a range of factors, including government policy and the availability and generosity of fallbacks outside the firm, such as unemployment benefits and social assistance. The respective value of being employed in either the state or the private sector, including restructured firms, as well as being unemployed will materially affect the decisions of workers and managers. We can think of agents in state firms weighing the values of staying employed in the state sector, and subject to the probability that their firm might ultimately close—full rent appropriation, after all, is hardly consistent with a long horizon—and that they will become unemployed, with an associated exit probability from unemployment. Alternatively, they may elect to restructure. Some proportion of workers will become unemployed at the time of restructuring, and face the exit probability from unemployment at that time. Decisions to restructure will then depend on outside labor market conditions as well as the distribution of bargaining power within the firm and the availability of severance or other mechanisms for compensating losers.

Restructuring will also depend on the fiscal regime and the incidence of taxation across the sectors. One reason this is important is that fallback schemes, such as unemployment benefits, must necessarily be financed through taxation. Different values of taxes and their incidence across sectors, as well as across capital and labor, will materially influence the transition. For instance, if the private sector largely manages to avoid taxation, there will be two important effects at work. First, by escaping the tax net, the value of employment in private firms will tend to increase; tax avoidance will likely stimulate private sector growth. But by shifting the burden to the state sector, tax pressure on state firms will work to force greater job losses, raising the inflow into unemployment. Depending on the timing, a rapid acceleration of flows into unemployment from state firms could risk collapsing the transition.[15]

The importance of these factors in configuring the transition is made clear in the empirical chapters. By offering a clearer sense of the scale of shocks and the responses of firms, these chapters provide critical information that can allow us to move to a more dynamic analysis, including a sensible calibration of general equilibrium models of the transition. The chapters by Commander and Tolstopiatenko and by Blanchard and Keeling are attempts to use this approach and the associated institutional

---

15. See Commander and Tolstopiatenko (1996) for a more detailed discussion of these conditions; also see Blanchard (1997) and Chadha and Coricelli (1995).

information to set up and calibrate large models of transition organized around two sectors—state and private—and three labor market states—employment in either sector or unemployment. They ask complementary questions, and give particular attention to the role of the labor market, the benefits regime, fiscal constraints, and taxation incidence on the path of the overall transition.

The model of transition laid out by Commander and Tolstopiatenko concentrates on explaining a feature that emerges from the country studies and other recent empirical work: the very different responses of firms and workers in Central Europe in comparison with Russia and the FSU. It is noted that in Central Europe, unemployment generally rose high early in the transition, with fallbacks being relatively generous; in Russia, unemployment and restructuring have remained much more restricted. Unemployment benefits have been very limited. The private sector's evolution has consequently been at a different pace, in part because of the differences in the speed of restructuring. How much of this has been the result of differences in the institutional regimes is an obvious question to ask, and it provides the basis for an interesting natural experiment.

What emerges is that the benefits generosity can indeed exert a strong influence on the unemployment peak and the path of output, as well as their respective degrees of persistence. This was surely predictable. Factoring in other appropriate considerations, particularly the financing constraint for unemployment benefits, not only provides some indication of the ways in which fiscal factors can undermine the transition, but also allows the model to approximate reality more closely. For example, it has become increasingly obvious that tax equivalence across the state and private sectors is not an assumption that meets reality in most transition economies; private firms face markedly lower effective tax rates. Thus, when the tax rate facing the private sector is reduced and the probabilities of closure and restructuring are lowered—features that correspond to the situation in Russia—it is found that because benefits generosity is so low, the financing constraint still does not dominate, and unemployment remains low through the transition. But the main cost is, of course, on the output side; the decline is not only large but also persistent, given the limited incentives for restructuring and associated job losses. By contrast, more generous benefits regimes, but also higher initial restructuring and closure probabilities, features that reflect Central European realities, result in high and reasonably persistent unemployment, but far smaller output losses and a much more rapid overall pace of transition.

The chapter by Blanchard and Keeling presents a numerical model of transition that explicitly incorporates both reallocation and restructuring mechanisms in relation to a pre-transition baseline in which firms received subsidies. This framework permits a better understanding of the combined effects of individual policies, including unemployment benefits and taxation, and the design of privatization procedures on the shape of the transition. Starting from a benchmark case of reallocation induced by a withdrawal of subsidies—with wages in both sectors equal to the reservation wage and capital accumulation constrained by earnings in the private sector—the model generates a U-shaped path of output and a sustained increase in unemployment.

Fiscal feedbacks are then introduced. Not only do such feedbacks affect the pace of transition, but their effects are also highly nonlinear. At given—reasonably large—values, the taxation required to finance generous benefits and pension regimes can actually derail the transition through its negative impact on profitability and capital accumulation in the private sector. Considering the range of tax instruments, assumed to be labor and capital taxation in both sectors, it can also be demonstrated that high relative taxation of capital may result in smaller consequences for employment in the short run, but not in the long run, because of lower capital accumulation. Further, it is clear that while an initially low tax rate on the private sector will result in higher unemployment given the tax pressure on state firms, it can have desirable longer-run consequences. In addition to directly stimulating capital accumulation in the private sector, it will raise the attractiveness of restructuring in state firms, and thus the pace of output and employment growth. In short, a case can be made for taxing the private sector relatively lightly at the start of the transition.[16]

When the wage setting between sectors is differentiated, as wages in the state sector become less sensitive to labor market conditions, unemployment will rise and output will fall at the start of transition. There is a simple asymmetry at work here; the greater the rigidity of state sector wages—in effect, the closer wages are to average product—the worse the outcome will be in unemployment, but the better it will be for output relative to the benchmark case. This asymmetry comes about because higher unemployment leads to lower private wages, and these elements feed back to the rate of private job creation.

Blanchard and Keeling also explicitly confront the factors that determine restructuring and the implications of the privatization procedure for restructuring and the transition path. Starting with the knowledge that

---

16. Of course, as Russian experience in 1996 vividly indicates, very low tax compliance by the private sector can have serious consequences for government, requiring very large fiscal adjustments with major macroeconomic consequences.

insider influence is important, restructuring will largely depend on its implications for insiders. They will be sensitive to conditions in the labor market and to the probability of being laid off in the restructuring process. Further, with the additional assumption that effective restructuring will normally require outsider investment and control, achieving this outcome in a context of insider influence will ultimately depend on the terms of the privatization. Thus, more generous terms offered to insiders will make it more probable that they will accept privatization and restructuring. Of course, if insider privatization initially dominates, restructuring will depend on the speed of resale, thereby letting in outsiders. Insofar as resale proceeds, the result will be more unemployment at the outset, but more rapid growth in output.

The Role of Unemployment

Unemployment has been shown to exert considerable influence on wage setting and the pace of restructuring in firms. However, among the assumptions made in constructing the general equilibrium models of transition is that the private sector grows by a combination of state firms restructuring and transforming themselves and by hiring directly from unemployment. These two routes have indeed been found to be important. In Central Europe, much of the contraction in employment has passed through into unemployment.[17] Regional disparities have remained large, and mobility has been constrained.[18] Further, the stark reality for those entering unemployment has been that exit probabilities to jobs have remained very small. Long-term unemployment has accounted for an increasingly large share—generally over 50 percent—of total unemployment. With the exception of the Czech Republic, monthly outflows from unemployment of 3 percent or less have implied steady-state mean unemployment durations of over three years. And even in Poland, which has experienced substantial growth since 1992, the probability of an unemployed person finding a job within a year has been roughly half that in North America.

But a close inspection of the way the private sector hires workers reveals a more complex picture. The evidence suggests that firms have

---

17. Movements to nonparticipation or to pensionable status have also been important. Indeed, these differences appear to be quite significant factors in explaining cross-country differences in unemployment, at least near the start of transition; see Commander and Coricelli (1995).

18. Regional disparities are addressed in OECD (1996)

more commonly hired workers from other firms than from unemployment. This begs the question of why job-to-job transitions have so clearly dominated flows from unemployment to jobs. Unraveling this puzzle is clearly important. The chapter by Boeri begins to address this issue.

One obvious candidate—the level of unemployment benefits—proves to be problematic on closer examination. The generosity of benefits and, in some cases, their duration has fallen sharply since the start of transition. In part because of expiration of benefits, the share of registered unemployed receiving benefits was reduced by at least one-half between 1991 and 1995 in Bulgaria, Hungary, and the Slovak Republic and has been substantially reduced in Poland. These changes in coverage and the associated decline in the reservation wage have not been accompanied by larger flows out of unemployment. Part of this lack of movement may be the consequence of duration; workers become discouraged and less effective in their job searches the longer they remain in unemployment. This would be plausible given the bunching of layoffs at or near the start of transition and the subsequent lag prior to resumption of hiring in the private sector. But it is also likely that the hiring preferences of employers is an important part of the puzzle. Further, the apparent absence of dynamic insider behavior suggests that the root of the problem is not an employment-constraining response.

The argument proposed by Boeri emphasizes information and screening problems inherited from the previous system. In the context of intense structural change and informational asymmetries, being unemployed carries a bad signal. Private employers, who cannot directly observe workers' characteristics, are likely to infer that the unemployed have the wrong attributes, and they will choose to hire directly from among those employed in the state sector. Workers in low demand in the private sector will then tend to be overrepresented in the unemployment pool because of firm screening procedures: firms will lay off workers with the "wrong" skills after a probationary period. This implies that the share of these workers among the unemployed increases beyond their share in the total population, while the share of workers with the wrong skills remains constant among state sector workers. Because this is common knowledge, the preference of private firms to hire only from among those in employment is reinforced.

The empirical evidence on labor market flows is, unfortunately, quite limited. The household data that are available suggest that state-to-private employment flows are of comparable magnitude to flows from unemployment to private employment. If the probability of recruiting low-productivity workers from the unemployment pool rose over time, it might be expected that the share of hires from unemployment would fall over time; this finding was not strictly verified. Alternatively, if private firms pay efficiency wages, this could account for the continuing small flows from unemployment relative to the size of reallocation. A further, detailed look at the respective roles of unemployment benefits, private sector wage setting, the characteristics of the unemployed, and the hiring preferences of the private sector will be needed to sort out this puzzle.

Conclusions

This volume is concerned primarily with the behavior of firms and governments—the latter mainly through the privatization procedures it sanctions, as well as the tax and benefits regimes it installs—in the early years of the transition. The empirical findings reported in this volume indicate that most firms faced a notable hardening of the budget constraint. In response to that challenge and the prospect of institutional change, the bulk of state and privatized firms began to adjust both wages and employment at the onset of transition. Despite evidence of considerable heterogeneity in response to shocks, employment declines have generally been substantial, and workers have accepted significant real wage cuts. Firm restructuring has thus been largely reactive. These results are consistent with the predicted response of insider-dominated firms: a willingness to trade off wages for employment stability and the persistence of an employment bias. Further, relative adversity in the product market has clearly created strong responses in terms of employment, although the response has been less severe in the area of wages.

Nevertheless, there appears to be a continuing employment bias in state and privatized firms. This can be traced to the structure of effective control in the bulk of these firms. Insiders have continued to dominate, and this has continued to limit the extent of restructuring, as well as the longer-run potential for renewal. The restructuring that has occurred has been sensitive to a combination of factors both inside and outside the firm. Decisions on restructuring in insider firms have depended on labor market conditions, the probability of job loss at restructuring, and the privatization procedure adopted. To date, insiders have been forced to behave defensively, which has limited the scale of job losses and/or greater outsider influence that would affect the rate of job destruction. This has contributed to some smoothing in the employment adjustment and has affected the overall pace of transition.

Not surprisingly, evidence of deeper restructuring in firms is largely limited to firms that have attracted outside—primarily foreign—investors. While by 1994 the effects of privatization had yet to work through the system, there is some evidence, particularly from Poland and Hungary, that privatization has begun to be associated with deeper restructuring and differing responses by privatized firms and the remaining state firms. Finally, what emerges beyond doubt are the costs of inconsistency in policy on ownership. By allowing firms to effectively remain in public hands, the Bulgarian experience testifies to the powerful ability of coalitions of insiders to decapitalize firms and plunder public resources.

There are a host of outstanding questions that need further attention. What are the longer-run prospects of privatized firms, and can we expect insider influence to wane sharply as growth in the new private sector accelerates? What governance procedures can be put in place for the remaining state firms? Why do private employers continue to show such strong preference for hiring workers already in employment rather than from among the unemployed? Is there more scope for active labor market policies, such as employment subsidies or retraining, that can improve the chances of the unemployed to regain work? At the least, this volume has attempted to chronicle and analyze the rude awakening that firms, governments, and individuals have confronted in the euphemistically termed *transition*.

References

Aghion, Philippe, and Olivier Blanchard. 1996. "On Privatization Methods in Eastern Europe and their Implications." Department of Economics, MIT, Cambridge, Mass. Photocopy.

Belka, M., M. Schaffer, S. Estrin and I. J. Singh. 1994. "Evidence from a Survey of State-Owned, Privatized and Emerging Private Firms." Paper presented at Workshop on Enterprise Adjustment in Eastern Europe, September, The World Bank, Washington, D.C.

Blanchard, Olivier. 1997. *The Economics of Post-Communist Transition.* Oxford, U.K.: Oxford University Press

Blanchflower, D., and A. J. Oswald. 1994. *The Wage Curve.* Cambridge, Mass.: MIT Press.

Carlin, Wendy, John Van Reenen, and Toby Wolfe. 1995. "Enterprise Restructuring in Early Transition: The Case Study Evidence from Central and Eastern Europe." *Economics of Transition* 3, 4 (December):427–58.

Chadha, B., F. Coricelli, and K. Krajnyak. 1993. "Economic Restructuring, Unemployment and Growth in a Transition Economy." *IMF Staff Papers* 40: 4.

Commander, Simon, and John McHale. 1996. "Worker Influence and Employment Bias in a Transitional Firm." EDI, The World Bank, Washington, D.C. Photocopy.

Commander, Simon, and Mark Schankerman. 1997. "Enterprise Restructuring and Social Benefits." *Economics of Transition,* June.

Commander, Simon, and Fabrizio Coricelli, editors. 1995. *Unemployment, Restructuring and the Labor Market in Eastern Europe and Russia.* Washington, D.C.: The World Bank.

Commander, Simon, Qimiao Fan, and Mark Schaffer, editors. 1996. *Enterprise Restructuring, and Economic Policy in Russia.* Washington, D.C.: The World Bank.

Estrin, Saul, Alan Gelb, and I. J. Singh. 1995. "Shocks and Adjustment by Firms in Transition." *Journal of Comparative Economics* 21: 31–53.

EBRD (European Bank for Reconstruction and Development). 1995. *Transition Report: Investment and Enterprise Development.* London.

Grosfeld, Irena, and Jean-Francois Nivet. 1997. "Firms' Heterogeneity in Transition: Evidence from a Polish Panel Dataset." Working Paper 47, The William Davidson Institute, University of Michigan Business School, Ann Arbor.

Hare, Paul, and Gordon Hughes. 1991. "Competitiveness and Industrial Restructuring in Czechoslovakia, Hungary and Poland." CEPR Discussion Paper 543, London.

Johnson, Simon, and Gary Loveman. 1995. *Starting over in Eastern Europe: Entrepreneurship and Economic Renewal.* Boston, Mass.: Harvard Business School Press.

Kollo, Janos, and Gyula Nagy. 1996. "Earnings Gains and Losses from Insured Unemployment in Hungary." *Labor Economics* 3 (3):279–98.

Konings, J., H. Lehmann, and M. E. Schaffer. 1996. "Job Creation and Job Destruction in a Transition Economy: Ownership, Firm Size and Gross Job Flows in Polish Manufacturing, 1988–1991." *Labor Economics* 3 (3):299–318.

Lindbeck, Assar, and Dennis J. Snower. 1988. *The Insider-Outsider Theory of Employment and Unemployment.* Cambridge, Mass.: MIT Press.

Nenova, Mariella, and Cecilia Ugaz. 1996. "The Behavior of Bulgarian State Firms." Agency for Analysis and Forecasting, Sofia, Bulgaria. Mimeo.

OECD (Organization for Economic Cooperation and Development). 1996. "Lessons from Labor Market Policies in the Transition Countries." *OECD Proceedings.* Paris.

Orazem, Peter F., and Milan Vodopivec. 1995. "Winners and Losers in Transition: Returns to Education, Experience, and Gender in Slovenia." *The World Bank Economic Review* 9 (2): 201–30.

Pinto, Brian, Marek Belka, and Stefan Krajewski. 1993. "Transforming State Enterprises in Poland: Evidence on Adjustment by Manufacturing Firms." *Brookings Papers on Economic Activity*: 213–70.

Rutkowski, Jan J. 1996. *Changes in the Wage Structure during Economic Transition in Central and Eastern Europe.* World Bank Technical Paper 340, Washington, D.C.

Schleifer, Andrei, and Robert Vishny. 1994. "Politicians and Firms." *Quarterly Journal of Economics* 108: 995–1025.

Spinnewyn, F., and J. Svejnar. 1990. "On the Dynamics of a Participatory Firm: A Model of Employer-Worker Bargaining." In R. Quandt, ed., *Micromodels for Planning and Markets.* Boulder, Colo: Westview.

World Bank. 1996. *World Development Report: From Plan to Market.* Washington, D.C.

2

The Effects of Output, Ownership, and Legal Form on Employment and Wages in Central European Firms

Saul Estrin and Jan Svejnar

This chapter will offer an assessment of how Czech, Hungarian, Polish, and Slovak industrial firms adjusted their employment and wages in response to changes in output, ownership, and legal form in the late 1980s and early 1990s. This analysis is of interest for several reasons. First, ours is one of the very few studies that analyze changes in the behavior of a large number of enterprises as they moved from the disintegrating centrally planned system into the first years of the transition. Second, since the former Soviet bloc economies suffered a sharp decline in aggregate output, and voters swiftly demonstrated their discontent with the socially painful aspects of the transition, it is important to understand how output changes affected employment and wages during this unique time period. Third, because enterprise commercialization and privatization are expected to be the main tools for inducing restructuring and growth, it is

The authors would like to thank Swati Basu, Nandini Gupta, Lubomir Lizal, and Chris Walters for valuable computer assistance.

essential to assess how the employment and wage effects vary with the legal form and ownership of firms. Finally, the economies of Central Europe were the first to enter the transition process and have differed dramatically from one another in their initial conditions, policies, and outcomes. Our comparative analysis of the pre-transition and transition behavior of firms therefore provides important information for the policymakers in these economies, as well as in those that began transition later.

With respect to the diversity of experiences of these economies, note that Poland and Hungary entered the transition with a significant private sector, especially in agriculture and services, while the Czech and Slovak economies were almost totally state-owned. In Poland and Hungary, the government gradually ceded some of its control over state-owned enterprises (SOEs) to workers and managers during the 1980s. In contrast, the Czech and Slovak economies remained highly centralized throughout the 1980s, and the supervisory ministries maintained strict control over their SOEs. Once the transition started in 1990, the relative situation changed dramatically. The Czech Republic and Slovakia have carried out massive privatizations of SOEs, while Poland and other economies, such as Bulgaria and Romania, have been slower in privatizing their state sectors. Hungary represents an intermediate case; it has avoided mass privatization but has sold a large number of firms individually. Hungary and Poland have also placed more emphasis than the Czech and Slovak Republics on commercializing their firms and have stressed adequate corporate governance. In this chapter, the labor market adjustment in the last years of the communist model will be compared with the first few years of the transition in this variety of economic circumstances and policy environments. Our findings are thus useful in identifying the labor market implications of alternative initial conditions and reform packages.[1]

The Conceptual Framework for Employment and Wage Setting

As we mentioned earlier, in the late 1980s the firms in Central Europe were subject to varying degrees of enforcement of output targets by the planners. Moreover, as the Soviet system collapsed in late 1989 and 1990, firms were exposed to a significant output shock brought about by the restrictive macroeconomic policies, the disintegration of the common trading system (Council for Mutual Economic Assistance: CMEA), and

---

1. For a detailed account of the principal labor market development in these economies, see Commander and Coricelli 1995.

the dramatic output decline in the Soviet economy. The behavior of firms is therefore likely to have been heterogeneous and to have changed dramatically during this period. It is important to adopt a methodological approach that allows for these differences across firms and for the changes over time. The heterogeneity across firms is controlled by using first-differences of variables. Variables are expressed in natural logarithms. Thus we are estimating the relevant effects as percentage changes over time. To allow for "changes in regimes" over time, a sequence of two-year (shortest possible) panels of data is used to estimate the first-difference logarithmic equations.

In estimating the employment equation, it is assumed that capital and labor are not easily substitutable within a one-year period. As a result, the traditional labor demand framework is not followed here; instead, the focus is on examining the relationship between employment and sales, without controlling for wages.[2]

In the wage equation, the focus is on (a) the relationship between wages and sales and (b) how this relationship varied across different kinds of firms and over time. The focus on the wage-sales relationship is particularly interesting in the sample analyzed. Under central planning, firms were expected to fulfill output targets; wages, while centrally set, were supplemented with bonuses that depended on the extent of plan fulfillment. Since our measure of wages is total annual earnings, we are able to capture this link between output and remuneration. As the central controls were gradually lifted and the transition unfolded, earnings depended on the nature and enforcement of wage controls, as well as on workers' power and the firm's ability to pay. While profit, calculated net of some reservation wage, would be an appropriate variable to measure the "pie" that workers might try to capture (see, for example, Prasnikar and others 1994), the profit data are relatively unreliable in the transition economies. As a result, we consider the firm's sales to be the best proxy for its ability to pay wages, especially since estimates are derived from a rate of change specification.

In order to capture the possible diversity of responses of different types of firms to changes in their output, we have divided the two-year panels of firms into two categories: firms that experienced increasing, and those that experienced decreasing, real sales during each two-year period. We then ran separate regressions on each set of firms, and used as explanatory variables the change in the firm's sales interacted with ownership and legal form (registration) dummy variables. In addition, we controlled

---

2. We are indebted to Olivier Blanchard for suggesting this approach to us.

for industry-specific effects by including a vector of industry-specific dummy variables. Within the two-year panel specification, the industry dummy variables also control for industry-specific price effects.

Formally, the logarithmic rate of change of employment and wage equations are specified as follows:

(2-1) $$L = L(QX, IND)$$

(2-2) $$W = W(QX, IND)$$

where L is the natural logarithm of the annual change in the number of employees of the firm, W is the natural logarithm of the annual change in real average annual earnings of employees in each firm, Q is the natural logarithm of the annual change in the sales of the firm, X is a vector of ownership and legal form dummy variables, and IND is the industry dummy variable.

There are two possible approaches to the issue of estimation in the context of our investigation. One is to assume that sales are exogenous and use ordinary least-squares (OLS) in estimating equations 2-1 and 2-2. This approach corresponds to the view that in the pre-transition years, output (sales) is set by the planners, and in the later years (the first phase of the transition), the negative demand shock constrained firms in their ability to sell. The other approach is to allow for the possibility of sales being endogenous and estimate equations 2-1 and 2-2 by instrumental variables (IV). The IV approach is also preferable when variables are likely to contain measurement error. We have carried out the estimation both ways and found the two sets of estimates to be similar. In the section entitled "Employment and Wage Determination," therefore, we report the IV estimates for all countries except for Hungary, where the IV estimates generate implausibly large elasticity coefficients.[3] Finally, in order to minimize bias that might arise from model misspecification, we have estimated equations 2-1 and 2-2 separately rather than as a system.

For all four economies, we used the firm's lagged capital stock, regional dummy variables, industry dummy variables, and ownership and legal form dummy variables as instruments. In Poland, we have used output in the neighboring industry (measured by standard industry classification) as an additional instrument.

---

3. The IV estimates have signs and statistical significace similar to the reported OLS estimates.

The Data and Summary Statistics

While for Hungary we use a sample of industrial firms, for the Czech Republic, Poland, and Slovakia we have data that cover the entire population of industrial firms with more than twenty-five employees. The data sets are therefore of interest in their own right, providing descriptive evidence about developments at the level of (almost) all industrial firms. The data come from the national statistical offices and they were provided to us in an anonymous format. Before estimating equations 2-1 and 2-2, we carried out consistency checks on the data and eliminated about 20–30 percent of firms because of missing or inconsistent data.

In table 2-1, we report summary annual statistics for the Czech, Slovak, Polish, and Hungarian data, respectively. For each variable we present

Table 2-1. Means (Standard Deviations) of Principal Variables, 1988–93

Variable	1988	1989	1990	1991	1992	1993
Czech Republic						
Average monthly wage	—	3.16	3.27	3.78	4.38	5.37
(thousand Kc)		(0.391)	(0.393)	(0.619)	(.927)	(1.22)
Consumer price index	—	1.5	9.6	56.7	11.1	20.8
(CPI)						
Producer price index (PPI)	—	0.1	4.3	70.4	9.9	13.4
Labor (number of	—	1,887	1,860	1,186	755	716
employees)		(4,901)	(4,753)	(3,106)	(2,220)	(1,966)
Sales (hundred million Kc)	—	2.23	2.28	2.21	4.53	5.01
		(7.21)	(7.24)	(11.2)	(15.7)	(18.6)
Ownership (percent)						
State	—	n.a.	n.a.	98.0	79.5	74.9
Private	—	n.a.	n.a.	n.a.	2.0	2.5
Cooperative	—	n.a.	n.a.	n.a.	15.6	18.4
Joint (domestic-	—	n.a.	n.a.	n.a.	1.9	2.7
foreign) venture						
Legal form (percent)						
State enterprise	—	n.a.	n.a.	77.5	55.6	46.7
Limited liability	—	n.a.	n.a.	n.a.	1.2	2.0
Joint-stock company	—	n.a.	n.a.	21.4	26.3	32.4
Cooperative	—	n.a.	n.a.	n.a.	n.a.	9.6
Industrial cooperative	—	n.a.	n.a.	n.a.	14.4	8.7
Number of enterprises (N)	—	781	761	1,053	1,455	1,030

(This table continues on the following page.)

Table 2-1 (*continued*)

Variable	1988	1989	1990	1991	1992
Slovak Republic					
Average monthly wage	—	3.11	3.22	3.73	4.28
		(0.32)	(0.344)	(0.559)	(1.07)
Consumer price index (CPI)	—	1.3	10.4	61.2	10.0
Producer price index (PPI)	—	–2.7	4.8	68.9	5.3
Labor (number of employees)	—	1,633	1,597	980	766
		(1,922)	(1,866)	(1,819)	(1,425)
Sales (hundred million Kc)	—	1.62	1.64	1.5	4.37
		(2.67)	(2.64)	(5.41)	(16.7)
Ownership (percent)					
State	—	—	—	98.5	79.4
Private	—	—	—	—	1.2
Cooperative	—	—	—	—	16.2
Joint venture	—	—	—	—	1.5
Legal form (percent)					
State enterprise	—	—	—	94.1	53.5
Limited liability	—	—	—	—	0.8
Joint stock company	—	—	—	4.4	27.9
Industrial cooperative	—	—	—	—	16.0
Number of enterprises (N)	—	315	311	476	592

	1988	1989	1990	1991
Hungary[a]				
Employment	1,311.837	1,215.787	1,069.369	864.137
	(1,871.54)	(1,704.06)	(1,497.54)	(1,256.61)
Real wages/head	105.939	115.014	119.795	127.433
	(36.86)	(45.39)	(51.40)	(64.46)
Nominal wages/head	110.424	136.009	173.956	237.595
	(39.33)	(53.05)	(75.07)	(116.08)
Real net sales revenue	2,140,001	2,088,615	1,783,214	1,393,149
	(5,067,098)	(4,950,942)	(4,553,419)	(4,018,924)
Nominal net sales revenue	2.295.528	2,495,832	2,664,403	2,786,349
	(5,659,240)	(5,944,303)	(6,888,380)	(8,282,690)
Industry price (1987 = 100)	104.053	118.443	145.520	187.806
	(3.84)	(5.99)	(11.61)	(18.06)
N	263	263	263	263

Table 2-1 *(continued)*

Variable	1988	1989	1990	1991
Poland				
Average annual wage, *W*	609.1	2,292.25	10,459.21	18,296.54
(thousand zloty)	(164.83)	(605.3)	(3,357.38)	(5,005.03)
Real consumer wage	609.1	652.88	434.421	446.26
(base = 1988)	(164.83)	(172.40)	(139.45)	(122.07)
Real product wage	609.1	714.36	510.49	614.41
(base = 1988)	(164.83)	(188.6)	(163.87)	(168.07)
Number of employees (*L*)	726.23	694.11	701.64	576.06
	(1,315.28)	(1,271.02)	(1,293.44)	(1,104.84)
Value of production (*Q*)	5,759.64	18,103.97	98,625.82	106,602.88
(million zloty)	(19,623.86)	(564,70.44)	(396,201.1)	(4,563,650.0)
Sales (million zloty)	5,836.03	18,504.83	100,474.67	—
	(19,719.09)	(57,004.19)	(398,740.59)	
Type of firm (percent)				
Basic unit with sub-	85	85	90	—
sidiaries	(0.36)	(0.36)	(0.30)	
State ownership	—	—	—	55.0
				(0.50)
Cooperative	—	—	—	41.0
				(0.49)
Private	—	—	—	0.26
				(0.05)
Mixed ownership	—	—	—	0.69
				(0.08)
Other	—	—	—	3.0
				(0.17)
Number of enterprises (*N*)	4,922	4,922	4,856	4,181

Note: Numbers in parentheses represent standard deviations.
a. The data refer to firms in industry and construction material branches only.

mean values and standard deviations. The data sets cover the period 1989–93 for the Czech Republic, 1989–92 for Slovakia, and 1988–91 for Hungary and Poland. Because Poland launched price liberalization, stabilization, and other elements of the transition in 1990, and Czechoslovakia in 1991, the earlier start and finish of the Polish data than the Czech and Slovak statistics is useful to the investigation. Similarly, Hungary started many features of the transition in the late 1980s; covering the 1988–91 period is hence appropriate. Overall, the data enable us to provide a fairly complete chronicle of the behavior of the Czech, Hungarian, Polish, and Slovak industrial firms immediately before and during the early stages of the transition.

Throughout the chapter we first present the findings for the Czech and Slovak economies, followed by those of Poland and Hungary. This sequencing of results makes sense, because the Czech and Slovak Republics operated under identical macroeconomic conditions and legal systems, both before and during the early phase of the transition. They also started market reforms relatively late, having generally adhered to the centrally planned system until 1990. It is thus of interest to compare the behavior of Czech and Slovak firms with that of the Polish and Hungarian enterprises.

The Czech and Slovak Republics

Commencing with the Czech and Slovak nominal monthly wages and consumer and producer price indexes, one observes that real consumer wages declined slightly in 1990, fell dramatically in 1991, and gained some of the lost ground in 1992. In the case of the Czech Republic (for which 1993 enterprise-level data are available), one can see that consumer wages also rose in 1993. The real producer wages held steady in 1990, experienced a sharper decline than real consumer wages in 1991, and registered a steeper rise thereafter. On the whole, the evolution of real consumer and producer wages was quite similar over the 1989–92 period.

The dispersion in interenterprise earnings was rising during the transition in the Czech and Slovak Republics. In the Czech Republic, for instance, the standard deviation started at 391 crowns in 1989 and reached 1,220 crowns in 1993. With the average wage in the Czech firms rising from 3,160 crowns in 1989 to 5,370 crowns in 1993, the coefficient of variation increased from 12 to 23 percent in this period.

The average number of employees in each firm held steady in the Czech and Slovak Republics in 1989 and 1990, but it fell substantially in 1991 and 1992. In the Czech Republic one observes a further moderate decline in 1993. The figures reflect the major wave of breakups of firms that took place in the Czech and Slovak Republics in 1990–91 (see Lizal, Singer, and Svejnar 1995), as well as the significant reductions of the labor force in many firms and the entry of a large number of smaller firms.

In the Czech and Slovak Republics, state and cooperative ownership of firms dominates private ownership and joint ventures in the periods for which data are available. The apparent paucity of private firms in our data is the result of timing: the first wave of large-scale privatization was carried out in 1992, the shares were transferred during 1993, and the Czech Statistical Office used ownership at the start of the year as the relevant variable. Firms were classified as privately owned only when they were 100 percent privately owned. For this reason, the legal registration of a firm (for example, joint-stock company or limited liability company) captures both a form of commercialization and the process of change of ownership (privatization).

Poland

As may be seen in table 2-1, Poland's real consumer and producer wages rose in 1989 and fell significantly in 1990. By 1991, real producer wages reached the level of 1988, but real consumer wages continued to lag behind. The phenomenon of producer prices lagging behind the consumer prices thus started much earlier and was much more pronounced in Poland than in the Czech and Slovak Republics.

On the wage side, the dispersion in interenterprise earnings remained unchanged between 1988 and 1991; the coefficient of variation was 27 percent in both years. This outcome contrasts markedly with the increased dispersion observed in the Czech Republic and Slovakia.

The average number of employees in each firm remained broadly constant in Poland during the pre-reform and early reform periods, but declined somewhat in 1991. The different employment pattern observed in Poland compared with the Czech and Slovak Republics is, in part, accounted for by Poland's decision not to create giant enterprises, as Czechoslovakia did in the 1980s.

The data for 1988–90 indicate that average sales tracked production very closely. This feature of the Polish transition is important for our analysis. While in the Czech and Slovak regressions we are able to use sales as an explanatory variable, in the Polish case the lack of sales data for 1991 has forced us to use output as a proxy for sales. The generally close relationship between output and sales in the 1988–90 period justifies this empirical approximation.

As may be seen from table 2-1, we do not have data on ownership for Poland prior to 1991. We do, however, have information on which firms were "basic units with subsidiaries," "basic units without subsidiaries," and "nonbasic units." The term *basic unit* refers to firms that were registered as independent enterprises and had a great degree of decisionmaking autonomy. The basic and nonbasic categories thus reflect a measure of government control over firms in the pre-transition period. For 1991, we have data on ownership, and we also know how firms with the basic and nonbasic status fit into the ownership categories. We use this information in our regression analysis.

Hungary

For Hungary we have a balanced panel of 327 industrial firms. As may be seen in table 2-1, employment fell by 34 percent between 1988 and 1991. The fall was very modest in 1988–89, but it averaged around 12 percent in 1989–90 and 19 percent in 1990–91. Despite the sizable declines, the average firm size in the sample remains rather large. Over the same 1988–91 period, real wages rose by slightly more than 20 percent. Almost half of the increase occurred between 1988 and 1989, but real wages in the sample rose by 5.8 percent even in 1991, the year when employment fell by almost 20 percent. Real sales fell by 35 percent between 1988 and 1991— slightly more than employment. The proportional fall in sales, however, was especially large in 1990 and 1991.

Employment and Wage Determination

In this section, we report our findings from estimating the first-difference employment and wage equations for the Czech Republic, Slovakia, Hungary, and Poland. In the first subsection, estimates of the employment equations are presented; the focus is then shifted to the wage equations. For each country, we present estimates for firms that were experiencing increasing sales and estimates for firms experiencing decreasing sales (see tables 2-2 through 2-9). In each table, we present estimates in column (1) that constrain all firms to have an identical elasticity, while in column (2) we present estimates that allow the elasticities to vary with ownership and legal form. Except for the Polish estimates, in columns (2) we use state ownership and state legal form as the base, and we estimate the effects of other types of ownership and legal form as a deviation from this base. In the 1988–90 Polish equations, we use basic firms as the base and estimate the effect of nonbasic firm as a deviation from this base. In the 1990–91 Polish equations, we use basic firms that were identified in 1991 as owned and registered by the state as the base. The effects of other types of ownership and legal form are measured as a deviation from this base.

Employment Equations

THE CZECH FIRMS. As may be seen from the estimates in table 2-2, Czech enterprises with increasing sales did not adjust employment together with sales in the pre-transition (1989–90) and early transition (1990–91) periods. Indeed, employment variation is found to be completely independent of changes in sales when the relationship is estimated jointly for all firms (columns (1) for 1989–90 and 1990–91). Moreover, as may be seen from columns (2) for 1989–90 and 1990–91, this lack of statistical relationship holds for all enterprise ownership categories (state, private, and joint ventures with foreign firms), as well as legal form (state, limited liability, and joint-stock company) during this period.

As the transition progressed during 1991–92 and 1992–93, the relationship between sales and employment became strongly positive; the overall elasticity of employment to sales is estimated in columns (1) of table 2-2 at 0.57 in 1991–92 and 0.44 in 1992–93. One also observes different patterns of this relationship across firms. The elasticity became positive and statistically significant for private firms and joint ventures with foreign partners, as well as for all firms registered as limited liability companies. The insignificant relationship between employment and sales continued for state-owned firms, joint-stock companies, and industrial as well as other cooperatives. The overall significant and positive elasticity is hence generated by a strong underlying employment-sales relationship on the part of the (relatively few) private joint venture and limited liability firms.

The estimates for Czech firms with decreasing sales show a very small but statistically significant positive elasticity of employment to sales before the transition; a much larger positive elasticity is seen during the transition (table 2-2). The joint estimate of the elasticity for all firms is 0.04 in 1989–90, 0.13 in 1990–91, 0.52 in 1991–92, and 0.4 in 1992–93. Moreover, while in 1990–91 the relationship is positive for all types of firms, but only significant for joint ventures, in 1991–92 and 1992–93 it is strongly positive and significant for all firms except (the few) limited liability companies in 1991–92.

Overall, the results in table 2-2 indicate that firms in private and joint venture ownership, as well as firms registered as limited liability companies, have spearheaded employment increases among firms with increasing sales, while all firms with decreasing sales reduced employment. The latter finding is important because it provides evidence against the argument that Czech firms have not been reducing employment in response to declining sales.

Table 2-2. The Czech Republic: IV Elasticities of Employment (*L*)
with Respect to Sales (*Q*)

Dependent variable is *dlnL*	1989–90	1990–91		1991–92		1992–93	
Category	*(1)*	*(1)*	*(2)*	*(1)*	*(2)*	*(1)*	*(2)*
Firms with increasing sales							
dlnQ (all firms)	0.01	–0.01		0.57[a]		0.44[a]	
dlnQ (state firms)			–0.02		–.08		0.05
dlnQ by ownership							
Private			0.01		0.90[a]		0.75[a]
Cooperative			—		–0.25		—
Joint venture			0.20		.42[a]		0.49[a]
dlnQ by legal form							
Limited liability			0.03		.29[a]		0.33[b]
Joint-stock company			0.01		.07		0.02
Industrial cooperatives			—		0.18		–0.17
Other cooperatives			—		.37		–.08
Industrial dummies	Yes	Yes	Yes	Yes	Yes	Yes	Yes
$\bar{R}^2$	0.08	0.06	0.05	0.17	0.40	0.16	0.31
N	556	779	779	646	646	472	472
Firms with decreasing sales							
dlnQ (all firms)	0.04[b]	0.13[a]		0.52[a]		0.40[a]	
dlnQ (state firms)			0.03		0.54[a]		0.41[a]
dlnQ by ownership							
Private			0.07		0.31		–0.34
Cooperative			—		–0.48[b]		—
Joint venture			0.23[c]		–0.42		–0.07
dlnQ by legal form							
Limited liability			0.18		–1.59[a]		–0.26
Joint-stock company			0.05		–0.15[a]		–0.07
Industrial cooperatives			—		0.70[a]		0.02
Other cooperatives			—		0.99[a]		0.01
Industrial dummies	Yes	Yes	Yes	Yes	Yes	Yes	Yes
$\bar{R}^2$	0.07	0.10	0.16	0.30	0.34	0.40	0.38
N	334	418	418	808	808	550	550

Note: State firms: state-owned and legally registered firms form the base.
a. Significant at 99 percent level.
b. Significant at 95 percent level.
c. Significant at 90 percent level.

THE SLOVAK FIRMS. As may be seen from the estimates in columns (1) of table 2-3, Slovak firms with increasing sales display an insignificant overall employment-sales elasticity in the pre-transition (1989–90) and early transition (1990–91) periods, and they yield a significant positive elasticity during the 1991–92 period. These findings are virtually identical to those observed for the Czech Republic in table 2-2. In the case of firms experiencing decreasing sales, one finds a significant positive elasticity of 0.10 in 1989–90, an insignificant one in 1990–91, and a strong, significant elasticity of 0.36 in 1991–92. Except for the insignificance of the 1990–91 coefficient, the overall Slovak estimates parallel those found in the Czech data.

Estimates of the elasticities by ownership and legal form suggest that except for the few joint ventures, there were no significant differences across all types of firms in 1990–91, because most coefficients are found to be insignificant at conventional statistical test levels. In 1991–92, the elasticity is insignificant for all firms with increasing sales except for joint-stock companies, which register a significant positive elasticity of 0.24. Virtually all firms with decreasing sales display significant positive elasticities, the exception being (the few) firms registered as limited liability companies—a finding that parallels that in the Czech Republic.

THE POLISH FIRMS. As may be seen from table 2-4, the overall elasticity of employment to output was positive in Poland's firms with increasing as well as decreasing sales, both before and during the transition. The point estimate of the elasticity is smaller (0.12) and less precisely estimated for firms with increasing sales than for those with decreasing sales (0.36) in the pre-transition (1988–89) period, but one cannot reject the hypothesis that the two coefficients are identical. For 1989–90 and 1990–91, the point estimates are virtually identical for both sets of firms, indicating that the overall effect was quite symmetrical. Unlike the Czech and Slovak firms, the employment decisions of Polish firms were already quite responsive to output in the pre-transition period.

During 1988–90, when we are able to distinguish basic and nonbasic firms, we observe that the positive output effect on employment is virtually identical in the two groups of firms, although elasticity is marginally higher in the nonbasic units in 1989–90. Hence, the firms that had more autonomy did not link employment more closely to output than firms that presumably operated under greater central control.

During the transition period of 1990–91, the overall strong positive elasticity is attributable to different sets of firms in the increasing and

Table 2-3. The Slovak Republic: IV Elasticities of Employment (*L*)
with Respect to Sales (*Q*)

Dependent variable is *dlnL*	*1989–90*	*1990–91*		*1991–92*	
Category	*(1)*	*(1)*	*(2)*	*(1)*	*(2)*
Firms with increasing sales					
dlnQ (all firms)	–0.01	–0.02		0.34ª	
dlnQ (state firms)			–0.01		–0.05
dlnQ by ownership					
Private			—		0.21
Cooperative			—		–0.18
Joint venture			3.48ª		0.13
dlnQ by legal form					
Limited liability			—		0.11
Joint-stock company			0.02		0.24ᶜ
Industrial cooperatives			—		–0.02
Other cooperatives			—		—
Industrial dummies		Yes	Yes	Yes	Yes
$\overline{R}^2$		0.07	0.07	0.22	0.46
N		312	312	214	214
Firms with decreasing sales					
dlnQ (all firms)	0.10ª	0.02		0.36ª	
dlnQ (state firms)			0.02		0.36ª
dlnQ by ownership					
Private			—		–0.18
Cooperative			—		—
Joint venture			—		0.45ᵇ
dlnQ by legal form					
Limited liability			—		–1.38ᵇ
Joint-stock company			–0.03		–0.03
Industrial cooperatives			—		0.03
Other cooperatives			—		—
Industrial dummies	Yes	Yes	Yes	Yes	Yes
$\overline{R}^2$	0.14	0.11	0.11	0.29	0.27
N	168	238	238	369	369

Note: State firms: state-owned and legally registered firms form the base.
a. Significant at 99 percent level.
b. Significant at 95 percent level.
c. Significant at 90 percent level.

Table 2-4. Poland: IV Elasticities of Employment (L)
with Respect to Sales (Q)

Dependent variable is *dlnL*	1988–89		1989–90		1990–91	
Category	(1)	(2)	(1)	(2)	(1)	(2)
Firms with increasing sales						
dlnQ (all firms)	0.12[b]		0.21[a]		0.35[a]	
dlnQ by firm type						
Basic unit (= base)		0.08[c]		0.11		
Not basic unit		0.01		0.02[b]		
Basic → state-owned (= base)						0.27[b]
Basic → cooperatives						−0.13[a]
Basic → private						−0.06
Basic → mixed ownership						0.25[b]
Not basic → state						−0.02
Not basic → cooperatives						−0.25[c]
Not basic → mixed ownership						—
Industrial dummies	Yes	Yes	Yes	Yes	Yes	Yes
$\overline{R}^2$	0.05	0.05	0.05	0.06	0.10	.012
N	2,078	2,078	514	514	932	932
Firms with increasing sales						
dlnQ (all firms)	0.36[a]		0.27[a]		0.44[a]	
dlnQ by firm type						
Basic unit (= base)		0.37[a]		0.25[a]		
Not basic unit		0.01		0.02[a]		
Basic → state-owned (= base)						−0.06
Basic → cooperatives						0.81[a]
Basic → private						0.33
Basic → mixed ownership						−0.64
Not basic → state						0.45
Not basic → cooperatives						1.15
Not basic → mixed ownership						1.36[a]
Industrial dummies	Yes	Yes	Yes	Yes	Yes	Yes
$\overline{R}^2$	0.10	0.10	0.11	0.11	0.12	0.11
N	2,834	2,834	4,338	4,338	3,247	3,247

a. Significant at 99 percent level.
b. Significant at 95 percent level.
c. Significant at 90 percent level.

decreasing sales groups. Among the firms that experienced increasing output, one finds a strong positive elasticity among firms that were registered as basic or nonbasic units and, in 1990–91, were identified as state-owned enterprises (0.27), as well as among those that were basic units, and in 1990–91 were revealed as having private or mixed ownership (0.25). These firms increased employment together with output more than the basic and nonbasic firms that were identified as cooperatives in 1990–91. The lower estimated elasticity for cooperatives is consistent with a model of an insider-dominated, labor-managed firm, which converts positive demand shocks into higher wages rather than higher employment (see, for example, Spinnewyn and Svejnar 1990).

In the group of firms with decreasing sales, one finds a significant and positive 1990–91 elasticity in basic firms that were revealed in 1990 to be cooperatives (0.81) and in nonbasic firms identified in 1990 as having mixed ownership (1.36). These are thus the only two sets of firms that were systematically reducing employment as they experienced declining output in the 1990–91 period. The cooperatives form a sizable group, and the present finding documents their willingness to reduce employment in the presence of decreasing sales.

THE HUNGARIAN FIRMS. As may be seen in table 2-5, the sample of firms with increasing sales contains 172 firms in 1988–89 but only 37 firms in 1989–90 and 1990–91. The overall constrained elasticity for all firms is insignificant, and it remains insignificant for state-owned and registered firms, as well as joint ventures and corporate firms, throughout the 1988–92 period. The few limited liability companies and cooperatives display first insignificant, and then (implausibly) large, elasticities in the later years.

All firms with decreasing sales show an insignificant relationship between employment and sales in 1988–89, but for most firms the elasticity becomes positive and significant in the following two years. In the case of state-owned and registered firms, the elasticity is in the 0.9 to 1.0 range in all three years, and it is statistically significant in 1989–90 and 1990–91. The coefficients of other firms are measured as deviations from this base. With the exception of limited liability companies, they are statistically insignificant, indicating that one cannot reject the hypothesis that the elasticity is the same as in the state firms.

Unlike the experience of the other three countries, the elasticity of employment with respect to output among firms with increasing sales is thus found to be insignificant. While the lack of significance may in part be brought about by the small sample size, it is nevertheless striking, for

**Table 2-5. Hungary: OLS Elasticities of Employment (L)
with Respect to Sales (Q)**

Dependent variable is *dlnL*	1988–89		1989–90		1990–91	
Category	*(1)*	*(2)*	*(1)*	*(2)*	*(1)*	*(2)*
Firms with increasing sales						
dlnQ (all firms)	1.51		0.37		–0.09	
dlnQ (state firms)		0.08		0.48		0.27
dlnQ by ownership						
Limited liability		—		44.01[c]		–13.19[a]
Cooperative		0.03		–0.29		10.63[a]
Joint venture		0.07		—		0.40
dlnQ by legal form						
Corporate		–0.10		0.43		–0.73
Cooperative		0.03		–0.33		11.33[a]
Industrial dummies	Yes	Yes	Yes	Yes	Yes	Yes
$\bar{R}^2$	0.35	0.41	0.23	0.39	0.20	0.22
N	172	172	37	37	37	37
Firms with decreasing sales						
dlnQ (all firms)	1.51		0.72[a]		0.66[a]	
dlnQ (state firms)		0.88		0.85[a]		1.01[b]
dlnQ by ownership						
Limited liability		—		–0.44[b]		0.03
Cooperative		–0.17		–0.37		–0.67
Joint venture		–1.39		0.58		–0.28
dlnQ by legal form						
Corporate		0.98		–0.11		–0.33
Cooperative		–0.17		–0.37		–0.68
Industrial dummies	Yes	Yes	Yes	Yes	Yes	Yes
$\bar{R}^2$	0.35	0.42	0.33	0.33	0.32	0.37
N	172	172	233	233	201	201

Note: State firms: state-owned and legally registered firms form the base.
a. Significant at 99 percent level.
b. Significant at 95 percent level.
c. Significant at 90 percent level.

Hungary has been thought to have been one of the most market-oriented countries in the transitional group, both before and during the early phases of the transition. The lack of significance in the 1988–89 elasticity estimate among the firms with decreasing sales also suggests that the Hungarian firms were not very responsive to economic stimuli before the start of the transition in Central Europe as a whole.

Wage Equations

The estimates of wage elasticities with respect to sales yield different behavioral patterns for firms in the four countries (see tables 2-6 through 2-9).

THE CZECH FIRMS. The estimates in table 2-6 point to a surprisingly small positive relationship between sales and wages in the pre-transition and early transition periods (overall elasticities of 0.04 to 0.1). Moreover, for firms with decreasing sales, the estimate becomes very small and statistically insignificant as early as 1991–92, while for firms with increasing sales the significance disappears in 1992–93. These overall findings are consistent with Czech government policies that have maintained government control over firms and denied worker-insiders formal channels for influencing firm policies, both under communism and during the pre-privatization phase of the transition.

An examination of the estimated wage-sales elasticities of individual categories of firms indicates that among firms with increasing sales, private firms increasingly displayed negative and growing elasticities; joint ventures produced positive elasticities in 1990–92, but a negative elasticity in 1992–93; limited liability companies had a negative elasticity in 1990–91, but no effect thereafter; and joint-stock companies turned up a positive elasticity in 1992–93, after registering zero elasticities in the preceding years. One thus observes a variety of short-term wage responses across firm categories and over time, with state-owned firms and cooperatives consistently showing no relationship between sales and wages.

Among firms with decreasing sales, one observes a positive elasticity for all firms in 1990–91, although joint-stock companies produced a somewhat smaller coefficient than other firms. All firms generate insignificant elasticities in 1991–92, and most do so in 1992–93 as well. In 1992–93, joint-stock companies display a small negative elasticity of −0.07, while limited liability companies yield a sizable positive elasticity (0.38).

Table 2-6. The Czech Republic: IV Elasticities of Wages (*W*)
with Respect to Sales (*Q*)

Dependent variable is *dlnL*	1989–90	1990–91		1991–92		1992–93	
Category	(1)	(1)	(2)	(1)	(2)	(1)	(2)
Firms with increasing sales							
dlnQ (all firms)	0.01	0.04[b]		0.10[a]		0.01	
dlnQ (state firms)			0.11		0.09		0.03
dlnQ by ownership							
Private			−0.08		−0.14[b]		−0.24[a]
Cooperative			—		0.41		—
Joint venture			0.31[c]		0.25[a]		−0.12[c]
dlnQ by legal form							
Limited liability			−0.42[a]		−0.01		0.02
Joint-stock company			0.01		0.01		0.15[a]
Industrial cooperatives			—		−0.39		−0.10
Other cooperatives			—		−.51		−.04
Industrial dummies	Yes	Yes	Yes	Yes	Yes	Yes	Yes
$\bar{R}^2$	0.06	0.17	0.16	0.01	0.13	0.05	0.07
N	556	779	779	646	646	472	472
Firms with decreasing sales							
dlnQ (all firms)	0.04[a]	0.09[a]		0.00		0.01	
dlnQ (state firms)			0.20[b]		0.00		0.03
dlnQ by ownership							
Private			−0.11		0.03		−0.16
Cooperative			—		0.12		1.38
Joint venture			−0.08		0.02		0.01
dlnQ by legal form							
Limited liability			−0.07		0.30		0.38[b]
Joint-stock company			−0.05[c]		0.00		−0.07[a]
Industrial cooperatives			—		−0.10		−1.43
Other cooperatives			—		−0.16		−1.39
Industrial dummies	Yes	Yes	Yes	Yes	Yes	Yes	Yes
$\bar{R}^2$	0.16	0.13	0.14	0.01	0.003	0.05	0.02
N	334	418	418	808	808	553	553

Note: State firms: state-owned and legally registered firms form the base.
a. Significant at 99 percent level.
b. Significant at 95 percent level.
c. Significant at 90 percent level.

In sum, Czech firms show a fairly consistent pattern of no, or only very limited, relationship between changes in their ability to pay (as proxied by changes in real sales) and changes in wages, both before and during the transition.

THE SLOVAK FIRMS. As may be seen in table 2-7, the Slovak firms display more positive overall elasticities, especially in firms with decreasing sales and for all firms in 1991–92. The joint elasticity for all firms rises for firms with decreasing sales, from zero in 1989–90 to 0.05 in 1990–91 and 0.37 in 1991–92, while it rises from zero in 1989–91 to 0.26 in 1991–92 in firms with increasing sales.

For firms with increasing sales, the 1991–92 elasticity is strongly positive for privately as well as cooperatively owned firms and for firms registered as limited liability companies. The effect of cooperatives is strongly positive because of ownership, but it is mitigated for firms that also have a cooperative legal form. In the case of firms with decreasing sales, the small overall 1990–91 effect is driven by state-owned firms, while the 1991–92 overall effect is not attributable to any given individual category of firms.

THE POLISH FIRMS. The overall joint elasticity of wages with respect to sales is positive and significant for firms with both increasing and decreasing sales in the pre-transition period (1988–89), as well as during the big bang period of 1989–90 (table 2-8). The elasticity remains positive and becomes stronger in firms with increasing sales, but it disappears in firms with decreasing sales in 1990–91.

As with employment elasticities, the 1988–89 and 1989–90 wage elasticities are attributable to the behavior of basic as well as nonbasic units. Similarly, among the firms with increasing sales, the positive overall 1990–91 elasticity is reflected in the elasticities of all kinds of firms; the highest elasticities are registered by basic units that were revealed to be private firms and cooperatives.

The Polish firms thus displayed significant and persistent rent-sharing behavior with rising sales, but the sales-wage nexus was gradually severed in firms facing economic downturn.

THE HUNGARIAN FIRMS. The overall elasticity estimates in table 2-9 indicate that Hungarian firms had no significant relationship between sales and wages during the 1988–91 period. The exception is firms with decreasing sales, which generated a negative elasticity of –0.3 in 1988–89,

Table 2-7. The Slovak Republic: IV Elasticities of Wages (*W*)
with Respect to Sales (*Q*)

Dependent variable is *dlnW*	1989–90	1990–91		1991–92	
Category	(1)	(1)	(2)	(1)	(2)
Firms with increasing sales					
dlnQ (all firms)	−0.01	0.01		0.26[a]	
dlnQ (state firms)			0.01		−0.13
dlnQ by ownership					
Private			—		0.48[a]
Cooperative			—		1.23[a]
Joint venture			0.42		−0.01
dlnQ by legal form					
Limited liability			—		0.36[b]
Joint-stock company			0.06		0.16
Industrial cooperatives			—		−0.78[b]
Other cooperatives			—		—
Industrial dummies	Yes	Yes	Yes	Yes	Yes
$\bar{R}^2$	0.41	0.11	0.10	0.19	0.51
N	200	312	312	214	214
Firms with decreasing sales					
dlnQ (all firms)	0.03	0.05[a]		0.37[a]	
dlnQ (state firms)			0.05[a]		0.10
dlnQ by ownership					
Private			—		0.08
Cooperative			—		—
Joint venture			—		−0.03
dlnQ by legal form					
Limited liability			—		−0.53
Joint-stock company			−0.05		−0.07
Industrial cooperatives			—		0.08
Other cooperatives			—		—
Industrial dummies	Yes	Yes	Yes	Yes	Yes
$\bar{R}^2$	−0.03	0.25	0.24	0.29	0.05
N	168	238	238	369	369

Note: State firms: state-owned and legally registered firms form the base.
a. Significant at 99 percent level.
b. Significant at 95 percent level.
c. Significant at 90 percent level.

**Table 2-8. Poland: IV Elasticities of Wages (W)
with Respect to Sales (Q)**

Dependent variable is $dlnW$	1988–89		1989–90		1990–91	
Category	*(1)*	*(2)*	*(1)*	*(2)*	*(1)*	*(2)*
Firms with increasing sales						
$dlnQ$ (all firms)	0.11[b]		0.22[b]		0.35[a]	
$dlnQ$ by firm type						
Basic unit (= base)		0.05		0.19[c]		
Not basic unit		0.01		0.01		
Basic → state-owned (= base)						0.30[b]
Basic → cooperatives						0.10[a]
Basic → private						0.27[b]
Basic → mixed ownership						–0.17
Not basic → state						0.14
Not basic → cooperatives						0.03
Not basic → mixed ownership						—
Industrial dummies	Yes	Yes	Yes	Yes	Yes	Yes
$\bar{R}^2$	0.07	0.08	0.03	0.03	0.03	0.05
N	2,078	2,078	514	514	932	932
Firms with decreasing sales						
$dlnQ$ (all firms)	0.42[a]		0.13[a]		–0.03	
$dlnQ$ by firm type						
Basic unit (= base)		0.43[a]		0.13[a]		
Not basic unit		0.03[b]		0.00		
Basic → state-owned (= base)						0.17
Basic → cooperatives						–0.20[b]
Basic → private						0.69
Basic → mixed ownership						0.43
Not basic → state						–0.05
Not basic → cooperatives						–0.85
Not basic → mixed ownership						–0.39
Industrial dummies	Yes	Yes	Yes	Yes	Yes	Yes
$\bar{R}^2$	0.07	0.07	0.12	0.12	0.01	0.02
N	2,834	2,834	4,338	4,338	3,247	3,247

a. Significant at 99 percent level.
b. Significant at 95 percent level.
c. Significant at 90 percent level.

Table 2-9. Hungary: OLS Elasticities of Wages (W)
with Respect to Sales (Q)

Dependent variable is dlnW	1988–89		1989–90		1990–91	
Category	(1)	(2)	(1)	(2)	(1)	(2)
Firms with decreasing sales						
dlnQ (all firms)	0.03		−0.21		0.03	
dlnQ (state firms)		0.01		−0.01		0.41
dlnQ by ownership						
Limited liability		—		−26.22[a]		−23.04[a]
Cooperative		−0.34[c]		−0.68[c]		−0.11
Joint venture		−0.20		—		−0.47
dlnQ by legal form						
Corporate		0.04		−1.13[c]		−0.74
Cooperative		−0.35[c]		−0.66[c]		−0.33
Industrial dummies	Yes	Yes	Yes	Yes	Yes	Yes
$\bar{R}^2$	0.18	0.17	0.01	0.13	0.12	0.06
N	107	107	37	37	37	37
Firms with decreasing sales						
dlnQ (all firms)	−0.30[c]		−0.08		−0.05	
dlnQ (state firms)		−0.24		−0.01		−0.07
dlnQ by ownership						
Limited liability		—		−.07		.49[c]
Cooperative		0.08		−0.10		0.11
Joint venture		−0.09		−1.11[a]		0.30[c]
dlnQ by legal form						
Corporate		−0.10		−0.08		−0.02
Cooperative		0.08		−0.11		0.12
Industrial dummies	Yes	Yes	Yes	Yes	Yes	Yes
$\bar{R}^2$	0.16	0.15	0.11	0.10	0.11	0.12
N	172	172	233	233	201	201

Note: State firms: state-owned and legally registered firms form the base. The effects of other forms of ownership and legal structure are measured as deviations from this base.
a. Significant at 99 percent level.
b. Significant at 95 percent level.
c. Significant at 90 percent level.

which points to the possible presence of soft budget constraints in the pre-transition period. State firms show no significant relationship between wages and sales throughout the period. In contrast, cooperatives with increasing sales generated negative elasticities in 1988–90, but the significance of the effect disappeared by 1990–91. The cooperative effect suggests that in the pre-transition and early transition periods, the cooperatives were reducing wages in firms with increasing sales, but that this was a temporary phenomenon that vanished as the transition progressed.

Among firms with decreasing sales, one finds insignificant elasticity estimates for virtually all firm types in the 1988–90 period, while in the 1990–91 period one observes a positive elasticity for limited liability companies and joint ventures.

Overall, the Hungarian results point to a very limited link between changes in sales and changes in wages. In this regard, the Hungarian firms resemble Czech companies. Nevertheless, the negative elasticity among firms with decreasing sales in the pre-transition period raises the possibility that Hungarian firms actually had softer budget constraints than firms in the other economies.

Conclusions

Our analysis of the large panels of Czech, Slovak, Polish, and Hungarian industrial firms in the pre-transition and early transition period leads to several important findings.

While the Polish and Hungarian firms are generally regarded as having had much more autonomy than their Czechoslovak counterparts in the pre-transition period, the estimated elasticities suggest that only Polish firms systematically adjusted employment and wages to changes in sales in the pre-transition period.

The transition generally brought about significant changes in the employment behavior of firms. In particular, the employment elasticities with respect to sales became larger and more significant as the transition unfolded. This effect is especially visible among firms with decreasing sales—they were evidently more ready to reduce employment in the face of falling sales. The main exception to the pattern of rising elasticities during the transition is the small sample of Hungarian firms with increasing sales, where the estimated elasticity remained insignificant.

In the Czech Republic, one observes that during the transition, firms with private and joint venture ownership, as well as firms registered as limited liability companies, spearheaded employment increases among firms with increasing sales, while all firms with decreasing sales reduced employment. The latter finding is important because it provides evidence against the argument that Czech firms did not reduce employment in response to declining sales.

The Polish data permit us to examine the behavior of cooperatives. We find that cooperatives tended to be more conservative in increasing employment than other firms with increasing sales, and that they were also more prepared to reduce employment than other firms when sales were falling. The behavior is consistent with a model of an insider-dominated firm.

The Polish and, to a lesser extent, Slovak firms yield a positive elasticity of wages to sales, indicating that rent-sharing may be an appropriate model to describe their behavior. In contrast, estimated elasticity is limited or zero in the case of Czech and Hungarian firms. In the case of the Czech firms, these findings are consistent with the Czech government policies that maintained government control over firms and denied worker-insiders formal channels for influencing firm policies, both under communism and during the pre-privatization phase of the transition. In the Hungarian case, the finding is quite surprising because the Hungarian firms have often been portrayed as operating with significant insider power. The one finding that is consistent with insider power (but also soft budget constraints) is that in the pre-transition period of 1988–89, one finds a negative elasticity of wages to sales in Hungarian firms with decreasing sales.

Overall, our study indicates that the transition has induced a more uniform and significant effect of firms' sales on employment than on wages in Central and Eastern Europe. This asymmetric link is consistent with the model of a competitive labor market, where individual firms accept (market) wages as given but adjust employment to demand shocks.

References

Commander, S., and F. Coricelli, eds. 1995. *Unemployment, Restructuring, and the Labor Market in Eastern Europe and Russia*. Washington, D.C.: World Bank.

Lizal, L., M. Singer, and J. Svejnar. 1995. "Manager Interests, Breakups and Performance of State Enterprises in Transition." In J. Svejnar, ed., *The Czech Republic and Economic Transition in Eastern Europe*. New York: Academic Press.

Prasnikar, J., J. Svejnar, D. Mihaljek, and V. Prasnikar. 1994. "Behavior of Participatory Firms in Yugoslavia: Lessons for Transforming Economies." *Review of Economics and Statistics* 76 (4): 728–41.

Spinnewyn, F., and J. Svejnar. 1990. "On the Dynamics of a Participating Firm: A Model of Employer-Worker Bargaining." In R. Quandt, ed., *Micromodels for Planning and Markets*. Boulder, Colo.: Westview.

World Bank. 1996. *World Development Report 1996: From Plan to Market.* New York: Oxford University Press.

3

Employment and Wage Setting in Three Stages of Hungary's Labor Market Transition

János Köllo

Despite years of research effort, the information available on the demand side of Eastern European labor markets is fragmentary, and the assumptions on employer behavior are uncertain. This study offers a step forward in the field with an analysis of the path of Hungarian firms in wages and employment during the transition. Short-panel samples are used that cover periods between 1986 and 1994.

A lengthy procedure of data cleaning preceded the analysis. To make the results available to the reader, an unusual number of technical comments are required. A Technical Notes section has been added at the end of the paper. A more detailed discussion of technical problems is available in Köllo (1996).

I am grateful to Gyõrgy Lázár and Judit Székely (National Labor Center, Budapest) for years of support with data. I thank Luca Barbone, Olivier Blanchard, Simon Commander, László Halpern, and Gábor Korõsi for comments on earlier versions of this study.

Employment and Wage Setting: Background

The State Firm under State Socialism

To locate the starting point of the firm—an indispensable step before defining paths—we briefly review the most important influences on wage setting and employment in traditional state socialist enterprises.

Graphs similar to figure 3-1 are used for illustration. The curves emanating from the bottom-left corner are iso-profit curves, the loci of wage-employment combinations that result in the same level of profit. If $R(n)$ is a revenue function and (w^*, n^*) is a point for which $R'(n^*) = w^*$ and $R(n^*) - w^*n^* = \pi^*$, then $R(n) - wn = \pi^*$ defines an iso-profit curve in the wage-employment plane with a slope of $\partial w/\partial n = [R'(n) - w]/n$, and thus it's turning point is at (w^*, n^*). The iso-profit curves serve as indifference contours, with lower curves representing higher profit.[1]

WAGE SETTING. Under central planning, the wage bill (or employment and the average wage) was determined by the planners. The wage plan was the single most stringent limit set for enterprises, as argued in detail in Chapter 16 of Kornai (1980).

Figure 3-1. The Wage-Employment Plane with Iso-profit Curves

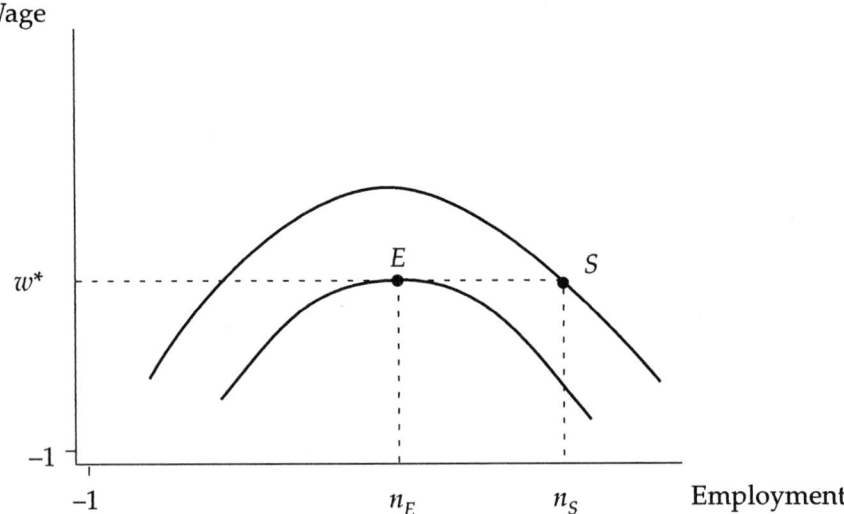

Wage

w^*

E S

-1

-1 n_E n_S Employment

---

1. The framework used here follows the introductory sections of McDonald and Solow (1982).

The case analyzed here is not that simple, because Hungary abandoned central planning in 1968; wages have been controlled by a tax-based incomes policy (TIP) since then. The firm was free to set wages within broad limits that had been suggested (rather than prescribed) for occupational categories. A tax was levied on the wage increment, and the rates depended on the relation of wage change to a reference indicator. The details of the TIP system changed rather frequently, but the typical setting might be formulated as

$$\text{tax} = \phi \Delta W = \phi[\Delta W / \Delta V] * \Delta W$$

where $W = wn$, V denotes value added, and ϕ is a steeply upward-sloping, convex function of $\Delta W / \Delta V$, which reached values up to 6 or 8 during fast wage bill growth relative to output.

Despite attempts to link wages to the firm's economic performance, empirical research by Böröczfyné Schmidt (1976) and Cukor and Kertesi (1987) suggested no strong relationship between these variables. Converting huge productivity gains into wage growth was prevented by prohibitive values of ϕ. Nevertheless, potential wage cuts in response to productivity losses were often averted by open wage subsidies, exemptions from TIP rules, or value added growth rates that were manipulated through transfers or prices (Kornai and Matits 1993). The distribution of subsidies followed relatively simple general rules. First, bargaining power increased with firm size, because the number of established communication channels between the firm and the Party—and hence the ability to bargain at all—was a function of size (as documented by Csanádi 1984 and others). Second, keeping firm size as measured by employment constant, the likelihood of subsidies increased with capital assets. Cukor and Kertesi (1987) provide empirical evidence of this, and they argue that the cost of refusing subsidies was higher, other things being equal, if low wages reduced the utilization of large assets of fixed capital. Third, keeping employment and fixed assets constant, subsidies were more likely when it became necessary to equalize nonpecuniary disadvantages.[2]

---

2. For instance, as the price of hard manual work increased—reflecting a general improvement of educational levels, the ceasing of massive flows from villages to industrial centers, and a consequent fall in the supply of unskilled labor—the wage levels generated by the "value added–wage growth rule" would have been insufficient to maintain staff levels at firms with predominantly unqualified jobs. Subsidies were often explicitly targeted to mitigate labor shortages of this kind.

The combined forces of prohibitive taxes and subsidies thus operated as an equalizing and preserving mechanism. With these elements in place, the risk that some firms would raise wages high above the industry average, or lag behind substantially, was actually rather small.

The special case of the tradeoff between employment and wages deserves a bit more discussion. An enterprise that is free to set employment and is taxed for the wage bill can raise wages, tax-free, by reducing labor hoarding.[3] The TIP rules encouraged a tradeoff between employment and wages, but other rules and incentives strongly discouraged such an arrangement, at least in the short run. First, and most important, severe political constraints were imposed on "firing without a cause": a firm that dismissed workers for wage gains risked serious political sanctions. Second, employment cuts resulting in lower output would have been an odd managerial strategy, given the rewards attached to growth, market share, and capacity utilization or the importance of fulfilling a responsibility to provide supplies or to meet the demands of export plans. It may be that the decades of wage bill control influenced the choice of technology in favor of capital-intensive production systems, but in the short or medium term, a firm's decision to move to lower employment and higher wage levels was strongly punished and/or incurred costs for the manager.

Taking into account a tendency to level off (nonequalizing, firm-specific wage differentials) and short-term employment rigidity, the assumption of a ruling wage, quoted by the state, seems to be a relevant assumption, even for the special and undoubtedly sophisticated case of post-1968 Hungary.

EMPLOYMENT. Under state socialism, firms employed more workers than similar capitalist enterprises that faced comparable wages and prices. The profit-maximizing firm (subject to w^* quoted by a union or government) is likely to choose $E(w^*, n_E)$, where the wage equals the marginal product and the firm is at the highest iso-profit curve available at w^*.[4] The choice of the socialist firm is $S(w^*, n_S)$, east of E.

E is an equilibrium point in the sense that, if other elements remain unchanged, the firm has no motivation to leave it. S is different. State socialist firms were always ready to expand employment beyond the current level. In the short run they might have been prevented from doing so

---

3. The intention of charging ΔW, rather that Δw, was to mitigate labor shortages.

4. The actual outcome may differ if both employment and the wage are set in a bargain, as shown by McDonald and Solow (1982).

by their budget constraint, but management continuously bargained for higher prices or fiscal transfers to make higher employment compatible with revenues. In this context, the assumption of a binding level of profit (setting a maximum for n_S at a given wage) would miss an important element of firm behavior. Kornai's notion of an unconstrained demand for labor (1980, Chapters 11 and 16) refers precisely to this point: irrespective of the wage level, in the absence of a binding level of profit, n_S had a tendency to move to the right of n_E (and, in a dynamic setting, to the right of *any* prevailing level of n).

DOES $S(w^*, n_S)$ EXHIBIT AN OPTIMUM FOR WORKERS? Many outside observers of Soviet-style systems interpreted the state socialist enterprise as *labor-managed*. At the same time, it was difficult to find a single piece of economic or sociological work (written by Hungarians) that shared this view. The apparent contradiction between the judgment of outsiders and insiders' calls for a choice, and a brief presentation of the arguments concerning enterprise behavior during and after socialism, follows.

For S to be at optimum, it has to lie in the tangency of an iso-profit curve regarded as momentarily binding by the management and the highest worker indifference curve available at that profit level. I would argue that such an optimum is not stable over time.

The representative worker's indifference curve with respect to wages and employment *in the firm* is one of the crucial points in understanding bargaining sets and possible outcomes. Of prime importance is that employment is full (time until reemployment is short), but job loss still implies non-zero cost because of the expenses of job search and the loss of seniority-related wage premiums. In a period between two jobs, income is $bw < w$. Expected income is $Y = pw + (1 - p) bw$, if p is the probability of staying employed in the firm. In case of random assignment, $p = \min(n/n_S, 1)$. The constant income curve is $w = \text{constant}/[b + (1 - b) - \min(n/n_S, 1)]$, which is flat for $n > n_S$, and downward-sloping elsewhere. For the representative worker, $n > n_S$ has no extra value, but employment cuts would imply some loss of utility because of the cost of job change. We may assume, therefore, that the indifference curve is kinked at the current level of employment.

Suppose that the point chosen by the firm, $S(w^*, n_S)$, accidentally provides the highest utility available for workers at profit π^*, as in figure 3-2. The agents will not be satisfied because they know they could gain further from state subsidies. We may think of subsidization as permission to move to a lower pretax profit rate—somewhere in the SAC area. Workers obviously prefer B to all other points and press the management to fight

Figure 3-2. A State of Bargaining

Wage

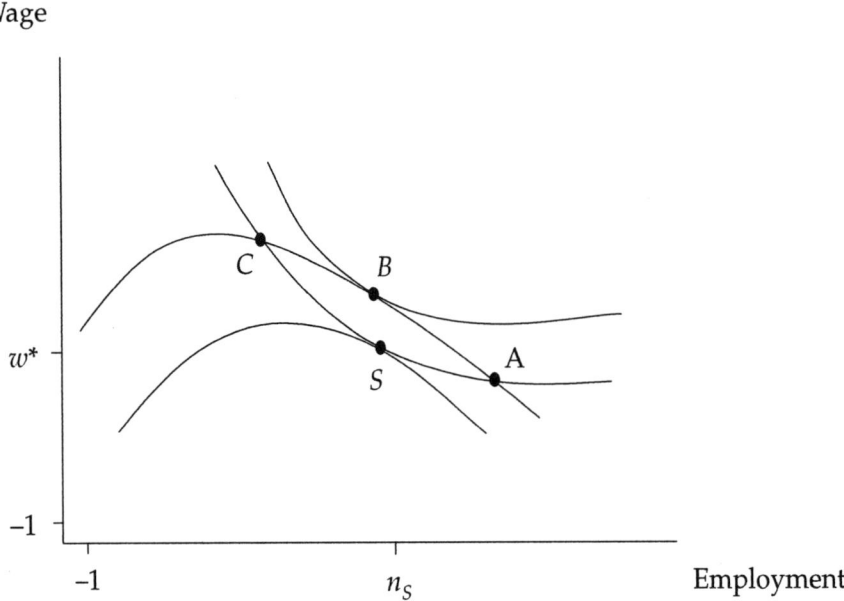

for *wage* subsidies. The difficult question is what managers want. They do benefit from higher wages for a number of reasons, but they could also benefit from higher output, as well as from higher profit (modest subsidy claims). Observations of success criteria applied by government and Party officials under socialism (Laki 1985) suggested that a proper mixture of a number of indicators—rather than a single criterion—was what mattered in evaluating managers. If we assume, accordingly, that managers strive for a combination of relevant success criteria—wage, employment, and profit in this presentation—the point they want to achieve is somewhere in the *SAB* triangle. If they have at least *some* bargaining power, the outcome will differ from *B*; the firm moves away from worker's optimum.[5]

_____

5. Note that after a shift to higher employment levels (for example, from *S* to *A*), the union indifference map should be rescaled. This is so because workers' utility is a function of the change, not the level, of employment. Preferences are transitive in the (w, p) plane, but not in the (w, n) plane.

The State Firm in the Immediate Pre-Transition Period

The *state socialist firm,* characterized briefly in the previous section, had virtually *disappeared* by 1989, which made it necessary to include the pre-transition period in the current analysis. This need was amplified by the 11 percent decline in paid employment (from 4.696 million to 4.169 million) between 1 January 1985 and 1 January 1990. Given that employment in the public sector grew rather than fell during these years, net job destruction is estimated to exceed 13 percent in the enterprise sector. The loss of jobs most probably reached 17 percent in medium-size and large firms.[6]

One is challenged to attribute these nontrivial changes to institutional reforms. In a period without major economic shocks—as was the case in Hungary, unlike Czechoslovakia, Romania, or the German Democratic Republic—the transition process was preceded by a stage of important reforms, and witnessed the apparent decay of the Communist Party state. Four reform measures were of particular importance to the labor market.

DELEGATION OF MANAGING RIGHTS TO FIRMS. The transfer of rights to manage was accomplished in both formal and informal ways. In the latter, Party and state control over enterprise decisions gradually weakened as the Party and state apparatus began to disintegrate. The establishment of elected enterprise councils, delegate assemblies, and general assemblies (instead of subordination to branch ministries) in 1985 created a legal framework for these changes. By the end of the period, most Hungarian firms could autonomously determine corporate structures, factor inputs, and the output mix.

INTRODUCTION OF DISPLACEMENT AND RETRAINING BENEFITS IN 1987. Under socialism, Hungarian firms were informally forbidden to fire large groups of redundant workers.[7] The introduction of the first elements of

---

6. Compare *Employment Observatory—Central and Eastern Europe,* CEC Bruxelles (pp. 27, 30, 33, 38) and *A nemzetgazdaság munkaerohelyzete a 80-as években,* KSH, Budapest (pp. 50–51). The estimate for large firms comes from the panel sample discussed later in this paper. For more detailed accounts, see Köllo (1997).

7. The post-1956 Hungarian media reported a single case between 1960 and 1986 where an attempt was made to fire hundreds of workers at a time, without offering them alternative employment (reported by Raba for the town of Gyor, 1995). The attempt incurred an enormous political burden for the enterprise and discouraged other firms from taking similar action.

an unemployment benefit system clearly signaled the end of political constraints on dismissals, challenged the taboo of full employment, and allowed managers to reduce employment without risking their own jobs.

GRADUAL HARDENING OF THE BUDGET CONSTRAINT. A series of market-oriented reforms contributed to the monetization of the economy and a gradual hardening of the budget constraint. These reforms included cuts in fiscal subsidies, wide-ranging price liberalization, tax reforms (Western-style value added and personal income taxes), commercial banks, an embryonic stock exchange, and a bankruptcy law. Although the reforms did not exclude the subsidization of huge loss-makers (most of them kept under government control even after 1985), they certainly confronted the system of paternalistic income redistribution. The nature of change is effectively demonstrated by time series presented in Kornai (1996, p. 18): the proportion of firms that blamed demand and lack of finance for capacity underutilization increased, while the frequency of complaints citing import shortages substantially decreased in 1985–90.

TIP. Compared with other fields, relatively little has changed in wage control. From 1985 onward, firms were allowed to choose between two systems of taxation (for details, see Ladó 1995). In system A, the tax owed at a given value added depended on the change in the *average wage*, while in system B it was a function of the change in the *wage bill* in relation to the change in value added.

These reforms did not leave the behavior of enterprises unchanged. With the end of stringent state control, and lacking private owners and unions, the role of managers and core workers could now become more important than ever before, and probably more important than it would ever be again. The decisionmakers had stronger motivation to find an optimum within the limits of revenues. Perpetual growth—previously both a prime value and a source of managerial reward—lost in importance. The firm now had a higher degree of freedom in cutting employment or trading off jobs for wages.

One can expect two kinds of employment and wage adjustment to have been initiated by the reforms and the resulting changes in corporate management:

- "Selfish" core workers and managers who gain control over the enterprise may agree to reduce labor hoarding. The elimination of low-productivity jobs has little impact on revenues, so both wages and profits can increase.

- The firm may want to move to an employment-wage combination that differs from S (in this case, output *is* affected). The targets may be different, depending on *who* makes the decisions, but the outcome is a cut in employment in most scenarios.

Some scenarios are based on *worker control*. Workers do not seek higher profit, but they do not want to drive the firm out of the market by pushing profit deep below zero. It is likely that they will try to maximize utility at close to zero profit. If the firm's profit was low at the outset (and we may assume this in state socialist firms), they look for points on, or left of, the current iso-profit curve. Apart from the special case that S is a tangency optimum, the union indifference curve crosses the iso-profit curve at S and C, as shown in figure 3-3. (Whether the worker's indifference curve is kinked or well-behaved has no importance from this point of view.) The points between the indifference curve and the profit curve are Pareto-superior to S. If workers have their own way, they will choose B.

A variant of this scenario is when decisions are made by, and in the interest of, a small group of m core workers. ($m << n_S$). With respect to profit, such a small group is likely to behave like the community of all workers, but its utility curve is kinked at m, as argued in Carruth and Oswald (1987). If decisions are made by such a group, the likely outcome

Figure 3-3. Possible Paths of the Firm

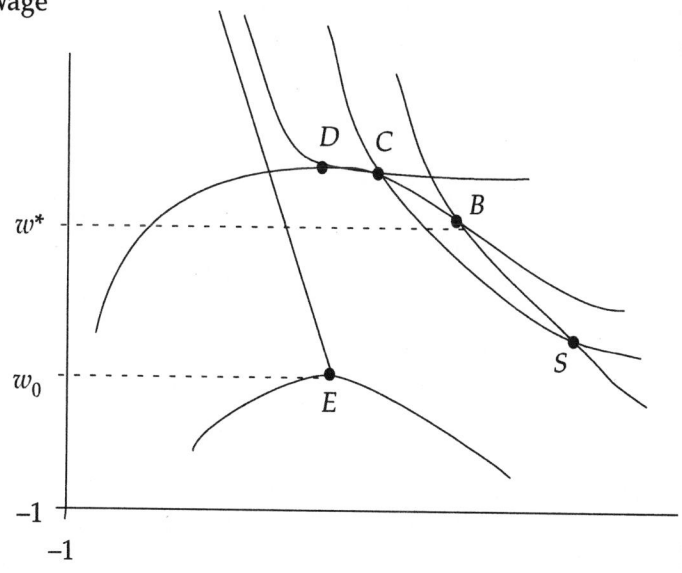

is D, the highest possible wage consistent with the prevailing level of profit. If m is small enough, D is an efficient choice in the sense that $R'(n) = w$. The position of D with respect to C is uncertain, but like C, it is northwest of S as well as B.

In other scenarios, control is taken over by *managers*. The manager, although not the agent of a private owner, may seek maximum profit for a number of reasons. Higher profits can improve his reputation in an emerging managerial labor market, make access to credit easier in the new commercial banking system, or improve the manager's prospect of becoming an owner in the future. If a profit-maximizing manager could make the decision on his own, he would choose E, a wage level at the reservation level w^0, and an employment level at which $R'(n^0) = w^0$. Whether or not the manager can reach this point is a matter of bargaining power, but he certainly wants to move west or southwest of S.

Finally, workers or managers *uninterested* in profit may try to maintain employment and raise wages at the expense of profit. We do not regard this as a highly relevant option, given the proximity of n_S to a level that would exhaust the firm's intakes at any given moment under socialism. In principle, this option would imply a move to the north of S.

A common corollary of the more relevant scenarios of pure worker control, profit-maximizing managerial control, or a mixture of the two is that *the reforms bring about labor shedding without any external market impetus.* Employment cuts can be accompanied by a wage increase, or not, depending on the nature of decisionmaking. Similarly, expectations concerning profits are uncertain, but the guess is that even under strong worker influence, profits do not change considerably.

Firms During the Transition

The major aggregate shocks of the early transition period made employment and/or wage cuts unavoidable.[8] Furthermore, the hardening of the budget constraint, the strengthening of the profit motive, and growing competition led many firms to continue the elimination of labor hoarding or to respond to negative shocks more quickly. One could observe a great variety of behavioral patterns in this period, depending on corporate management, goals, constraints, and other factors, but a *general trend in*

---

8. We do not discuss Hungary's general economic problems and reforms during the transition period, because these have been thoroughly analyzed in a series of books and papers and are most probably well-known by the readers of this study.

the early stage of transition and a real or apparent *regime change at the end of 1992* are not difficult to identify.

It is well known from macroeconomic statistics that the burden fell on employment rather than wages in Hungary. Of all the reforming countries in 1989–92, the decline of employment relative to gross domestic product (GDP) was among the highest, and the rate of real wage cuts by far the lowest, in Hungary.

Depending on the statistical source used, one may set the beginning of a new stage of labor market transformation at the end of 1992 or at the beginning of 1993.[9] The GDP stopped declining in 1993. Employment (measured on the basis of the International Labor Organization and Organization for Economic Cooperation and Development definition) was nearly stabilized at its early 1993 level. Alternative employment figures (of firms employing more than ten workers) indicate ongoing net employment destruction in this period, but at a diminished rate. (For the GDP and employment trends, see figure 3-4.) While employment was almost stabilized, the previous trend of slow and steady real wage decline was replaced by wide-ranging fluctuations: annual real wage growth exceeded 7 percent in 1994, followed by cuts of similar magnitude in 1995 and 1996.

An obvious suspicion raised by the macroeconomic figures is that firms were—and remained—under insider control. What we are witnessing is a gradual move toward *wage adjustment* of the kind assumed in Carruth and Oswald (1987) or Blanchard and Summers (1992). If the decisions are made, or heavily influenced, by core workers, who account for only a portion of the firm's pre-transition staff, a transition process started with major employment cuts, followed by enhanced wage adjustment, is a likely outcome. Firms initially respond to the shock by shedding marginal workers, whose welfare is unimportant to core workers. (It may be that some firms also have to fire core workers in response to the drastic shocks of the early transition period.) Labor shedding unrelated to market signals may also continue for a while, but the remaining core workers

---

9. The Labor Force Survey (LFS) suggested a huge drop in employment (by 265,000) between 1992.Q4. and 1993.Q1. A closer look at the raw LFS files suggested that this is a major overestimation caused by suspiciously large differences in the composition of cohorts leaving and entering the survey and by a change in the evaluation of casual work (see reference in Galasi and Kertesi 1996). The officially published figures on employment in 1993 relative to 1992 (on a year-on-year basis) are biased. Employment decline probably slowed down at the end of 1992, at latest, as suggested by the NLC Forecast Survey or by unemployment inflow rates.

Figure 3-4. GDP, Employment, and Real Wage

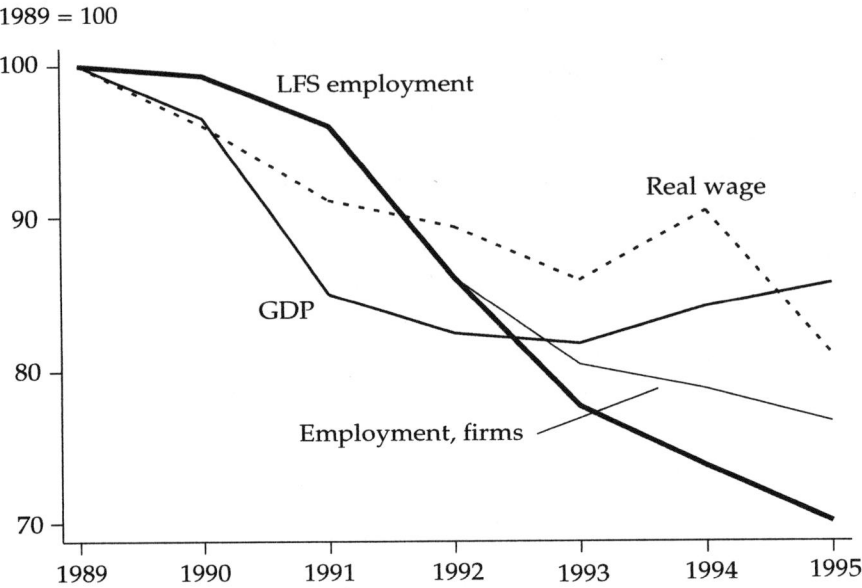

Note: Employment, firms: establishment-based figures. LFS employment: figures based on the Labor Force Survey.

become increasingly concerned with the level of employment as time passes, and they adjust wages to absorb (expected) negative shocks.

This story seems consistent with the macroeconomic trends, but that is not a sufficient condition for relevance. Several factors call for caution. First, the macroeconomic figures can be strongly affected by developments in the budget sector, which accounts for over 20 percent of employment and wages in Hungary. Second, a generally stable employment level after 1993 may reflect an accidental equilibrium of massive job destruction in some sectors and job creation in others, rather than the stabilization of enterprise-level employment. An investigation at the microeconomic level thus seems indispensable for a clear understanding of macroeconomic trends.

Despite the caveats presented later, some simple indicators may offer an insight into the character of the change. Nonincreasing elasticity of employment to output and increasing wage flexibility would provide support for the assumption of insider power. In contrast, if we find $\partial n / \partial R$

largely increasing, and $\partial w / \partial (R/n)$ and $\partial n / \partial w$ steeply decreasing, we may suspect that insider power (of the kind assumed here) is losing importance and the role of cost-minimizing owners is gaining ground. An attempt can be made to verify this hypothesis by testing whether these trends are stronger in private and privatized firms, or not.[10]

Before starting the discussion, it should be mentioned that important pieces of information are missing for a thorough analysis of enterprise behavior. The decisions of the firm are influenced by the softness of its budget constraint, the strength of the profit motive, unionization, and the firm's path preceding the period under examination. We face major difficulties in observing and measuring these important factors.

- Firms that cut employment substantially in the pre-transition period need less adjustment during the transition. Unfortunately—through the lack of long panels—we are not able to control the estimates for past history.
- Very little is known about unionization in Hungary. We therefore miss an important predictor of worker behavior.
- Like most analysts, we use private ownership as a proxy for the importance of the profit motive. This is clearly a second-best solution. On the one hand, as argued in McMillian (1996), or shown by Pinto and van Wijnbergen (1995), the maximand of the *state firm* can change substantially when a new generation of managers assumes the leading position or profound changes take place in government control and commercial banking. On the other hand, privatization often means title change rather than the shifting of assets to profit-maximizing owners. By comparing firms titled "private" or "state," we can make both Type I and Type II errors.
- Finally, it is difficult to identify the loci of soft budget constraints. After 1989, subsidies were typically latently channeled to the firm through the banking system (or in the form of tax arrears) rather than by easy-to-observe fiscal transfers, as had been done in the past (see Commander, Kollo, and Ugaz 1995 on subsidies to huge loss-makers and Schaffer 1995 on arrears).

---

10. The coincidence of large employment fluctuations and a stable wage is also consistent with the McDonald-Solow framework, where the union bargains about both wages and employment. The relevance of this approach is partially tested by a comparison of state firms with the private sector, where this kind of bargaining is rather unlikely.

Considering these problems, a modest aim was chosen for the empirical analysis that follows. We start by studying the immediate pre-transition period (1986–89) and test the alternative scenarios. Second, we check whether the patterns characteristic of 1986–89 survived after 1989. In the likely case that they did not, an attempt is made to identify some characteristic symptoms of typical development paths.

Data, Estimation, and Restrictions

Data

Three data sets are used, as shown in table 3-1. The first is labeled the Wage Survey (WS), the second the Wage Survey Firm Panel (WSFP), and the third the Forecast Survey (FS). For technical reasons we begin with the WS.

The *Wage Survey* was carried out in 1986, 1989, and 1992–94 by Hungary's National Labor Centre (NLC). The survey used a two-step sampling procedure. First, a random sample of firms that employ more than twenty workers is selected. Second, within each firm a random sample (about 10 percent) of the workers is drawn. In addition, all budget institutions and their workers are observed. The original WS samples contain the data of about 1 million public sector employees and 100,000–300,000 firm sector workers. The WS samples used here have been adjusted and

Table 3-1. The Samples Used

	1986	1989	1992	1993	1994
Wage survey (WS)	145,450 workers	145,453 workers	131,288 workers		151,408 workers
Wage survey firm panels (WSFP)	3,250 firms (2,666 after cleaning)				
		2,353 firms (1,235 after cleaning)			
			4,589 firms (2,387 after cleaning)		
Forecast survey (FS)			827 firms		

reweighted by Kertesi and Köllo (1995a) to ensure that they are representative. The final samples comprise 140,000–150,000 workers, representing employees in firms with twenty or more workers or in budget institutions. The weighting procedure is briefly presented in Technical Note 1 (for further details, see Kertesi and Köllo 1995a). The data on employers in the WS come from the financial database of the Ministry of Finance (MoF).[11]

The *Wage Survey Firm Panels* have been built by selecting nonbudget employers that reported data for the Wage Survey in two consecutive waves. For each firm we have a record for wave t as well as for wave $t + k$ containing financial data and summary statistics about workers (provided the firm is large enough). A comparison with figures from the Central Statistical Office (CSO) in Technical Note 2 suggests that the panel sample of 1986–89 comprised nearly two-thirds of the firms in the target population and covered four-fifths of their employment. The other two panels cover about one-third of all firms and half of employment. The loss is attributable to a lower enterprise sampling quota in 1992 and to more frequent dismantling, which made many firms unavailable for longitudinal observation. We know the level of sales, value added, employment, fixed assets, profit, and wages in t and $t + k$ and have estimates of the producer price index (PPI) between the two dates. We also know industry attachment, geographical location, and ownership (in 1992 and 1993).[12]

The *Forecast Surveys* (FS) comprise the data of roughly 4,000 firms interviewed by the NLC in March and August of each year since 1992. The sample is nonrandom, albeit the firms are selected on the basis of quotas given to local labor offices. The quotas are designed to ensure representativity of region and industry, but the selection of particular firms within the quota is biased by the almost arbitrary choice of persons in charge of the local surveys. Not all firms are interviewed regularly, and rotation is, again, not strictly random.[13]

We selected 827 of the firms interviewed in all waves between March 1992 and August 1994. It is important to add that the FS has been

---

11. The MoF and the NLC cooperated in merging the files and removed identification codes to ensure anonymity.

12. We shall not use the 1993 wave of the WS for analyzing wage differentials because we lack information on workers' education in the budget sector. The wave, however, is used to draw the firm panel because we do not need this information for the enterprise-level investigation.

13. Detailed descriptions of the FS are available in Székely (1992–96).

designed for purposes of short-term forecast rather than research. The poor measurement level of sales—and the observation of expectations rather than actual changes—makes it less attractive for analytical purposes. A small number of relatively reliable variables from this source will be used. (The composition of the four enterprise panels by some basic characteristics is shown in Technical Note 4.)

Estimations

In this section the contents of tables 3-2 through 3-7, the main source of information used during the discussion, are summarized. The aim of the calculations is to clarify what happened to employment, wages, and profitability during the transition. It follows from the exploratory nature of the investigation that we end up with an unusual volume of statistics, but

Table 3-2. Employment and Sales, Univariate Regressions
$\Delta\log n = b\Delta\log q + c$

Dependent: employment	1986–89	1989–92	1992–93
All firms			
Sales	0.127[a]	0.328[a]	0.225[a]
c	–0.269[a]	–0.124[a]	–0.127[a]
aR^2	0.0499	0.3442	0.1823
F	134.4[a]	648.7[a]	530.8[a]
Number of observations (N)	2,666	1,235	2,387
Firms increasing sales			
Sales	0.012	0.037	–0.041
c	–0.227[a]	–0.069	–0.044
aR^2	0.0000	0.0000	0.0031
F	0.4	0.4	3.2
Number of observations (N)	1,293	133	733
Firms decreasing sales			
Sales	0.209[a]	0.346[a]	0.333[a]
c	–0.252[a]	–0.102[a]	–0.085[a]
aR^2	0.0596	0.3219	0.2510
F	86.9[a]	523.6[a]	551.8[a]
Number of observations (N)	1,373	1,102	1,645
Percentage with falling sales	50.4	90.5	66.6

a. Significant at the 5 percent level.

we prefer to show the sensitivity of the results to changes of viewpoint and specification.

We start with estimates of employment flexibility. Table 3-2 sums up equations regressing the log change of employment on the log change of value added, deflated with the branch-specific PPI (q). The results are presented for subsamples of firms with increasing and decreasing output:[14]

$$\Delta \log n = b \cdot \Delta \log q + e.$$

In table 3-3 the employment-sales relationship is estimated in a two-equations model of simultaneous employment and wage setting:

$$\Delta \log n = b_{11} \cdot \log q + b_{12} \cdot \Delta \log (w/ppi) + b_{13} \cdot X + e_1$$

$$\Delta \log w = b_{21} \Delta \log(q/n) + b_{22} \cdot \log(ppi) + b_{23} \cdot Z + e_2$$

where X and Z are vectors of controls, and q, X, Z, and ppi are exogeneous. It is important to note that b_{12} does not necessarily reflect a substitution effect in the case of the post-socialist state enterprise. Shedding redundant labor may leave the firm's output unchanged and can finance wage growth without any change of technology. In this case, the increase of the capital/labor ratio is a statistical artifact rather than a signal of substitution.

Wages are examined in a number of ways to reveal aspects of their evolution and their relationship to sales and productivity. Table 3-4 presents univariate real wage equations for various subsamples:

$$\Delta \log (w/cpi) = b \cdot \Delta \log q + e$$

$$\Delta \log (w/cpi) = b \cdot \Delta \log (q/n) + e.$$

Table 3-5 sums up estimations of enterprise average wage *levels* in year t and $t + k$ for firms observed in wave t as well as in wave $t + k$. The average wage is related to value added per worker and variables in X, including the share of rouble and dollar exports, ownership, industry, the local unemployment rate, and some other variables. For 1989 we have two estimates (one from the 1986–89 panel and another from the 1989–92 panel),

---

14. The terms *output* and *sales* are used in the same sense. In both cases, gross sales minus material cost and the purchase price of materials sold (called 'ELÁBÉ' in the reports) is meant.

Table 3-3. Simultaneous Equations Model of Employment and Wage Adjustment

(Two-stage least squares)

Employment equation: $\Delta \log n = b_{11} \cdot \Delta \log q + b_{12} \cdot \Delta \log (w/ppi) + b_{14} \cdot X + e_1$

Category	1986–89		1989–92		1992–93	
	b	*t*	*b*	*t*	*b*	*t*
Sales	0.190	18.7	0.352	26.6	0.228	22.7
Wage/ppi	−0.564	−11.9	−0.165	−2.8	−0.253	−3.1
Exporter (Rbl)	−0.006	−0.5	−0.032	−1.0	–	–
Exporter ($)	0.082	7.2	−0.054	−1.9	0.047	4.0
Small firm	0.087	2.8	0.180	5.2	0.100	9.0
Large firm	0.125	12.3	−0.126	−5.4	0.041	2.6
Constant	−0.197	−15.4	−0.064	−3.6	−0.189	−21.8
aR^2 , *N*	0.365	2,666	0.449	1,230	0.260	2,367

Wage equation: $\Delta \log w = b_{21} \cdot \Delta \log(q/n) + b_{22} \cdot \Delta \log(ppi) + b_{23} \cdot Z + e_2$

Category	1986–89		1989–92		1992–93	
Productivity	0.060	6.2	0.120	9.5	0.035	4.5
ppi^i	0.064	1.7	0.314	9.9	0.008	0.2
Unemployment	–	–	−0.031	−1.6	−0.039	−1.3
Manual (log ratio)	−0.068	−7.0	−0.031	−1.2	−0.039	−1.3
100% nonmanual	0.086	0.6	–	–	0.021	1.5
Private	–	–	−0.018	−1.0	−0.029	−3.8
Foreign	–	–	0.344	3.2	−0.010	−0.7
Mixed	–	–	0.023	0.9	−0.015	−1.7
Constant	0.790	17.2	0.637	4.9	0.183	16.6
aR^2, *N*	0.092	2,666	0.210	1,230	0.041	2,367

and the same applies to 1992. We restrict the cross-sectional analysis to firms in the panel samples to ensure that the estimates for t and $t + k$ deal with the same set of enterprises.

$$\log w_t = b_{1t} \log (y/n)_t + b_{2t} X_t + e_t$$

$$\log w_{t+k} = b_{1t+k} \log (y/n)_{t+k} + b_{2t+k} X_{t+k} + e_{t+k}.$$

Table 3-4. Real Wage, Univariate Regressions

$\Delta\log (w/cpi) = b\Delta\log q + c$

Dependent: real wage	1986–89	1989–92	1992–93
All firms			
Sales	0.046[a]	0.049[a]	0.022[a]
c	0.148[a]	−0.181[a]	−0.028[a]
aR^2	0.0103	0.0215	0.0052
F	28.7[a]	28.1[a]	13.4[a]
N	2,666	1,235	2,378
Firms increasing sales			
Sales	0.054[a]	0.069[a]	0.032[a]
c	0.146[a]	−0.112[a]	−0.016[a]
aR^2	0.0071	0.0043	0.0054
F	10.2[a]	1.6	5.0[a]
N	1,293	133	733
Firms decreasing sales			
Sales	0.034[a]	0.029[a]	−0.009
c	0.144[a]	−0.209	−0.046[a]
aR^2	0.0035	0.0055	0.0000
F	4.8[a]	7.1[a]	0.9
N	1,373	1,102	1,645
All firms			
Productivity	0.131[a]	0.141[a]	0.071[a]
c	0.113[a]	−0.161[a]	−0.032[a]
aR^2	0.0948	0.1206	0.0481
F	279.9[a]	169.9[a]	117.9[a]
Firms increasing sales			
Productivity	0.133[a]	0.078[a]	0.043[a]
c	0.117[a]	−0.098[a]	−0.005
aR^2	0.0606	0.0148	0.0112
F	128.4[a]	4.2[a]	12.3[a]
Firms decreasing sales			
Productivity	0.028	0.110[a]	0.020
c	0.072[a]	−0.194[a]	−0.062[a]
aR^2	0.0038	0.0556	0.0023
F	2.6	55.9[a]	2.8

a. Significant at the 5 percent level.

Table 3-5. Cross-Sectional Estimation of Enterprise Average Earnings

	Data source					
Dependent: log (wage bill/average number of employees)	*1986–89 panel*		*1989–92 panel*		*1992–93 panel*	
Item	*1986*	*1989*	*1989*	*1992*	*1992*	*1993*
Value added/worker (log)	0.2749	0.3587	0.3711	0.2891	0.3304	0.3156
	(42.4)	(51.7)	(32.1)	(25.6)	(31.7)	(30.2)
Highly monopolized industry[a]	0.0358	−0.0554	−0.0016	0.1594	0.1288	0.1629
	(1.4)	(−1.9)	(−0.1)	(2.2)	(2.9)	(3.5)
Rouble sales/sales	0.1969	0.2466	0.1581	–	–	–
	(5.1)	(6.1)	(2.9)			
Dollar sales/sales	0.2257	0.0095	0.0769	−0.0948	−0.0807	−0.1251
	(−4.7)	(0.3)	(1.3)	(−2.6)	(−2.9)	(−4.4)
Unemployment rate (log)[b]	–	–	−0.0511	−0.1541	−0.1056	−0.1154
			(−3.6)	(−8.8)	(−6.3)	(−6.7)
Private[c]	–	–	−0.0270	−0.0432	−0.0747	−0.0760
			(−2.1)	(−2.6)	(−5.2)	(−5.1)
Foreign[c]	–	–	−0.0366	0.2537	0.0499	0.0376
			(−0.5)	(2.9)	(1.8)	(1.3)
Mixed, unknown[c]	–	–	−0.0273	−0.0316	0.0119	0.0053
			(−1.5)	(−1.4)	(0.8)	(0.3)
One-digit industry dummies	yes	yes	yes	yes	yes	yes
Dummy for firms with very low value added	0.3557	0.7859	0.7709	0.8815	0.7276	0.8575
per worker (< 50,000 Ft)	(12.9)	(17.7)	(11.6)	(14.5)	(10.2)	(10.0)
Parameter, *t, n*	(33)	(20)	(8)	(8)	(11)	(8)
Number of observations	2,666		1,208		1,498	
F- ratio	216.9	271.9	89.9	79.0	101.5	97.2
aR^2	0.4711	0.5285	0.5249	0.4798	0.4847	0.4755
Root MSE	0.1499	0.1778	0.1671	0.2096	0.2185	0.2264

Note: t-values in parentheses.

a. Petroleum mining, petroleum refining, energy, mail, railways, and public transport.

b. For 1989 the local unemployment rate of December 1992 is used.

c. For 1989 and 1992 the majority ownership in 1992 is considered.

Table 3-6. Cross-Sectional Estimation of Individual Earnings

Dependent: log (monthly wage + 1/12*previous year's bonuses) Category	1986	1989	1992	1994
Male	0.279	0.288	0.215	0.227
Age 16–20	−0.257	−0.307	−0.261	−0.269
Age 21–25	−0.184	−0.200	−0.165	−0.165
Age 26–30	−0.072	−0.079	−0.056	−0.062
Age 31–35	0	0	0	0
Age 36–40	0.051	0.058	0.078	0.053
Age 41–45	0.104	0.106	0.125	0.096
Age 46–50	0.116	0.134	0.157	0.127
Age 51–55	0.129	0.139	0.184	0.161
Age 56–60	0.120	0.138	0.209	0.188
Age 61 and older	0.084	0.150	0.305	0.225
0–7 classes	−0.098	−0.063	−0.109	−0.067
Primary	0	0	0	0
Vocational, manual	0.096	0.099	0.108	0.096
Secondary	0.118	0.143	0.200	0.188
Higher	0.344	0.426	0.501	0.458
Job: manual	0	0	0	0
Job: nonmanual	0.087	0.156	0.184	0.269
Job: managerial	0.477	0.795	0.677	0.823
Regional dummies (15)	yes	yes	yes	yes
Industry dummies (35)	yes	yes	yes	yes
Constant	8.38	8.77	9.36	9.76
Number of observations	145,450	145,453	131,288	151,408
aR^2	0.4642	0.4688	0.4900	0.4751

Note: All parameters are significant at the 0.01 level.

In Table 3-6, wage relativities are examined. The log gross monthly earnings of workers observed in the WS are regressed on a series of demographic and human capital variables (X), job classification (Z), regional (R), and two-digit industry (I) dummies. All workers in the WS of the relevant year are included:

$$\log w_i = b^*(X, Z, R, I)_i.$$

Table 3-7. Estimation of Profit Change and/or Loss-Making

Category	1986–89 OLS		1989–92 Probit		1992–93 Probit	
Profit/sales 1989 (log)	Dependent					
Profit/sales 1986 (log)	0.388	18.6				
Loss-maker 1992	–	–	Dependent			
Loss-maker 1993	–	–	–		Dependent	
Loss-maker 1992	–	–	–		0.429	18.8
Sales ((log)	0.152	2.9	–0.225	–.7.4	–0.271	–10.7
Employment ((log)	–0.030	–0.3	–0.001	0.0	–0.047	–1.0
Wage ((log)	0.191	1.8	–0.078	–1.1	–0.187	–2.5
Construction	–0.186	–3.0	0.020	0.3	–0.005	–0.1
Agriculture	0.279	6.3	0.272	7.9	–0.069	–2.4
Transport	–0.372	2.9	–0.137	–1.2	–0.056	–0.9
Trade	–0.375	–7.5	–0.033	–0.8	–0.078	–2.6
Services	0.327	2.4	–0.071	–0.7	–0.053	–1.0
Industry not available	0.389	1.3	0.120	0.4	–0.115	–2.0
Private	–	–	–0.019	–0.5	–0.060	–2.2
Foreign	–	–	0.327	2.2	–0.021	–0.041
Mixed, unknown	–	–	0.055	1.0	0.031	1.0
c	0.097	1.4	–	–	–	–
Predicted P	–	–	0.641		0.360	
aR^2, pseudo R^2	0.237		0.164		0.203	
F, χ^2	73.7	0.00	264.5	0.00	639.2	
–Log likelihood	–		685.2		1254.9	
Number of observations	2,342		1,235		2,378	

We will not interpret all the parameters in the earnings functions. A detailed analysis of changing differentials by gender, age, education, and region is given in Kertesi and Köllo (1995a), which also deals with the problem of selectivity bias. Here the attention is restricted to results directly relevant to the study of wage setting at the enterprise level.[15]

Finally, table 3-7 presents profit equations. In 1986–89, after-tax profit/gross sales is measured as a continuous variable and OLS is used. In 1992 and 1993, profit figures became increasingly unreliable; we therefore restrict ourselves to the meaningful difference between loss-making firms

---

15. The reader may have realized that the discussion of fixed assets is missing from the plan summarized here. The technical problems arising from revaluations and the changing composition of capital proved too difficult to solve.

and those with positive or zero profit ($\pi = 1$ if the firm was loss-maker, and 0 otherwise). For 1989–92 and 1992–93, the probability of loss-making is estimated with binary probit.

$$\pi_t = b^*(\pi_{t-k}, \Delta\log q, \Delta\log n, \Delta\log w, ppi, X).$$

The major aim is to observe how profits were affected by changes in employment and wages; revenues are held constant. For a brief overview, the profit margin or the loss-making dummy is regressed on a lagged term, the branch-specific price index, real output change, employment and wage change, and one-digit industry dummies to capture subsidies or other fiscal effects that do not appear in prices. Because the number of loss-makers was very small in 1989, the lagged term has been omitted in the estimation for 1992. In the probit equations we present the marginal effects evaluated at the mean (or default value) of the right-hand-side variables.

Sampling Bias and Measurement Errors

The firm samples used in the paper are potentially biased; there are at least two reasons for this. On the one hand, we observe firms under the condition of the possibly nonrandom event that they survive in period *(t, t + k)*. On the other hand, after detecting measurement error with some variables, the panel samples were reduced to enterprises that met selected criteria; doing so introduced another source of bias.

By looking at longitudinal samples, closing and newly established firms are automatically excluded. This is a severe restriction in a transforming economy where thousands of firms are dismantled or merged with others in search of more efficient organizational forms, to seek rents, to avoid taxes, or to hide from creditors. Not only *de novo* and dying firms are ignored, but also all enterprises involved in spin-offs, dismantling, mergers, or any other change that affected their legal personality (and hence their identification code).

Unfortunately, the magnitude of bias could not be precisely measured, but an attempt was made to ascertain its direction. Figure 3-5 shows the path of employment in all firms and institutions observed by the CSO. The curve depicts the level of employment (1989 = 100). The employment paths observed in our samples were fitted to the macroeconomic path. The gap between the two curves at the end of a panel period shows net job creation in the rest of the economy (in the world outside the panel). It is clear that *we observe faster employment decline in the longitudinal samples*

Figure 3-5. Employment: CSO and Longitudinal Samples

1989 = 100

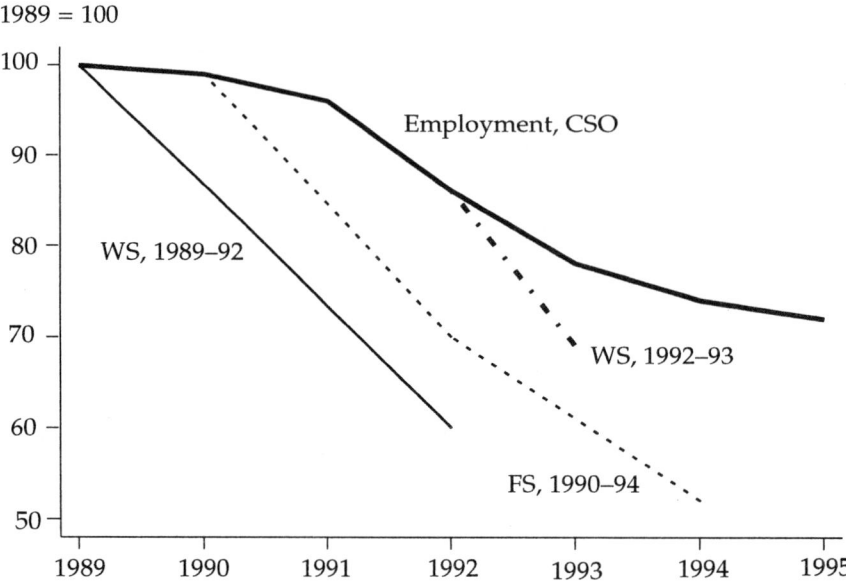

than in the economy as a whole. The gap is attributable to the budget sector, and primarily to the net balance of birth and death of businesses. The analysis of the short panels biased the samples toward firms *destroying* jobs.

The panel is also biased toward less-efficient firms in 1989–92. Analysis of variance suggested no difference in revenue per worker between firms followed in the panel and firms not followed in 1986 ($F = 0.0$) or 1992 ($F = 0.9$). In 1989, however, $F = 26.3$ (0.000), with a 33 percent difference in productivity in favor of firms not followed in the 1989–92 panel. Here again, the sampling bias toward the *collapsing sectors* of the economy is apparent.

In analyzing the firm panels, we rely on data from CSO financial reports. As demonstrated in Technical Note 3, using these data without cleaning leads to a *crucial* overestimation of the elasticity of wages with respect to productivity, and this results in standard errors biased downward in both employment and wage equations. The main reason for this bias is that payments to workers *not employed* by the firm are occasionally included as part of the firm's wage bill. Therefore, a shift to more outside labor leads to the illusion of growing productivity and average wage, even if labor input and the price of an hour of work did not change.

Thanks to wage data from another source, the problem can be eased by excluding firms that posted considerably different wage figures in the financial report (FR) and the WS. This paper presents findings on firms meeting the criterion:

$$abs[\Delta(w^{FR} - w^{WS})] < Ft\ 5,000.$$

Table 3-8 presents calculations to assess whether the exclusion of wrong cases leads to substantial bias along important dimensions. The probability that a firm is retained for analysis is estimated with logit. The FR-based wage measure has an obvious impact because the higher this figure, the higher the probability that the selection criterion is not met. Large firms had a higher probability of remaining in the sample in 1986–89 and 1992–93. Productivity and ownership had no statistically signifi-

Table 3-8. The Effect of Cleaning: Estimating the Probability That a Firm in the Panel Sample Is Selected for the Cleaned Sample (Logit)
$Prob(s_{t,t+k}) = \Lambda(bX_t)$ where $s_{t,t+k} = 1$ if $abs[\Delta\ (w^{FR} - w^{WS})] < Ft\ 5,000;$ 0 otherwise.

Variables	1986–89		1989–92		1992–93	
(levels, base year)	Coeff.	z	Coeff.	z	Coeff.	z
Average wage (FR)	−0.00019	6.6	−0.00008	−6.2	−0.00042	−12.1
Employment	0.00049	5.5	0.00002	0.7	0.00040	5.3
Sales/worker	−0.03172	−1.8	−0.33177	−1.8	−0.00852	1.5
Construction	−0.14639	−0.8	−0.34933	−2.0	0.17423	1.5
Agriculture	−0.42291	−3.5	−0.00444	−0.0	0.28204	3.2
Transport	−0.50183	−1.1	0.22932	0.6	−0.03069	−0.2
Trade	0.32661	1.9	0.38162	2.9	0.29069	3.1
Services	1.6766	1.6	2.1015	3.4	−0.11562	−0.9
Industry not available	−0.51044	−0.8	−0.16268	−0.2	0.16587	1.0
Private[a]	..	..	−0.11131	−1.1	−0.06018	−0.8
Foreign[a]	..	..	−0.15234	−0.3	0.24289	1.7
Mixed, unknown[a]	..	..	−0.00285	−0.0	0.06852	0.8
c	2.7898	13.5	1.1653	8.0	0.92001	9.6
−Log likelihood	1397.3		1543.9		2991.1	
Pseudo R^2	0.0503		0.0485		0.0574	
chi^2, significance	147.9	0.00	157.3	0.00	364.0	0.00
Number of observations (N)	3,250		2,353		4,589	

a. Ownership dummies refer to majority ownership in 1992.

cant effect. Compared with industrial firms, trade and service ventures had a higher probability of passing the criterion. The other industry dummies are insignificant, except for agriculture, with significant coefficients changing in size, and even sign. The general impression is that the effect of cleaning is not drastic—the composition of the sample is not greatly distorted by retaining cases with meaningful wage statistics. Köllo (1996) presents a more detailed analysis that uses a variety of selection criteria and gives estimates for the uncleaned sample and various subgroups.

Results: Chronological Overview

The Pre-Transition Period, 1986–89

EMPLOYMENT, 1986–89. The evolution of employment and its relation to output can best be examined in figure 3-6. The graph plots firms by their changes in output and employment using log scales; the circles denoting enterprises are proportional to their size in 1986.[16] It is clear from the plot that almost all firms reduced employment in the immediate pre-transition period, but this process had little relationship to changes in output. Net hiring seems more frequent in expanding firms, but even in this group, the majority reduced employment.

When summarized in numbers rather than graphics, the estimated elasticity of employment to output is 0.127 in the univariate model and 0.190 in the two-equations model. The difference is not as striking as in the single-equation model; the coefficient combines the direct effect with an indirect effect of opposite sign—growing output leads to higher wages through increasing productivity and reduces employment. The relationship between output and employment seems stronger in the case of decreasing output: the downward elasticity is 0.201, while the upward elasticity is not significantly different from zero.

The constants of the employment equations hint at massive labor shedding unrelated to sales (a magnitude of 20–27 percent in all subgroups). There is no difference between firms increasing, and those decreasing, sales in this respect.

The rate of job destruction was the highest in medium-size firms. Enterprises that employ more than 1,000 workers had a 12.5 percent higher level of employment than medium-size firms in 1989 relative to 1986, other

---

16. The scatterplots in this paper exclude heavy outliers. Graphs showing all firms are available in Köllo (1996).

Figure 3-6. Change of Output and Employment (left panel) and Change of Productivity and Wage (right panel) in the WSFP Samples

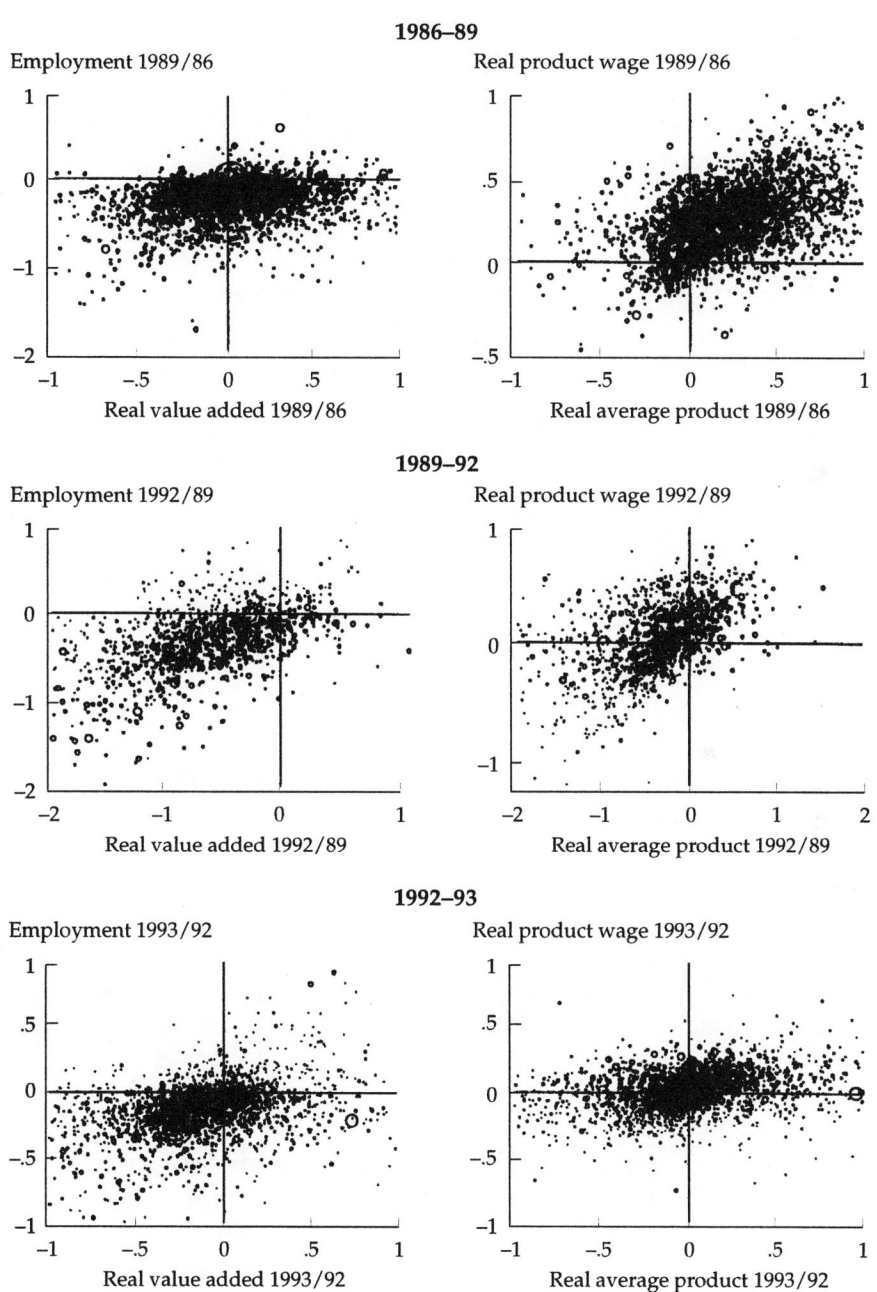

1986–89

Employment 1989/86   Real product wage 1989/86

Real value added 1989/86   Real average product 1989/86

1989–92

Employment 1992/89   Real product wage 1992/89

Real value added 1992/89   Real average product 1992/89

1992–93

Employment 1993/92   Real product wage 1993/92

Real value added 1993/92   Real average product 1993/92

Note: Log scales. The circles are proportional to firm size in the base year.

things being equal (see table 3-3). The parameter for small firms ($n < 100$) is also positive and significant. The result is consistent with expectations— the largest employment cuts occurred in the size category most affected by pre-transition reforms. (Many large firms remained under state control until 1990, and small ones had more freedom before 1986, so the magnitude of change may have been the largest in the medium-size category.)

The employment equations in table 3-3 suggest a strong tradeoff between wages and employment: a 1 percent higher average wage appears to reduce employment by more than half a percent. The causation might be reversed, of course, because this is a simultaneous equations system, with one of the equations normalized for employment by choice. The coefficient is three times as high as in 1989–92, and higher by a factor of two than in 1992–93.

Although the interpretation of this parameter may be a matter of debate, in the case of the pre-transition firm, assuming direct linkage between the reduction of employment and a fast-growing average wage is supported by intuition and experience. Firms with an accumulated stock of low-productivity jobs and workers could trade off employment for higher wages without a major effect on output, and hence with a positive effect on productivity. In addition, such firms could move to lower output and employment levels with the aim of achieving higher wages, as discussed earlier. Accordingly, we find the employment-wage tradeoff to be the strongest in firms decreasing both output and employment. The b coefficients in simple employment equations of the form $n = aq + b(w/p) + c$ (n, q, and w in change of logs) are 0.077 in the case of q, $n > 0$; –0.206 if $q < 0$, $n > 0$; –0.384 when $q > 0$, $n < 0$; and –0.643 in firms where q, $n < 0$.

WAGES, 1986–89. The results suggest that changes in employment had a marked, adverse effect on the average wage, while sales had virtually no effect. The role of employment cuts is also demonstrated by the relatively low number of firms increasing output (49.6 percent) and the high proportion increasing productivity (76.9 percent). As a result, no major wage adjustment or change in labor's share was required to avert the adverse impact of negative shocks.

As shown in table 3-3, wages were not significantly affected by the sales record of the employer: we get positive, significant, but very low elasticities (around 0.05). The effect of productivity change was not very strong either. The wage equation in table 3-3 indicates $dw/d(q/n) = 0.06$, and shows a similarly weak connection with the branch-specific ppi. The univariate estimate of the wage-productivity relationship hints at a slightly closer correlation (an elasticity of 0.131). This is consistent with the finding of a highly significant tradeoff between employment and wages: the parameter in the univariate estimate combines the effect of a "sharing rule" (productivity to wage), with a feedback effect that leads from higher wages to lower employment at given sales revenues, and hence to higher productivity and back to wages.

Existing nonlinearities are easy to check in table 3-4 and figure 3-6. While decreasing productivity did not necessarily imply wage cuts, most firms increasing average productivity raised wages, and most of the firms raising wages did so by increasing productivity.

The productivity-wage relationship is also dealt with in the wage-level estimations in table 3-5. The elasticity of the firm's average wage with respect to value added per worker increased from 0.275 to 0.369 between 1986 and 1989.

WAGE DISPERSION, 1986–89. Wage differentials substantially increased in 1986–89; the Gini coefficient rose from 0.217 to 0.263 (Kertesi and Köllo 1995a). That was actually a larger increase than the one observed during the early stage of transition. The earnings functions presented in table 3-6 reveal that the differentials generally grew along with education and position. The advantage held by secondary school graduates over workers with only a primary school education rose by a modest 3.5 percent, but the advantage of university graduates increased from 34.4 to 42.6 percent. The advantage of nonmanual workers over blue-collar employees increased from 8.7 to 15.6 percent after controlling for education. Managers of all ranks raised their wage advantage over workers from 47.7 to 79.5 percent, a rate that is substantially higher than those observed after the collapse of Communism.

PROFITS, 1986–89. The profit equation of table 3-7 calls attention to strong price and industry effects, but it does not suggest that the changes in employment and average wage are effective predictors of changes in profit. The test applied here is elementary, but the low and insignificant parameters do not promise robust coefficients from more sophisticated models. We interpret the results as an indication that employment cuts left the profit rate unchanged, while wage increases had a weak *positive* rather than negative effect.[17]

---

17. The latter result is consistent with those presented in Halpern and Korösi (1995)

SUMMARY, 1986–89. The immediate pre-transition years do not give the impression of a motionless world waiting for the "big bang." Considerable cuts are observed in employment for almost all firms covered in the panel. The development of small and medium-size firms and a rise in self-employment and public sector employment could offset the effect of job destruction in larger firms. Open unemployment could stay below 1 percent until 1990, but the transition seems to have started several years before the political reforms began.

These findings are consistent with the expectation presented earlier: firms began to shed labor, irrespective of external market signals. They typically did so without undermining productivity, and the productivity gains helped maintain or increase wages, especially those for managers and more qualified workers.

The Transformational Crisis, 1989–92

EMPLOYMENT, 1989–92. Figure 3-6 leaves no doubt that output and employment changes were more closely correlated in this period than they had been earlier. More than 90 percent of the firms had lower output in 1992 than in 1989, and the overwhelming majority of enterprises cut employment, including most firms that increased production. In the small set of firms that expanded employment, there is no observable connection between output and staff levels. Output *decline* and employment *decline*, however, were rather closely correlated.

The impressions from the graph are reinforced by tables 3-2 and 3-3. The 2SLS estimation suggests that the elasticity of employment with respect to output was more than doubled by increasing from a range of 0.19 to 0.35. The single-equation estimate is similar (0.33). The reaction of the firm is asymmetric: the downward elasticity is 0.346, but the statistical upward elasticity is zero.

The estimates also suggest that employment cuts unrelated to output were less typical than they had been in 1986–89. The equations for constant terms of employment are in the range of 6–12 percent, as opposed to 20–27 percent in the pre-transition period. The coincidence of output and employment cuts is also shown by the fit of the simplest univariate model $n = f(q)$ in 1986–89 ($R^2 = 0.0499$) and in 1989–92 ($R^2 = 0.3442$).

The tradeoff between employment and wages that was so strong in 1986–89 seems to fade away after 1989 (the estimated parameter is –0.165, as opposed to –0.564 before 1989). In an environment where practically all firms are hit by strong negative shocks, we would expect such a tradeoff to emerge if some firms reacted to the fall in output by cutting wages, while others cut employment instead. The former was a common practice in some Eastern European countries, such as Romania, and particularly in Russia, but was uncommon in Hungary. As shown in table 3-4, the elasticity of the real wage with respect to output was only 0.049, a level not significantly different from that estimated for 1986–89.

Table 3-4 shows that the large firms hit hardest by the systemic change cut employment faster—by 12.6 percent at a given output—than those employing 101–1,000 workers. Small firms kept employment high relative to output in 1989–92. We interpret this finding with caution because, as suggested by the interview-based analysis of Laki (1994), small firms typically regard dismissals as a measure of last resort, and they will generally cut working time instead. It may be that *hours* relative to output did not remain higher in small firms.

WAGES, 1989–92. The equations suggest no dramatic change in the responsiveness of wages to sales or productivity. The elasticity of wage on sales remained unchanged. The relationship between changes in wage and productivity remained weak (coefficients of 0.120 from 2SLS and 0.141 from univariate regressions). It is important to note, however, that real average product decreased in three out of four firms in this period. Therefore, the same weak connection now reflected correlations between productivity *loss* and wage *cuts*, unlike 1986–89. In addition, *as a group*, firms that decreased productivity had slower wage growth than the *group* that improved their records, as shown by the constants in table 3-4.

The relationship between the *dynamics* of w and q/n was not powerful enough to further strengthen the linkage between the *levels* of productivity and wages. Table 3-5 suggests that the explanatory power of productivity in the cross-sectional wage equation was actually lower in 1992 than in 1989, after controlling for industry and other effects.

A NOTE ON INDUSTRY WAGE EFFECTS, 1989–92. Table 3-5 suggests that the variation in wage change in 1989–92 was largely explained by *industry affiliation* rather than firm-level characteristics (branch-specific *ppi* was found to have a strong effect). This is consistent with observations presented in Kertesi and Köllo (1995b), which suggest that industry effects were highly important in shaping individual wages in the WS sample in this period.[18] They find that the pure industry-specific wage returns—those controlled for gender, age, education, position in the hierarchy, and

---

18. Analysis of variance of wages by industry yields $F = 205$ in 1986 and $F = 98$ in 1989, but $F = 262$ and $F = 205$ again in 1992 and 1994, respectively.

region—grew fastest in *petroleum mining, petroleum refining, energy, mail and telecommunications, railways,* and *public transport.* The relative earnings of workers employed in these sectors improved by 15–30 percent in 1989–92 after controlling for human capital, demographic attributes, and region.

The industries in question were—and most still are—dominated by a small number of large firms. This group includes one firm in petroleum mining and refining, two noncompeting firms in railways, one firm in mail and telecommunications, and local monopolies in public transport. Competition is constrained in several ways: import competition is limited or impossible, prices are controlled by the central or local governments, and entry into the market is very costly. Not all the constraints apply to all industries, but one or more of the factors are present in each industry.[19] Furthermore, we propose that these constraining factors do not apply outside this group, with perhaps a single exception.[20] It may also be of significance that the group of monopolized industries had higher than average *ppi* in 1989–92, lower than average output fall, and lower than average employment loss.[21]

These results are supported by table 3-5, where a dummy for the group of highly monopolized (two-, three-, or four-digit) industries is presented alongside one-digit industry dummies, on the right. A spectacular 16 percent jump on the wage ladder is observed in monopolized sectors, even after controlling for productivity.

A NOTE ON LOCAL WAGE CURVES, 1989–92. Transition brought about an increase in unemployment, which rose from zero to 12.9 percent by the end of 1992. Evidence from Mincer-style earnings functions (Kertesi and Köllo 1995) supports the conclusion that wages were strongly affected by this major change. Wage curves relating the region-specific components of wages to regional unemployment (as measured in 1994) are already

---

19. Mail and telecommunications is no exception. Competition in the telephone market received a strong impetus only at the end of the period discussed here, with the entry of mobile phone networks. The mail service was dominated by Magyar Posta throughout this time.

20. The exceptions are bauxite mining and aluminum processing. Unfortunately, it is not possible to separate this branch from other sectors in the *Other Mining* category.

21. Prices grew by 214 percent in the monopolized group, as opposed to 182 percent in other industries (calculated as an average weighted with sales in the base year). Output fell by 25 as opposed to 62 percent, and employment fell by 19 as opposed to 42 percent. The figures relate to the WSFP sample.

easy to observe in 1986 or 1989, but they turned markedly clockwise as unemployment appeared and increased.

The cross-sectional estimates at the firm level in table 3-5 tell a similar story. Firms operating in regions hit by high unemployment in 1992 already had lower wages in 1989, when national unemployment was still below 1 percent. The parameter for (the log of) the March 1992 rate of unemployment is –0.051 in the 1989 wage equation. The parameter for the same firms and the same unemployment rates is three times that high (–0.154) in 1992.[22]

We also get a negative but insignificant coefficient in the wage equation in table 3-3. This coincides with the observation that enterprise average wages were loosely correlated with (future) unemployment rates before the transition.

WAGE DISPERSION, 1989–92. The transition period brought about further differentiation by education. The return to secondary education grew further, from 14.3 to 20 percent (over return to primary schooling). The advantage of workers with a higher education background grew from 42.6 to 50.0 percent. These figures are controlled for differences in job classification. The earnings of nonmanual workers relative to the blue-collar workforce increased by an additional 6 percent, while managerial earnings (having increased substantially in 1986–89) now decreased relative to manual workers, after controlling for education and other characteristics (see table 3-6). The Gini coefficient for gross monthly earnings, starting from a value of 0.21 in 1986, grew to 0.29 by the end of the second stage of transition.

PROFITS, 1989–92. For reasons presented earlier, we estimated the probability of loss-making in 1992 with a binary probit. The results, shown in table 3-7, demonstrate that employment and wage change during 1989–92 had no significant impact on the probability of loss-making.[23] It seems that even huge employment and/or wage cuts proved insufficient to avert a general decline in profitability during the transformational crisis.

---

22. We measure the rate of unemployment recorded in 170 labor office areas by dividing the number of registered unemployed in December 1992 and 1993 with the labor force in 1990.

23. It was also observed that firms with majority foreign ownership had a greater chance of making losses, but we remind readers that there were only seventeen firms in the 1989–92 panel.

SUMMARY, 1989–92. The tremendous shock of the transition led to massive job destruction in almost all firms. The connection between output and employment became much stronger during this time. The rate of job displacement was generally insufficient to avoid the fall in productivity, and required downward adjustment of wages as well.

It seems, however, that enterprise-level variables are not particularly successful in explaining wage change in this period. The wage-productivity relationship at the enterprise level remained rather weak, but both considerable aggregate wage cuts and significant differences by regions, industries, and job categories were observed.

Given the size of the shock, and that practically *all* firms had to reduce both output and employment tremendously, it is difficult to determine if the employment and wage setting patterns characteristic of the 1986–89 period survived. The post-1992 period provides a better opportunity for testing.

The Later Stage of Transition: 1992–93, 1992–94

EMPLOYMENT, 1992–93. Figure 3-6 and table 3-2 suggest that in 1993, downward elasticity did not significantly differ from the value prevailing in 1989–92. Firms that increased their output did not necessarily expand employment, and we again get zero elasticity in this group. The regression line for the whole sample becomes flatter because the proportion of such firms increased from 1/10 to 1/3. No major change in output elasticity can be observed as the new stage of transition starts. Similarly, the constant terms of employment equations remain negative and are roughly equal to the levels for 1989–92. The coefficient of the wage term in the employment equation (see table 3-3) is higher than it was in 1989–92, but much lower than it was in 1986–89.

WAGES, 1992–93. Wages seemed to be less responsive to the firm's productivity in 1993 than in 1989–92; the estimated parameters all fall close to zero. The effect of the *ppi* completely disappears. The cross-sectional estimates of table 3-5 hint at no change in the productivity-wage relationship.[24]

---

24. A stronger relationship is seen between value added and wages in 1992 if it is estimated from the 1992–93 panel (0.33), and lower (0.29) when the 1989–92 panel is used. This is arguably so because the panel for 1992–93 includes more small and medium-size firms, and it already covers enterprises established during the transition.

WAGE DISPERSION, 1992–93. The transformation of the wage hierarchy seemed to settle down after 1992. The differences based on education diminish as the extreme groups (workers with 0–7 classes and university graduates) move inward. The differences between manual and office workers, however, increased further; the advantage of nonmanagerial office workers reached 27 percent, and that of managers amounted to 82 percent (after controlling for education) by 1994. The Gini coefficient for gross monthly earnings also increased, and reached 0.32 in 1994.

An overview of the observations suggests that the combined effect of education and job characteristics on relative wages during the transition was substantial. The net advantage of a middle-level manager with a university degree over an unqualified manual worker increased from 82 percent in 1986 to 128 percent in 1994. An office worker with a secondary school background earned more, by 20 percent in 1986 but by 46 percent in 1994.

PROFITS, 1992–93. The probability of loss-making in 1993 was higher by 42 percent if the firm had been a loss-maker in 1992. The equation in table 3-7 reveals the strong impact of the year's sales record and suggests a 6 percent lower probability of negative profit in private firms. There appears to be no connection between employment dynamics and profitability; higher wages are associated with a lower probability of loss-making.

EMPLOYMENT, 1992–94 (FS). There is additional information on the evolution of employment from the FS firm panel for the post-1992 period. As mentioned previously, the FS data on economic performance are not measured on the interval level and capture the manager's evaluation rather than actual changes. Table 3-9 details two measures that allow the changes in employment to be examined. The first is the firm's sales revenue over the previous year as reported by the responding manager in August. The other is the volume of orders given to the firm in the third quarter compared with the previous year's orders, evaluated on a rough scale (of "more," "same," "fewer"). The employment figures are observed on the interval level and reflect actual values, except for the 1994 year-end value, which is an estimate by the manager in August 1994.

In 1992, 40 percent of the enterprises in the sample foresaw decreasing orders, and less than 20 percent expected a rise. Employment decreased in all categories of sales and orders, except for a small minority of firms that increased sales by more than 20 percent (table 3-10).

In 1993 the proportion of firms that faced decreasing sales and/or orders declined, but employment, at best, remained unchanged. The fig-

Table 3-9. Employment and Wage Elasticities by Ownership (WSFP)

Category	State	Private	Privatized (in 1993)	Foreign	Other
1989–92					
Employment/sales	0.351		0.347	–	0.473
(percent, falling sales)	(90.8)		(94.4)	–	(94.1)
Wage/productivity	0.215		0.351	–	0.317
(percent, falling productivity)	(74.9)		(80.0)	–	(76.2)
1992–93					
Employment/sales	0.241	0.290	0.108	n.s.	0.240
(percent, falling sales)	(71.3)	(67.9)	(65.2)	(45.1)	(66.1)
Wage/productivity	0.061	0.151	0.068	0.099	0.196
(percent, falling productivity)	(53.4)	(55.4)	(43.0)	(45.3)	(52.1)
Employment/sales					
Rising sales	n.s.	0.235	n.s.	n.s.	0.161
Falling sales	0.321	0.289	0.293	0.664	0.225
Wage/productivity					
Rising productivity	n.s	0.115	n.s.	0.035	n.s.
Falling productivity	0.101	0.129	0.107	0.250	0.129

n.s. Not significant at the 0.05 level.

Note: Univariate estimations on full samples weighted with $1/abs[\Delta(w^{FR} - w^{WS})]$. Ownership defined by majority stockholding at the end of the period. Privatized: majority state in 1992, majority private or foreign in 1993. Producer real wage.

ures do not suggest a clear pattern of change: the employment/sales relationship appears to be weaker in the range of successful firms, but the connection between employment and orders seems stronger.

The suggestions for 1994 are less uncertain. The relationship between employment and sales, as well as orders, became stronger. Like the WSFP, we find no evidence in the FS sample of a weakening connection between the firm's economic performance and employment. As far as the poor proxies at hand allow any conclusion to be drawn, the opposite seems to be true in 1994.

SUMMARY, 1992–94. The link between output and employment became stronger rather than weaker in 1993–94. Again, positive shocks did not imply hiring, but negative shocks were associated with massive labor shedding. The downward elasticity was close to the level that prevailed

Table 3-10. Sales, Orders, and Employment in the FS Sample, 1992–94
(percentage over previous year)

Sales and orders	Employment			Cumulative distribution of firms by sales/orders		
	1992	*1993*	*1994*	*1992*	*1993*	*1994*
Sales						
80 or fewer		69.0	54.7		9.6	9.9
80/90	78.9	79.0	75.6	47.0	16.7	16.9
90/100		88.2	81.0		28.0	22.6
100	92.6	89.7	85.8	70.8	52.5	46.2
100/105		94.1	91.2		64.5	58.8
105/110		95.9	96.4		80.1	79.1
110/115	96.2	90.4	101.4	87.8	88.3	87.4
115/120		98.8	100.0		93.2	92.2
120 or more	110.5	100.8	126.7	100.0	100.0	100.0
Orders						
Fewer	80.5	80.3	72.0	39.3	35.0	27.0
Same	94.2	90.1	87.1	80.1	68.5	62.5
More	95.7	100.2	105.5	100.0	100.0	100.0

in 1989–92. We find no evidence of enhanced wage adjustment in either direction in 1993. On the contrary, the elasticity of average wage change to productivity change was estimated to be markedly lower than in earlier years. The link between the levels of productivity and average wage was also slightly weakening, rather than strengthening, in 1993.

With a lack of data from recent years, as well as comparable evidence from other researchers, it is too early to make strong statements about the nature of post-1992 development. But the findings are sufficiently consistent in that they all cast doubt on the assumption of continuing worker control. Instead, they raise the suspicion of a move toward more flexible setting of employment and less revenue sharing.

Differences by Ownership

The discussion of ownership-specific differences is restricted to the relationship between employment and output on the one hand, and the

Table 3-11. Employment and Sales by Ownership (FS, 1992–94)

Sales	Change of employment (percent)			
	State	Private	Privatized (by end of the year)	Coop
1992				
Sales over previous year				
"Decreased"	−11.6	−19.2	−19.9	−24.9
"Did not change"	−14.7	−13.3	−16.4	−15.5
"Increased by 1–20%"	−10.7	5.8	−5.5	−14.3
"Increased by 20 or more %"	−4.6	16.6	−6.4	−8.4
Employment/sales elasticities[a]				
Unweighted				
1993	0.279	0.388	0.136	0.163
1994	0.273	0.839	0.688	0.627
Weighted				
1993	0.183	0.199	n.s.	0.172
1994	0.315	0.846	0.694	0.446

n.s. Not significant at the 0.05 level.

a. The elasticities reported here are the slopes of the best-fitting linear curves on figure 3-7. Unweighted: ds_j compared to $\Sigma_i \, (n_t/n_{t-1})/k_j$; weighted: ds_j compared to $\Sigma_i \, n_t/\Sigma_i \, n_{t-1}$.

impact of productivity on the producer real wage (labor's share) on the other. The most important figures are summarized in tables 3-9 (WSFP) and 3-11 (FS).

Employment by Sector

The WSFP numbers for 1989–92 do not hint at large differences between state firms and firms that were private from the onset, or those privatized early in the transition. It should be noted that the panel for 1989–92 is likely to include firms that belong to this last group, because the number of genuinely private firms that employed more than twenty workers in 1989 was probably very small (ownership was not recorded in 1989, hence the uncertainty). The output-elasticity of employment is 0.351 for state firms, 0.347 for private/privatized firms, and 0.473 for firms with unknown ownership or without a majority owner. These figures virtually designate the downward elasticity, because the proportion of firms that increased output was below 10 percent in each group. [25]

The data for 1993 reveal considerable differences based on ownership. Here we can distinguish between firms that remained state-owned at the end of 1993, those privatized in 1993, and enterprises already in private hands in 1992. The differences in sales records varied: 70 percent of the state firms, 66 percent of the nonstate firms, and less than 50 percent of the foreign firms reduced output. The reaction of employment to output was asymmetric in state and newly privatized firms: the upward elasticities were zero, while the downward elasticities were 0.321 and 0.293, respectively. The relationship between output and employment appears to be very strong in the group of foreign firms hit by a negative shock (0.664), but firms that increased production seemed to do so without additional hiring.[26]

Unlike state-owned, newly privatized, and foreign firms, Hungarian private enterprises had significant, although not particularly high, elasticities in both directions: 0.290 in the case of increasing output and 0.289 in the case of decreasing output. The results for firms of unknown or mixed ownership (these are likely to be private rather than state-owned) are similar, although not as highly symmetric: the estimated elasticities are 0.161 upward and 0.225 downward.

In the FS sample, where firms were followed between 1992 and 1994, the assessment of employment elasticities needs more preparation—and courage, given the problem with measurement levels. For each firm we know a range of sales relative to the previous year, and we have interval-level data on the change of employment. The ranges for sales are very broad in 1992; table 3-11 presents the mean change of employment in each sales range and ownership group. In 1993 and 1994, when the ranges were narrower, we used the following procedure: (a) graphs were drawn (figure 3-7) that related the midpoint of each range of sales to the mean change of employment in that sales category; (b) the revenue figure considered in the open ranges ($dR < 75$ and $dR > 125$) was taken from the WSFP of 1992–93 by calculating $E(dR \mid dR < 75)$ and $E(dR \mid dR > 125)$; and (c) a linear curve was fitted to each employment-sales curve. The slope of

---

25. Because we only have a dozen firms privatized by foreigners in the 1989–92 panel, calculating measures of association would make no sense. These firms are excluded here.

26. The parameter $q > 0$ is –0.187 because of two heavy outliers, but increases to 0.076 ($t = 1.2$) if the outliers are excluded.

Figure 3-7. Change of Employment by Change of Sales over Previous Year (FS)

State Firms Compared with Private Firms

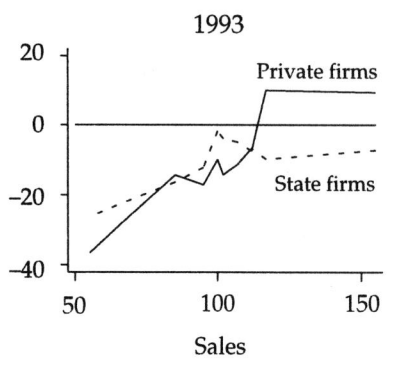

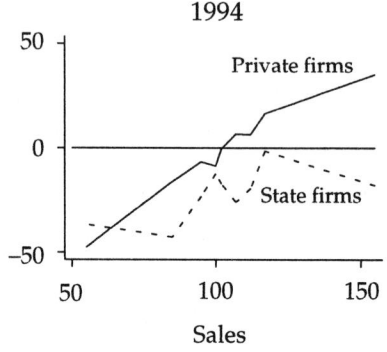

Privatized Firms Compared with Private Firms

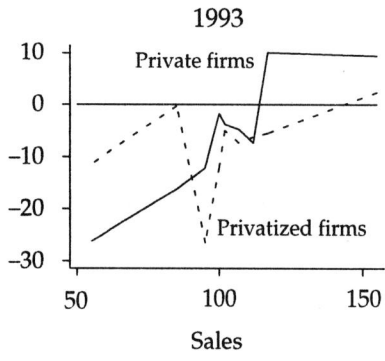

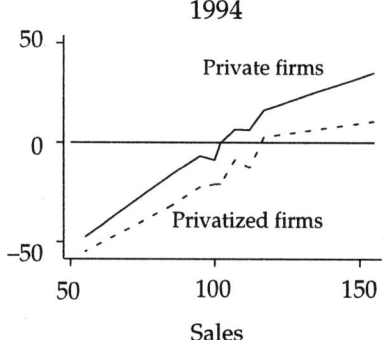

Cooperatives Compared with Private Firms

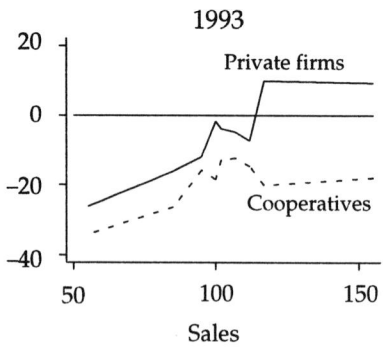

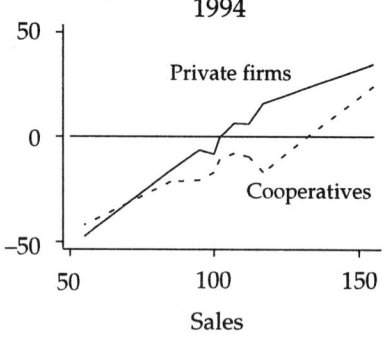

the best-fitting linear curve has been reported as a proxy for the employ-ment/sales elasticity in table 3-11.

The first of the two sets of indicators in table 3-11 (unweighted) comes from the relation of dR to $\Sigma_i(n_t/n_{t-1})/k$, or the average employment change of the k enterprises in a sales range. The second (weighted) set reports how dR is related to $(\Sigma_i\ n_t)/(\Sigma_i\ n_{t-1})$, or the change of total employment in a sales category. Ownership in the FS is defined in a slightly different way than in the WSFP. We can make a distinction between state-owned firms and cooperatives. A firm is regarded as priva-tized in 1994 if it had majority state ownership in 1992 but reported priva-tization in the FS in, or before, 1994.

The data for 1992 depict an already familiar picture: state firms, newly privatized enterprises, and cooperatives cut employment even if they performed well in the market. Job destruction unrelated to output is also important everywhere, except for genuinely private firms.

In 1993 state firms and cooperatives continued to cut employment in all sales categories. Not surprisingly, changes of employment were unrelated to output in firms privatized during the year. In private firms, the sales-employment curve is nearly linear, steeper than in other firm categories, and hints at net hiring where sales grew rapidly. A comparison of the weighted and unweighted measures, however, reveals that the favorable employment record in this category can be attributed to rapid growth in some firms rather than to a general recovery of labor demand in the pri-vate sector as a whole.

The year of 1994 brought major changes in the patterns of the sales-employment relationship in the FS sample. The relationship became rather strong in both private and privatized firms (the slopes are 0.839 and 0.688). The unweighted employment measure hints at similar change in cooperatives, but a comparison with the result from the weighted sam-ple (0.446, as opposed to 0.627) suggests that this may not apply to the average cooperative. In contrast, the weighted and unweighted measures are almost equal in the private and privatized sectors. The elasticity of employment to output remained low in state firms (0.273), and these firms continued to decrease employment in all categories of sales.

The weak evidence we can draw from our two sources of information suggests that in the private sector, which is slowly becoming dominant in the Hungarian economy, the relationship between employment and out-put is becoming closer over time. Cutting employment, irrespective of output, was highly important in the early stages of transition in the pri-vate sector as well. The data, however, suggest net hiring by successful private firms in 1992 (FS), 1993 (FS, WSFP), and especially in 1994 (FS).

The employment record of privatized firms does not seem to have been bright during, or right after, privatization (WSFP 1993; FS 1992, 1993), but their pattern in the sales-employment relationship became very similar to that observed in private firms in 1994 (FS), and the most successful privatized firms started to (net) hire in 1993, and increased hiring in 1994.

Wages by Sector

Calculations by Kertesi and Köllo (1995b), using individual earnings data from the 1993 wave of the WS, suggested that the effect of ownership on wages was very modest, except in the case of foreign enterprises. Earnings in Hungarian-owned private firms were not different from those paid by state firms at conventional levels of significance, after controlling for human capital variables, region, industry, and firm size. Wages in mixed (private-state, private-foreign, and state-foreign) firms were higher by 8 percent, and those in majority foreign-owned firms were higher by 20 percent. In the latter case, the statistical findings coincide with the experience—validated by the media rather than research—that foreign firms entering the Hungarian labor market used higher wage levels as a screening device, especially in the case of executives and qualified office staff. Kertesi and Köllo (1995b) found that the 1993 adjusted wage gap between foreign and Hungarian firms was 17.5 percent for manual workers, 25.4 percent for nonmanual staff, and 44.1 percent for managers.

Because private firms tend to employ a less-educated work force, and foreign firms a more educated group than the state sector, the differences between average enterprise wages are biased downward in the former and upward in the latter (see the unadjusted deviations in table 3-12). By

Table 3-12. Unadjusted Deviation of Mean Enterprise Average Wages from the State Sector Mean, Compared with Adjusted Deviations Derived from the Cross-Sectional Estimations
(percent)

Ownership (end of the period)	1992 (from WSFP 1989–92)		1992 (from WSFP 1992–93)		1993 (from WSFP 1992–93)	
	Unadjusted	Adjusted	Unadjusted	Adjusted	Unadjusted	Adjusted
Private	−10.1	−4.3	−3.1	−7.5	−8.7	−7.6
Foreign	+84.2	+25.3	+45.7	+5.0	+30.4	+3.8
Mixed, n.a.	−3.0	−3.2	+7.4	+1.2	+2.9	+0.5

Note: Cross-sectional estimations are presented in table 3-5.

comparing these unadjusted deviations with the regression parameters of ownership dummies in table 3-5, conclusions can be drawn that are similar to those for individual wage data.

Wage differentials between private and state firms are not substantial. The mean enterprise average wage in the private sector is lower by a few percentage points. Controlling for productivity does not alter the sign or order of magnitude of the difference.[27] The data on *foreign firms* make it clear that their wage advantage is supported by considerably higher productivity. The unadjusted advantage of the few new foreign firms in the 1989–92 sample was 84 percent, but the adjusted advantage was only 25 percent. In 1992–93 the unadjusted difference amounted to 30.8 percent, but the adjusted deviation was a mere 3.8 percent.

Finally, let us briefly look at wage responsiveness (see table 3-9). During the transformational crisis, productivity decreased everywhere. Wages were responsive to the fall in the state sector (an elasticity of 0.215), but even more so to the reduction in the private sector (0.351, and 0.317 with mixed/unknown ownership).

The period 1992–93 brought a growing differentiation of firms by productivity change. Wages did not grow with increasing productivity except in the private sector, where the upward elasticity was significant (0.115). Downward wage adjustment was observed in all sectors, but the parameters are low (around 0.1) except in foreign firms, where—alongside a strong tendency to adjust employment to negative shocks—downward wage adjustment seems to be more important (0.250).

Conclusions

The post-1989 transition process was preceded by nontrivial changes in the employment and wage setting behavior of state enterprises. Most cut employment substantially, and the cuts were not strongly related to output. A strong tradeoff between employment and wages was observed. Relative wages within the firm began to grow for office workers, managers in particular. The patterns of employment and wage change were consistent with the forecast of labor shedding induced purely by institutional reforms. There was evidence of massive employment cuts at unchanged output and a strong tradeoff between employment and wages in firms that were cutting output. These findings were consistent with the expec-

---

27. The difference in the composition of the samples warns that the minor relative movements of adjusted and unadjusted figures may have no tractable message.

tation that core workers, managers, or both groups may have been interested in reducing labor hoarding and/or shifting to higher wages and lower output (employment) after taking over the enterprise.

Because Hungary implemented some important reforms before the years of the aggregate shock, this component of the decline in employment was relatively easy to observe. In most former Soviet-bloc countries, where the reforms and the shocks came together, their effects were almost impossible to separate.

The tremendous shock of the transition led to output decline and massive job destruction in almost all firms. The connection between output and employment became stronger, and labor shedding unrelated to output lessened in importance. The speed of employment adjustment usually was insufficient to avoid a fall in productivity, and required the downward adjustment of wages as well. The differences along the job hierarchy increased.

From 1993 onward, one could observe the recovery of GDP, a major slow-down of the employment decline, and large fluctuations of the real wage. These developments raise the suspicion that we are witnessing an insider-effect, which gives increased emphasis to wage adjustment and a stable employment level. Under strong insider influence, however, one would expect that $\partial w / \partial (q/n)$ or $\partial w / \partial q$ would increase over time, and $\partial n / \partial q$ would fall. This is quite clearly *not the case* in the firms analyzed here. The relationship between employment and output is strengthening rather than weakening, a result of behavioral change and a compositional effect. The elasticity of employment with respect to sales or orders seems to have increased in 1994 in all sectors, especially in privatized firms. The expansion of the private sector, which adjusted employment more promptly in response to external shocks, adds the compositional effect.

The relationship between wages and the firm's productivity became almost insignificant in 1993; more wage adjustment and revenue-sharing were observed in private than in state-owned firms in that year. On the basis of these findings, we may consider the possibility that the stable macro level of employment hides an accidental equality of job destruction and job creation, and real wage fluctuations are brought about by forces other than firm-level wage adjustment to expected shocks.

It should be emphasized that the results presented here come from data collected until 1994 (1993 for wages), and the conclusions are based on an elementary overview of the most important correlations. The extension of research in both time and depth is required for an understanding of the apparent contradiction between macro-level developments and enterprise-level findings after 1992.

An important final comment is a warning: this study dealt with a collapsing sector of the Hungarian economy. Since the start of transition, most of the new jobs have been created by new firms, or at least by new "legal personalities." Self-employment and the black economy were—and are—also of prime importance in Hungary, but they were neglected here. What this study tried to capture is how the process of job destruction started, peaked, and settled in a part of a diversifying economy that is decreasing in importance.

Technical Notes

Note 1. The Wage Survey

The Wage Survey was carried out by the National Labour Centre in 1983, 1986, 1989, 1992, 1993, and 1994. The target population of the survey was workers in firms with more than twenty employees, plus budget sector employees. In the nonbudget sector, all firms were approached and asked to provide information on workers born on selected days (before 1992 a stratified sampling procedure was used). In the budget sector, institutions were asked to provide information on all workers. The computer files contain frequency weights attached to each worker. The weights (WEIGHT1) show the number of workers represented by the respondent, given the sampling quota within the firm.

Both the weights and the sample size had to be modified before the analysis. First, the original files did not contain any information on nonresponse, although many small and medium-size firms refused to answer in 1993 and 1994. Therefore we checked the composition of the target population and the samples (by firm size) and attached weights (WEIGHT2) to firms as well. Second, the sampling quotas were sharply different in the budget sector and the firm sector (8–15 percent with firms, 100 percent in the budget sector). Therefore, we drew random samples from the budget subsample using the sampling quota in the firm sector. Third, in some years the files were far too large to allow computations on a PC. We drew random samples to reach the 20–25 mbyte file size that fit the memory of our computers. The final weight we used was WEIGHT3 = WEIGHT1*WEIGHT2. The weights restore representativity under the assumption that nonresponse is not correlated with variables in the equations. In the final computations, carried out with Stata, cases were weighted with Stata's analytical weights to avoid an artificial improvement of standard errors, except in tables, where only frequency weights were allowed.

Note 2. Coverage in the Wage Survey Firm Panels

Table 3-13. Coverage in the WSFP

Characteristic	1986–89	1989–92	1992–93
Number of firms[a]			
CSO	5,156	8,463	13,690
Sample	3,250	2,353	4,589
Sample/CSO	63.0	27.8	33.5
Employment[a]			
CSO	3,384,161	3,630,327	3,069,984
Sample	2,639,602	1,648,377	1,488,400
Sample/CSO	80.0	45.4	48.5

a. Base year, firms employing twenty or more workers.

Note 3. Measurement Errors and Resulting Bias in Financial Reports—
The Payroll Problem

In this note we present evidence that using the FR data without cleaning leads to biased estimation of the output elasticity of employment, as well as to a drastic overestimation of the elasticity of average wage with respect to productivity. The effect of wages on labor demand also appears stronger than it actually is. In an uncleaned sample, we also get downward-biased standard errors.

These are aggravating threats, because the concepts above are central to the analysis of employer behavior. The value of the FR—the *single* data base where figures on employment, wages, and economic performance are jointly available—calls for an effort to diagnose and cure the bias.

The problem is rooted in the laxity of the notion of "payroll" in Hungary: firms can settle a payment from their wage bill by paying workers they do not employ. This payment will be part of their wage cost, but the payee will not appear in the FR as the firm's employee.[28] This is the core of the problem. The far-reaching consequences can be examined first in a simple example.

Imagine four firms with identical characteristics: employment is 100, output is 1,000, and the average wage is 5. Firms A and B are hit by a

---

28. At the same time, not all the employees are paid. Workers on maternity aid, in military service, or on unpaid leave appear as full-time employees in the FR. The bias from this source is not crucial, because the incidence of these events is not closely correlated with economic performance.

Table 3-14. The Story of Firms A–D

Category	Output	Employ-ment	Wage bill	Average wage	Productivity
Before (A–D)	1,000	100	500	5	10
After				5	10
True and reported values				After/before (reported)	
A (true)	800	80	400		
A (reported)	800	80	400	1.00	1.00
B (true)	800	80	400		
B (reported)	800	60	400	1.33	1.33
C (true)	400	40	200		
C (reported)	400	40	200	1.00	1.00
D (true)	400	40	200		
D (reported)	400	30	200	1.33	1.33

minor shock—they have to decrease output by 20 percent. For the sake of simplicity we assume that they cut labor input proportionally, by 20 percent, but they do not cut wages. The difference between A and B is that A displaced twenty workers and bought no outside labor after the adjustment, whereas B displaced forty workers, but kept paying a wage for the services of twenty outside workers. Firms C and D are hit by a major shock—they cut output and labor by 60 percent. C dismissed sixty workers and bought no outside labor, whereas D laid off seventy workers but kept buying ten units of labor from outside.[29] The example is summarized in table 3-14.

Let us now estimate the elasticity of employment to output and the elasticity of average wage to productivity with linear regression using the panel sample of firms A–D. It is easy to check that although the true elasticity of labor input (L) on output (Y) is $dL/dY = 1$, we will estimate $dN/dY = 0.875$. The case is much worse on the wage side. Productivity and the average wage did not actually change at all, but we will posit a robust estimate of $dw/d(Y/N) = 1$. We will also detect a strong negative correlation between dN and dw, while the true value is zero.

---

29. The firm may want to follow the strategy of B or D in order to save fixed costs associated with inside workers, to minimize labor hoarding in the face of fluctuating demand, or simply to demonstrate restructuring to banks, owners, or state officials.

How strong is the real bias? Fortunately, because we have two independent data sources, we can check with acceptable precision. Let W^{ws} be the average wage of workers in a firm reporting individual wage data for the Wage Survey (WS). Let W^{fr} denote the average wage calculated from the Financial Report (FR) by dividing the annual wage cost by the average number of employees. The two figures will not necessarily be equal. In firms hiring labor from outside at the expense of their wage bill, $W^{ws} < W^{fr}$ will hold. In firms with unpaid workers on their payroll, the contrary will be true.[30]

Indeed, a comparison of W^{ws} and W^{fr} in our samples reveals large differences, reaching hundreds of thousands of forints in extreme cases, even with large firms. The main statistics for $D = W^{fr} - W^{ws}$ are the following (expressed in forints, for firms employing 200 or more workers):

1986: mean = –256; median = –247; standard deviation = 1,319.
1989: mean =   670; median = –116; standard deviation = 6,139.
1992: mean = 1,945; median = 1,522; standard deviation = 7,569.
1993: mean = 3,087; median = 2,594; standard deviation = 7,770.

How does the deviation affect the FR-based estimates of labor and wage elasticities? To test this, we first estimate a univariate regression for firms where abs(dD) = abs($D_{t+1} - D_t$) < 2,000 *Ft*. We then extend the sample step by step, including firms with higher or lower dD, respectively. That is, we first estimate for firms where the relation of inside and outside labor—or paid and unpaid employees—did not change over the observation period, and than we repeat the estimation for samples containing increasing numbers of firms with biased data.

The results for 1993/1992 are summarized on figures 3-8 and 3-9. The points (a, dD^*) and (b, dD^*) on figure 3-8 show the value of the parameters a and b gained from:

$$n_i = a \cdot q_i + c \quad \text{and} \quad w_i - ppi = b \cdot q_i/n_i + c$$
$$\text{subject to } dD_i < dD^* \text{ if } dD_i > 0 \text{ or } dD_i > dD^* \text{ if } dD_i < 0.$$

---

30. It should be mentioned that the two figures also differ because the WS data come from April or May, while the FR data include the whole year. More important, because each firm has at least one top manager, the FR average wage should generally be higher than the WS average wage, because the WS makes a random selection of individuals within each firm. If the proportion of top managers is 5 percent in the economy, only one in twenty firms will be observed with its top managers in the WS. Further differences exist, but they bear no great importance for the comparison we are making here.

Figure 3-8. Regression Coefficients from Subsamples Defined on the Basis of $dD = \Delta(w^{FR} - w^{WS})$ in 1992–93

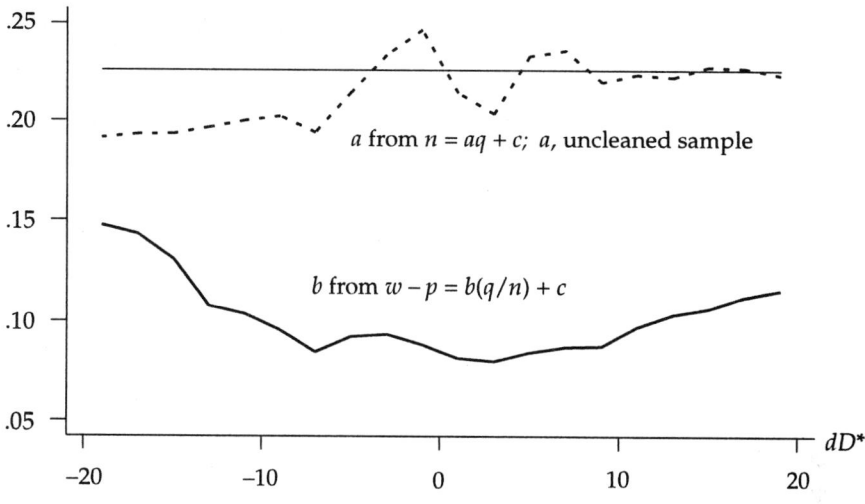

Note: b for the uncleaned sample is 0.2032.

Figure 3-9. Standard Errors from Subsamples Defined on the Basis of $dD = \Delta(w^{FR} - w^{WS})$ in 1992–93

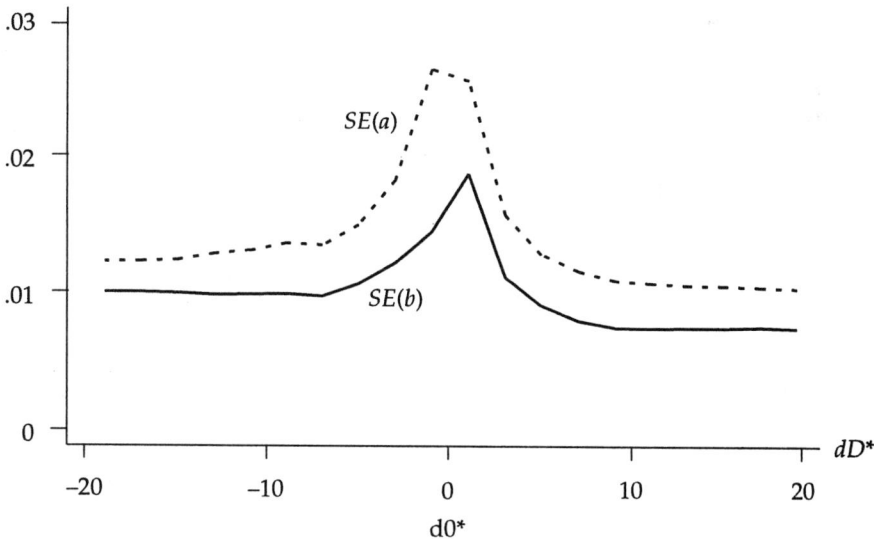

Note: b for uncleaned sample is 0.2032; *a* from $n = aq + c$; *a*, uncleaned sample; *b* from $w - p = b(q/n) + c$.

The estimated output elasticity of employment increases as we extend the sample by including firms that (probably) shifted to more outside labor in 1993. The elasticity decreases as we include firms that (probably) stopped paying a portion of their workers without displacing them. The results are fully consistent with the expectation elaborated in the naive example of table 3-14. We get high estimates where employment dropped more steeply than actual labor input, and we get low estimates where the opposite is likely to hold. The results also confirm the conjecture that the estimates are not overly biased. For the whole sample, dN/dY is 0.226. This is not so different from the "true" value we get for firms where $abs(dD) < Ft\ 2{,}000$.

The results on wages are dreadful, as expected. Because we include firms shifting to more outside labor ($dD > 0$), the estimate sharply increases. The same thing happens if we include firms, step by step, where the number of unpaid workers grew ($dD < 0$). Productivity appears to fall, and so does the average wage, although those actually providing services to the firm may do so with unchanged efficiency, and for the same wage. We may not be bothered by the bias in this case because the productivity and average wage of active and idle workers *together* decreased. The grave problem is on the other side, where we base the estimation on an illusion of growing productivity and wage.

The consequence of the use of the whole FR data set in assessing wage elasticity is severe. The estimate for the overall sample is 0.203, higher by a factor of *three* than the probable true value.

Figure 3-9 shows the standard errors of the estimates. If one works with the uncleaned FR, the standard errors will appear to be very low (t-values 30.0 or higher). One can restrict oneself to a smaller sample with reliable data, but that incurs less reliable parameters, and also implies a further step away from representativity.

Overall, we have a set of three options to choose from: (1) restricting the analysis to firms where $abs(dD)$ is below selected limits at the cost of a substantial cut of sample size; (2) replacing W^{fr} for W^{tws} (the cost is that we have wages for a selected period rather than the annual figures, including productivity-related premiums, that we need); and (3) weighting the observations with $1/abs(dD)$ or a similar, vaguely defined importance weight.

In Köllo (1996), a series of estimations are available on data sets modified in keeping with the three options. In this study the data refer to firms meeting the following criterion (exceptions are indicated in the text).

$$abs(dD) = abs(D_{t+1} - D_t) < 5{,}000\ Ft\ ,\ \text{where}\ D_t = W^{fr}_t - W^{tws}_t.$$

Note 4. A Comparison of the Four Panel Samples

Table 3-15. The Composition of the Samples by Industry, Size, and Ownership

Composition	WSFP 1986–89	WSFP 1989–92	WSFP 1992–93	FS 1992–94
Industry type				
Industry	31.9	35.2	35.9	36.7
Construction	8.9	8.0	8.9	6.9
Agriculture	38.9	37.9	20.7	30.7
Transport	1.5	1.3	3.1	1.5
Trade	17.2	15.9	19.3	15.6
Services	1.2	1.2	8.2	1.8
Other, unknown	0.4	0.4	3.8	6.8
Size				
$n < 100$	2.6	14.5	45.2	29.6
$n > 1000$	32.1	28.0	11.9	4.7
Ownership (at $t + 1$)				
State + coop	n.a.	70.3	36.0	51.2
Private	n.a.	19.2	48.2	37.3
Foreign	n.a.	0.7	7.0	–
Mixed, unknown	n.a.	9.9	8.8	0.0

n.a. Not available.

References

Böröczfyné Schmidt, K . 1976. "Analysis of the Wage Subsidy System" (in Hungarian). Pénzügykutató Intézet Kiadványai, Budapest.

Blanchard, O. J., and L. H. Summers. 1992. "Hysteresis in Unemployment." In P. Garonna, P. Mori, and P. Tedeschi, eds., *Economic Models of Trade Unions*. London, New York, Tokyo, Melbourne, and Madras: Chapman and Hall.

Carruth, A., and A. Oswald. 1987. "On Union Preferences and Labor Market Models: Insiders and Outsiders." *The Economic Journal* (June): 431–45.

Commander, S., Janos Kollo, and Cecilia Ugaz. 1995. "Firm Behavior and the Labor Market in the Hungarian Transition." Policy Research Working Paper No. 1373, World Bank Economic Development Institute, Washington, D.C.

Cukor, E., and G. Kertesi. 1987. "Inter-enterprise Wage Differentials in Hungary: Causes and Implications" (in Hungarian). Gazdaság No 4.

Csanádi, M. 1984. "Dependence, Selection, Mutual Adjustment" (in Hungarian). Institute of Financial Research, Budapest.

Galasi, P., and G. Kertesi, eds. 1996. *Report on the Hungarian Labor Market 1995*. ILO-Japan Project. Budapest: ILO.

Halpern, L., and G. Korösi. 1995. "Market Power and Firm Size Effects in Transition" (econometric analysis of Hungarian exporting firms, 1985–93). Institute of Economics Discussion Paper No. 27, Budapest.

Kertesi, G., and J. Köllo. 1995a. *Wages and Unemployment in Hungary, 1986–94*. ILO-Japan Project. Budapest: ILO.

———. 1995b. *Inter-firm Wage Differentials in Hungary*. ILO-Japan Project. Budapest: ILO.

Kornai, J. 1980. *The Economics of Shortage*. Amsterdam: North-Holland.

Kornai, J., and Á. Matits. 1993. "On the Softness of the Budget Constraint on the Basis of Enterprise-level Data" (in Hungarian). Gazdaság No. 4.

Köllo, J. 1996. "Employment and Wage Setting in Three Stages of Hungary's Labor Market Transition." Paper presented at the workshop Unemployment, Restructuring, and the Labor Market in Eastern Europe and Russia, World Bank, EDI, Washington, D.C., May 6.

———. 1997. "Transformation before the Transition." Institute of Economics, Budapest.

Ladó, M. 1995. "Moves Towards Free Wage Bargaining in Hungary." In D. Vaughan-Whitehead, ed., *Reforming Wage Policy in Central and Eastern Europe*. Geneva: ILO.

Laki, M. 1985. "Economic Policy and the Practice of Outstanding Firms." Report on a Workshop Held in Gyor, 28–29 May 1985 (in Hungarian). Közgazdasági Szemle 12.

———. 1994. "Firms after Socialism" (in Hungarian). Dissertation, Hungarian Academy of Sciences, Budapest.

McDonald, I., and R. Solow. 1982. "Wage Bargaining and Employment." *American Economic Review* 71: 896–908.

McMillan, J. 1996. "Restructuring Enterprises in Central and Eastern Europe." Paper presented at the workshop Policy Studies to Promote Private Sector Development, EBRD, London, April 26–27.

Pinto, B., and S. van Wijnbergen. 1995. "Ownership and Corporate Control in Poland: Why State Firms Defied the Odds." CEPR Discussion Paper No. 1273, London, December.

Schaffer, M. E. 1995. "Tax Arrears in Transition Economies." IMF Research Department Seminar, Washington D.C., October 3.

Székely, J. 1992–96. "Short-term Labor Forecast" (in Hungarian). National Labor Centre, Budapest.

4

Enterprises in the Polish Transition

Simon Commander and Sumana Dhar

Over seven years have now passed since Poland embarked on a dramatic stabilization program. In that time, initially large declines in output have given way to a new phase of growth. Table 4-1 indicates that both GDP and industrial output have gradually expanded, so that by end-1996, GDP had more than recovered, and industrial output was only slightly below, pre-transition levels. And despite slow progress in the privatization of state enterprises, over 60 percent of GDP was accounted for by the private sector.

Given the initial and large shocks to output and trade, unemployment predictably rose high early in the transition, and it exceeded 12 percent of the labor force by end-1991. More recently, even in the presence of strong aggregate growth, unemployment has declined only gradually. In part, this is because of some increase in the inflow rate, but it is also attributable to the rising, although still low, exit rates from unemployment, particularly to jobs (see Boeri 1995; Gora 1995). In short, aggregate growth

We thank Olivier Blanchard for very detailed comments on an earlier draft of this chapter, as well as Samuel Bentolila, Brian Pinto, and Mark Schaffer. Piotr Mazurowski and Krzysztof Rybinski helped us collect and understand the data.

Table 4-1. Poland, Summary Indicators, 1989–96

Year	GDP	Total employ- ment	Industry output	Industry employ- ment	Prices (cpi)	Prices (ppi)	Average wage	Un- employ- ment	Private sector (% of GDP)
1989	0.2	−0.2	−1.4	−0.5	251.1	212.8	291.8	0.1	29
1990	−11.6	−4.2	−26.1	−5.9	585.8	622.3	398.0	3.4	31
1991	−7.6	−5.9	−11.9	−8.0	70.3	48.1	70.6	9.7	45
1992	2.6	−4.2	3.9	−8.7	43.0	28.5	38.8	13.6	48
1993	3.8	−4.3	5.6	−2.9	35.3	32.2	33.8	14.9	54
1994	5.0	−1.5	13.0	−3.9	32.2	30.1	34.7	16.1	56
1995	7.0	0.8	7.4	1.1	28.1	25.5	41.4	15.3	60
1996	6.3	−0.4	8.9	−0.5	18.5	12.1	25.6	14.1	n.a.

n.a. Not available.
Note: All expressed as percentage changes, except unemployment, which gives registration rate as percentage of labor force and private sector, which gives its estimated share in GDP.
Source: GUS, World Bank, and EBRD Transition Report.

has yet to exert a strong effect on employment. While part of the persistence in unemployment and the associated growth in long-term unemployment can be attributed to persistent spatial mismatch, it must also be related to the job creation process in Poland and to the wage and employment decisions being made by firms. Although most of the job creation in Poland is now taking place through the private sector, the state and privatized sectors—the main focus of this chapter—remain a sizable presence in industry, and their decisions on separations and accessions continue to be critical in explaining the overall path of employment.

This chapter is concerned with the behavior of the enterprise sector in Poland since 1989, particularly the state-owned enterprises. These firms generally entered the transition with excess employment and low productivity levels. Performance incentives were skewed, not only by the structure of taxation and other incentives, but also by the ability of loss-makers to extract compensating finance from the government. Previous work with firm-level datasets has clearly shown that while Polish firms did indeed respond rapidly to the new environment—cutting employment and relating wage behavior more closely to the financial status of the firm—the variation in response was nevertheless not that significant. In short, macroeconomic policy was not sufficient to induce a radical break in behavior. Bank lending initially kept the budget constraint soft, while inflation allowed for major revaluation of assets and inventory that temporarily boosted profitability in the first year of stabilization. One result was that firm financial performance was—at first—best explained by sectoral provenance. By 1992/93, these firm surveys showed that the links from sector to performance had been weakened; that there was a positive link between profits and investment; that bank lending was a smaller factor in sustaining a soft budget constraint; and that loss-makers were beginning to take tough decisions, particularly in the realm of employment, in response to their financial difficulties (Belka and others 1994; Estrin and others, in this volume; Pinto, Belka, and Krajewski 1993; Schaffer 1993). Even so, several years into the transition, overmanning was rampant, particularly in state and privatized firms. Wage settlements were often guided largely by firm liquidity, but for some of the financially distressed state firms, excess wage tax payments seemed to indicate the presence of decapitalizing behavior.

In sum, the picture that emerged from these earlier studies was one of adaptation among state-owned firms, alongside a significant core of loss-making, highly indebted, larger enterprises that continued to rely on forms of soft finance—and were not permitted to fail. Further, while a predictable link from financial performance to employment was emerging quite strongly, evidence still pointed to significant overmanning, and wage data showed surprisingly little variation across firms as graded by their profitability. Despite large job destruction and persistently high unemployment, average consumption wages for industrial workers and unit labor costs have clearly drifted upward, and by 1995, both were both 20 percent higher than in 1990 .[1]

This chapter not only retraces the key parts of these stories using a more comprehensive dataset, but also carries the story forward. We focus on the wage and employment decisions of Polish firms over annual short panels and also over a longer span, from the start of transition to end-1994. We not only trace out the response of firms and, through the financing link, of government and the financial system, but also look closely at the internal bargaining arrangements particular to firms, paying close attention to the likely importance of insiders in the decisionmaking process.

Data Description

To undertake the analysis of firm behavior, we have constructed a set of year-to-year short panels, as well as a longer panel covering the period

---

1. However, related to 1989, real consumption wages in industry were still nearly 25 percent lower in 1995, although unit labor costs were broadly constant.

from 1990 to end-1994. To do this, we have merged several datasets collected by the Polish Statistical Office. These comprise the standard GUS (Glowny Urzad Statystyczny) F-01 financial information on firms, as well the DG-1 data covering wage and employment information for the period 1991–94 and, for 1989 and 1990, the Z-07 data on employment and wages. In all cases, the information relates to the two-digit level of industry, with disaggregation over all the regions or *voivods* in Poland. Both the financial and employment datasets cover all large firms in the country, with an additional 10 percent sampling of medium-size enterprises.[2] Large firms are defined as having more than 500 employees for construction and more than 200 for other branches; medium-size firms are defined as employing between 50 and 500 workers in construction and 20 to 200 in other branches. Ownership indicators are available from 1991 onward. For prices, we use a two-digit producer price series. For consumer wages, the deflator is the consumer price index provided by GUS.

One striking property of our dataset is that it comprises all firms that have completed the basic F-01 or balance sheet questionnaire, even when the number of firms for a given record was equal to one. Consequently, in a significant number of cases we are indeed working with firm-level information. In putting together the financial (F-01) and the employment and wage datasets (DG-1 and Z-07), we used the number of firms and the wage bill as the main matching variables for the same two-digit industry identifier and region. Wage-rate data are generated using the average of the current and lagged year's employment. The merged dataset has retained a high share of individual firm observations, ranging from 20 percent in the 1989/90 and 1990/91 short panels to 33–40 percent in the remaining short panels. The size of these short panels is quite large, ranging from 550 to 1,030 observations. The long panel contains nearly 600 firm observations.

The dataset clearly will give us a biased view of firm behavior. First, it contains observations primarily on large firms, generally those that have remained in the state sector or at some point undergone privatization. By concentrating on surviving firms, we obviously ignore the question of firms that exit in this period. This may, however, not be as serious as it appears: in the universe of large and mid-size firms, closures or bankruptcies have remained rather scarce, in part because of delays in implementing bankruptcy legislation. We also largely bypass the major source

----

2. Where large firms are classed as > 500 employees in construction and industry and > 200 elsewhere; medium is < 500 > 50 in construction and industry and < 200 > 20 elsewhere.

of growth in the Polish economy—new starts and small de novo firms. Despite these limitations, we think that a close look at the larger state and privatized firms has value, in part because of the initial conditions, and in part because—given the major hemorrhaging of jobs in the Polish economy—we are interested not only in the response of the larger firms to adverse shocks, but also to the subsequent improvement in the external environment.

Aggregate or Reallocation Effects?

A starting point for any discussion of Polish firm behavior is to ask whether the significant changes that we have observed since 1989/90 have been consistent with restructuring. As already noted in earlier studies, the decline in output in 1990 was surprisingly common. A crude test with principal components indicated that the first component explained as much as 50 percent of output variability in the period 1990/91. While the variation in employment was rather larger, the variation for wages was smaller than that for output. This common effect was interpreted as indicating an absence of structural change and the likely dominance of aggregate effects (Borensztein, Demekas, and Ostry 1993). These exercises were carried out on quite aggregated data, however, and may have camouflaged the degree of variation over branches.

Table 4-2 provides summary information from our panels. Because of some extreme values, we report median as well as mean values, and also the coefficients of dispersion and variation, respectively. In the absence of direct information on changes in output, we report changes for sales. The table shows substantial declines in real sales across the long panel. In the short panels, the initial upturn in 1989/90—largely prompted by a revaluation of stocks—gave way to significant declines in all years. Median sales values continued to fall as late as 1993/94. Real wages also experienced a consistent decline in the short panels, although this tapered off quite significantly. Indeed, mean changes were either positive or very slightly negative post-1991. In the long panel, we observe an unambiguous increase in real product wages over the period 1994–90. For employment, both long and short panels indicate substantial declines, with the exception of 1993/94, when both median and mean values are positive. In variability, it is evident from both the coefficients of variation and dispersion that there was significant increase over time. This is true for all three variables reported in table 4-2. The size of the coefficients is large, pointing to major disturbances.

Table 4-2. Change in Real Sales and Employment, 1989–94

| | Long panel | | Short panels | | | | | | | | | |
| | 1990–94 | | 1989–90 | | 1990–91 | | 1991–92 | | 1992–93 | | 1993–94 | |
Item	Median	cd	Median	cd	Median	cd	Median	cd	Median	cd	Median	cd
Real sale	-70.30	-60.5	29.82	117.0	-64.90	-57.5	-40.49	-123.1	-18.73	-354.7	-11.70	-393.4
Real wage	25.39	465.9	-36.98	-57.6	-24.94	-211.9	-1.66	-3,484.4	-13.86	-402.6	-12.12	-422.3
Employment	-54.74	60.8	-14.70	-89.9	-3.36	-1,422.7	-37.10	-96.7	-15.38	-349.4	3.70	1,605.3
	Mean	cv	Mean	cv	Mean	cv	Mean	cv	Mean	cv	Mean	cv
Real sale	-46.70	-152.8	24.86	169.5	-48.40	-107.5	-25.95	-275.8	7.30	1,410.0	-6.62	-976.2
Real wage	79.19	206.3	-40.55	-61.8	-10.29	-672.7	6.88	1,083.9	-3.17	-2,406.8	-2.85	-2,551.2
Employment	-44.42	-112.7	-16.09	-137.5	18.64	401.5	-30.61	-157.1	3.48	2,419.3	33.85	278.3

Note: cd, coefficient of dispersion; cv, coefficient of variation.
Source: GUS.

114

Larger variability can be taken as one indicator of the restructuring process and the relative weight of structural, as against aggregate, shocks. But we can also directly observe shifts in sectoral composition. Indeed, using one-digit data, Jackman and Pauna (1996) have argued that little of the change in employment in Poland since 1989 has been associated with restructuring. Using Organization for Economic Cooperation and Development (OECD) comparators for composition, they argue that the ultimate restructuring effect has been weak, in part because of changes in the OECD comparators. They conclude that aggregate shocks have continued to dominate. This conclusion is misleading, not least because of the level of aggregation. Table 4-3 uses data from the complete sample for the end-points—1989 and 1994—and therefore allows for exit and entry of firms. It shows that there have been some significant changes in the composition of sales, employment, and the wage bill over the period 1989–94. Further, most of the changes are predictable, with a large expansion in the relative shares of the service and energy or fuel sectors and a clear decline in the shares of heavy industrial branches across all three variables. For the industrial branches, the change is generally weakest in employment, which is again predictable, given the differences in average firm size across industrial and service sector firms. These shifts would be difficult to explain purely in terms of aggregate shocks.

To what extent have these changes been consistent with underlying viability or advantage? Figure 4-1 provides a weak test of the association

Table 4-3. Shares of Sales, Wage Bill, and Employment

	1990			1994		
Branch	*Sales*	*Wage bill*	*Employ-ment*	*Sales*	*Wage bill*	*Employ-ment*
Fuel	14.5	16.5	10.5	24.8	13.3	8.5
Metallurgy	12.1	6.7	6.3	9.7	8.6	6.4
Engineering	14.1	13.8	15.3	8.2	7.6	9.7
Chemicals	10.0	6.3	6.5	6.7	5.0	7.4
Light industry	10.2	12.1	15.0	9.4	12.0	17.1
Agroindustry	12.7	7.8	8.7	12.8	12.6	10.6
Construction	8.2	11.4	10.1	2.3	4.4	5.7
Transport	8.1	12.3	13.2	3.7	5.5	6.6
Trade	6.2	7.3	9.0	0.7	3.5	3.3
Services	4.0	5.6	5.3	21.6	26.9	24.8

Note: Yearly raw data are used to construct the panels.
Source: GUS.

Figure 4-1. Change in Sales and Viability

Sales index 94 (90=100)

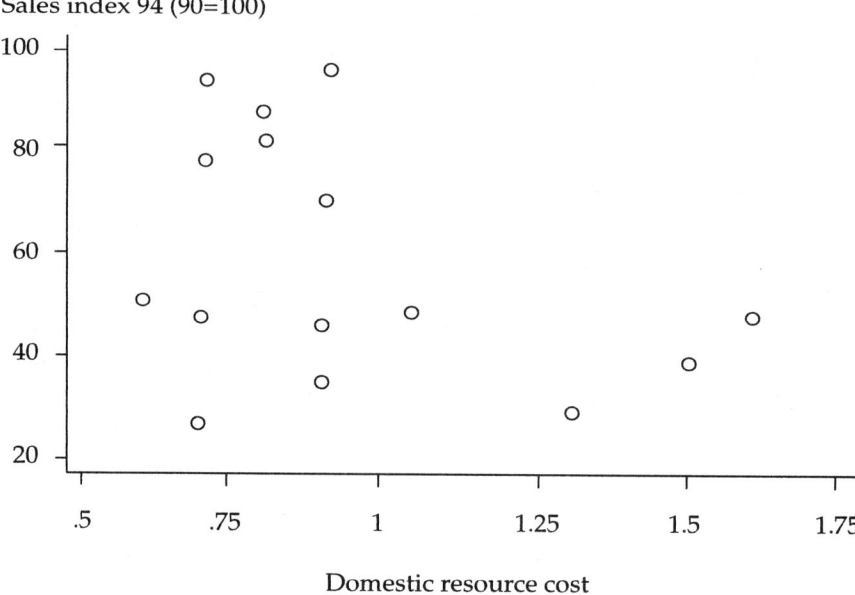

Domestic resource cost

between ex ante viability, as measured by the domestic resource cost (DRC), which related the level of value added at world prices to domestic prices at the start of transition, and the change in real sales (the DRCs are taken from de la Calle 1990). Plotting the change in real sales for the period 1994–90 against this viability measure, we find that there is, at best, some weak evidence of a predictable association of sales with value added. The same exercise using the change in prices shows no apparent relationship.

Despite evidence of this larger variation in the changes, table 4-4 indicates that an examination of wage levels alone overlooks a very significant increase in measures of inequality over the period. The Gini coefficient was strikingly high at the outset of the transition and has shifted only gradually. Wage inequality in this sample is significantly higher than in more aggregate data. At the end of the period, however, we do see a clear shift in the decile ratio, which indicates a larger gap between the poles of the remuneration scale and increased dispersion. When disaggregating further, we also find that while private wages appear to be more dispersed, the difference relative to the state sector has remained quite small over time. This appears to be consistent with earlier

Table 4-4. Wage Distribtution, 1989–94

	1989	1990	1991	1992	1993	1994
Gini	0.6	0.5	0.5	0.5	0.5	0.5
cv	184.9	102.7	89.5	92.9	93.0	108.5
cd	180.0	113.5	98.1	85.7	84.2	105.5
Decile ratio	18.4	15.5	17.9	12.1	12.7	29.5
Quartile ratio	4.8	4.9	5.9	4.5	3.8	5.9

Source: GUS.

evidence that pointed to the stability of the wage distribution until 1992 (Coricelli, Hagemejer, and Rybinski 1995).

In short, we are able to observe nontrivial shifts in the composition of sales, employment, and the wage bill, as well as clear evidence of growing variability in the changes to these variables as the transition proceeds. The impression is of considerable heterogeneity and of quite powerful reallocation effects at work.

Financial Performance

Aggregate data suggest that Polish firms have indeed experienced large adverse shocks to profitability over the course of the transition. Between 1991 and 1993, roughly 40 percent of enterprises surveyed by the statistical agency reported gross losses. For firms in our long panel, the median decline in real sales between 1990 and 1994 was, as we have seen, around 25 percent. Figure 4-2, which is based on the long panel, plots the ratio of gross profits to sales in 1990 against that for 1994. It shows quite unambiguously the way in which profits have largely evaporated. By the end of the period, the bulk of firms are reporting roughly zero profits.

While ideally we might like to gain a more detailed view of the evolution of profitability, this is made quite complex by changes in reporting standards and definitions. We generally avoid possible mismeasurement through recourse to a far simpler—but revealing—classification of firms that relies only on the direction of change in sales revenues over a given period. With both the long and short panels, status is given by the position at the end of the period.

The first and obvious point to make is that the substantial decline in sales and a widespread shift into loss-making occurred only after 1990 (Schaffer 1993). Part of this decline can be attributed to the fall in inflation over the period. Because costs were in historical prices, with high infla-

Figure 4-2. Profitability

1994 gross profit/sales

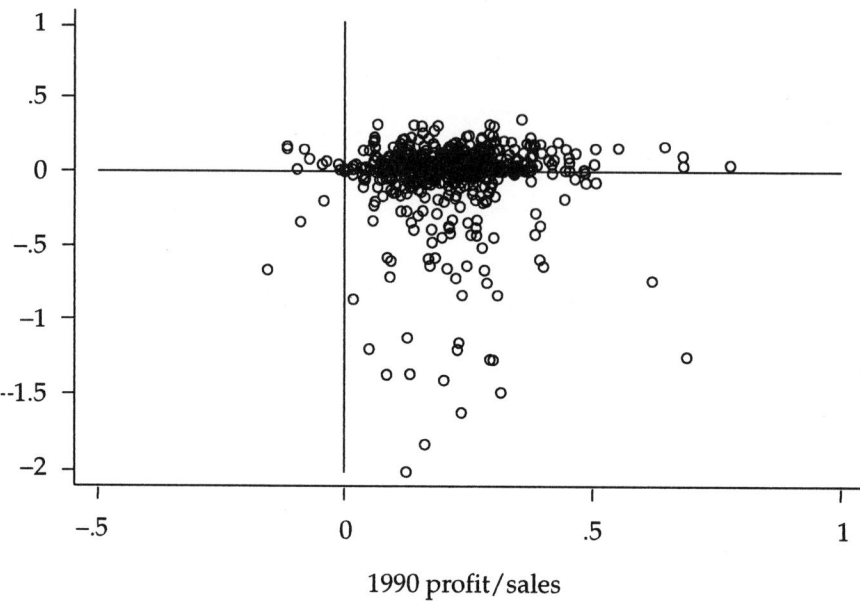

1990 profit/sales

tion there was a persistent tendency for costs to be understated relative to sales, thereby artificially inflating profits. This point was well established by Schaffer (1993) when looking at the collapse in profitability between 1990 and 1991. With suitable caveats regarding measurement, it appears that while barely 4 percent of firms made negative gross profits in 1990, this figure jumped to just over 50 percent in 1992, before declining to around one-third in 1994. Turning to our simpler indicator—the direction of change in real sales—we find that while over 70 percent of firms in 1990/89 experienced increased sales, this percentage fell sharply, to below 15 percent, in the following year. Thereafter, the share of firms with increased sales in the short panels rose, averaging around 36 percent after 1992.

Table 4-5 breaks the changes down by branch, and it can easily be seen that by 1993/94, almost all branches were reporting that 30–40 percent of firms were experiencing positive sales increases. By this time, there is not only some unambiguous decline in the share of loss-makers in almost all branches, but, with the exception of fuels and chemicals, there was relatively little variation in the size of that share across branches. While the numbers point to a reasonably common upswing in performance across

Table 4-5. Number of Firms by Branch and Change in Real Sales

	Short panels									Long panel		
	1990			1992			1994			1994		
		Change in real sales from 1989			Change in real sales from 1991			Change in real sales from 1993			Change in real sales from 1990	
Branch	Total	>= 0	< 0	Total	>= 0	< 0	Total	>= 0	< 0	Total	>= 0	< 0
Fuel	20	19	1	40	14	26	34	23	11	32	13	19
Metallurgy	27	24	3	21	5	16	30	15	15	28	1	27
Engineering	99	85	14	69	16	53	75	30	45	57	10	47
Chemical	58	54	4	40	10	30	28	6	22	35	4	31
Light industry	229	204	25	148	38	110	151	63	88	144	35	109
Agroindustry	122	91	31	61	8	53	71	29	42	22	2	20
Construction	98	79	19	96	21	75	113	34	79	104	3	101
Transport	77	42	35	47	15	32	89	40	49	64	8	56
Trade	67	7	60	27	18	9	61	22	39	25	11	14
Service	148	77	71	45	5	40	184	55	129	68	10	58
Total	945	682	263	594	150	444	836	317	519	579	97	482
Share (%)	100	72	28	100	25	75	100	38	62	100	17	83

Source: GUS.

119

Table 4-6. Change over 1990–94
(percent)

	Long panel					
	Change in real sales from 1990 > = 0			Change in real sales from 1990 < 0		
	Mean	*Median*	*cv*	*Mean*	*Median*	*cv*
Real sales	73.8	38.9	131.7	–70.9	–79.1	–37.9
Real wage rate	194.1	134.7	93.9	56.1	3.3	266.1
Employment	–9.2	–10.6	–541.7	–51.5	–61.3	–91.3
n	97			482		

Source: GUS.

branches, it is striking that by 1994 a very significant majority of firms in our sample had failed to achieve real sales growth. Indeed, over one-quarter of the industrial firms were making negative gross profits at a time when aggregate industrial output was growing substantially. This heterogeneity is not surprising, however, particularly because our sample is concentrated on the larger state and privatized firms.

Perhaps most interesting is the financial performance of our long panel. Here it appears that roughly one-third of firms were loss-makers in 1994. Only 16 percent of the panel had experienced an increase in real sales since 1990.[3] The branch effects appear fairly uniform, with heavy industry, primarily chemicals and metallurgy, experiencing little positive sales growth. Table 4-6 lists the magnitude of both mean and median changes to sales in the period. For the minority of firms experiencing a sales increase, that expansion involved a 40–75 percent growth in real sales over the period. For the bulk of firms experiencing a decrease in sales, the mean and median values lay closer together, in the range of a 70–79 percent decrease. These clearly are large-order negative shocks. We later look in more detail at how these have been distributed in the employment and wage choices open to insiders.

The impact of product market shocks is partly captured by the evolution of inventories. Inventory accumulation peaked in 1991, albeit with large branch variation.[4] By 1994, loss-making firms had significantly higher inventory to sales ratios than were seen in the other categories.

---

3. This share would have been significantly higher if 1989 had been the base year.

4. Note that we have inventory numbers at annual end-period.

Continuing weak sales performance thus continued to appear in stocks accumulation. Nevertheless, the ratio to sales, even in loss-makers, and even at the start of transition, was not that large, and not very different from OECD levels.[5]

Normalizing profits, costs, and investment by sales in table 4-7, we can observe the respective trends over time. Again we distinguish over firms experiencing real sales increases and those recording decreases, and we report these ratios for three of the short panels as well as the long panel. Several features stand out. First, looking at the short panel information, we find that the gross profit to sales ratio declined very significantly across all types of firms between 1990 and 1994. By 1994 we observe some stabilization for firms with sales growth, while for firms with sales decline, there was some improvement. Even so, the mean ratio remained negative for the latter. Not surprisingly, the ratio of total costs to sales jumped significantly over the period for firms with declining sales. By 1993/94, total costs still exceeded sales for this category. Labor costs to sales rose across the board, but again to a larger extent in firms experiencing sales declines, and this ratio remained broadly stable after 1992. In the case of the long panel, we can see a clear deterioration in profitability. By 1994, we again find a negative mean profit to sales ratio for the bulk of firms with sales declines, and total costs exceed sales. While labor costs had risen in relation to sales in both categories, the expansion was significantly larger for firms with declining sales. In these cases, the labor cost ratio doubled between 1990 and 1994.

Finally, with respect to investment, the long panel indicates a striking difference in behavior between firms with increasing sales over the period and firms with sales declines. The latter maintained an investment to sales ratio of 0.04. By contrast, firms with increasing sales reported investment ratios nearly three times larger and expenditures on investment goods double the ratios reported for declining sales firms. This clearly shows that positive sales profiles have increasingly been associated with higher investment. This investment upswing among both state and privatized firms—56 percent of these investment-intensive firms were still state-owned—is undoubtedly one major factor behind the growth in output that emerges from the aggregate data on industrial output.

---

5. A point made in Commander and Coricelli (1993). For all Polish industry, finished goods inventory amounted to no more than 3.7 percent of sales in 1989.

Table 4-7. Ratio of Costs and Profit to Sales, 1989–94

Short panel

Item	1990 Change in real sales from 1989 >= 0 Mean	sd	< 0 Mean	sd	1992 Change in real sales from 1991 >= 0 Mean	sd	< 0 Mean	sd	1994 Change in real sales from 1993 >= 0 Mean	sd	< 0 Mean	sd
Gross profit/sales	0.19	0.11	0.15	0.17	0.06	0.18	−0.14	0.58	0.05	0.21	−0.07	0.38
Total cost/sales	0.87	0.14	0.91	0.27	0.79	0.29	1.08	0.45	0.90	0.31	1.03	0.44
Labor cost/sales	0.19	0.09	0.30	0.17	0.28	0.15	0.42	0.32	0.32	0.21	0.42	0.30
Depreciation/sales	0.04	0.05	0.04	0.04	0.05	0.05	0.07	0.09	0.04	0.05	0.05	0.06
Investment outlay/sales					0.07	0.30	0.07	0.47	0.05	0.09	0.05	0.14
Investment goods/sales									0.03	0.06	0.02	0.06

Long panel

Item	Change in real sales over 1990–94 >= 0 Mean	sd	< 0 Mean	sd	Change in real sales over 1990–94 >= 0 Mean	sd	< 0 Mean	sd
Gross profit/sales	0.22	0.1	0.22	0.113	0.07	0.1	−0.07	0.4
Total cost/sales	0.81	0.3	0.84	0.133	0.79	0.3	1.03	0.3
Labor cost/sales	0.20	0.1	0.19	0.103	0.28	0.2	0.39	0.2
Depreciation/sales	0.04	0.06	0.04	0.05	0.05	0.05	0.05	0.05
Investment outlay/sales					0.11	0.38	0.04	0.09
Investment goods/sales					0.04	0.07	0.02	0.05

Note: All classification is "end of period," except 1990 in the long panel.
Source: GUS.

Budget Constraint

Given the fall in profitability and declining sales over the period, an obvious question arises (given the legacy of public financial supports to the firm sector): have firms in distress been able to extract transfers from government or other sources of soft finance? In other words, have Polish state firms come to face hard budget constraints? We know from aggregate data that there was a very substantial contraction in subsidies from the budget to the firm sector. While in 1989 producer subsidies amounted to around 13 percent of GDP, by 1994 they had declined to no more than 2 percent. Budget-financed bail-outs of firms certainly have declined in frequency, and this was confirmed by earlier firm-level evidence that indicated that most firms were continuing to operate as if under a hard budget constraint.

The explicit subsidy measure is somewhat misleading, however, in part because firms have managed to find alternative sources of soft financing, whether from the banking system or through effective default on tax and other obligations, such as social security payments, to government. Schaffer (1996) shows that at end-1994, the stock of tax arrears was around 5–7 percent of GDP, with the flow at a maximum of 1 percent. Both reflected declines since 1993. Firm-level evidence for 1993 indicated that as much as 75 percent of reported tax arrears was concentrated in financially distressed firms, which comprised no more than 13 percent of the sample. Thus, while soft finance has flowed through diverse channels, the picture from both aggregate and firm data is that government-related supports—subsidies and tax arrears—have been of fairly limited incidence. We now try and get a better idea of how hard the budget constraint for the firms in our dataset has been, and to pick up the changes in financing and their concentration over time.

The evolution of explicit subsidies in our dataset is clear. Table 4-8 shows that in 1989, the ratio of subsidies to sales was quite high, between 0.11 and 0.08 for firms classified by sales. Thereafter, subsidies tended to decline. Nevertheless, we do find that in both 1993 and 1994, firms with increasing sales still managed to extract subsidies that ranged between 8 and 10 percent of sales in that year, and while firms with declining sales did have generally higher subsidy ratios, this was not a systematic difference, nor was the difference between these firms and firms experiencing sales increases that large. Part of this can be explained by the concentration of subsidies. Table 4-8 also shows that the Gini coefficient, already high in 1989, shifted to between 0.7 and 0.8 after 1991. Much of the subsidy story was concentrated on one branch—transport. Subsidies to other

Table 4-8. Ratios of Subsidy, Credit, and Payables to Sales, 1989–94

	1989, change in real sales over 1989–90		1990, change in real sales from 1989		1991, change in real sales from 1990		1992, change in real sales from 1991		1993, change in real sales from 1992		1994, change in real sales from 1993	
	≥ 0	< 0	≥ 0	< 0	≥ 0	< 0	≥ 0	< 0	≥ 0	< 0	≥ 0	< 0
Subsidy/sales	0.114	0.077	0.057	0.056	0.022	0.043	0.006	0.059	0.104	0.048	0.084	0.108
n	158	72	101	77	51	212	15	42	46	57	45	59
0 or nonreporting	715		767		771		537		430		732	
Gini coefficient	0.60	0.59	0.67	0.65	0.87	0.82	0.80	0.87	0.80	0.86	0.73	0.68
Overall Gini coefficient	0.61		0.66		0.83		0.88		0.83		0.70	
Bank credit/sales					0.088	0.116	0.167	0.221	0.126	0.274	0.176	0.296
n					109	686	107	259	141	195	168	262
0 or nonreporting					239		228		197		406	
Overdue bank credit/sales					0.027	0.049	0.207	0.228	0.072	0.345	0.129	0.156
n					19	227	18	79	37	46	23	42
0 or nonreporting					788		497		450		771	
Net payables/sales	−0.059	−0.018	−0.045	−0.003	0.011	0.051	0.024	0.252	0.072	0.169	0.108	0.233
n	682	263	682	263	155	879	150	44	194	339	317	519
0 or nonreporting	0		1		4		12		6		15	
Overdue net payables for goods/sales							−0.014	−0.006	−0.014	−0.057	−0.018	0.021
n							103	270	142	201	178	253
0 or nonreporting							221		190		405	

Note: All classification is "end of period," except 1989; means do not include "0 or nonreporting."

124

branches have generally remained very small and have declined over time. Subsidies have also continued to be directed primarily to state firms; those directed to privatized firms have fallen off sharply.[6]

While there has been a clear reduction in subsidies as well as significant branch concentration, it is also clear that Polish firms have actively sought out other financing channels. A measure of their behavior with respect to bank financing is also given in table 4-8, which shows that both the better performing firms and the worst performing firms have maintained quite high bank credit to sales ratios. In the former case, this presumably reflects financing for investment and restructuring. But in the case of firms with declining sales—where bank credit to sales approached 0.3 in 1994—this would be an improbable explanation. It does, however, point to the ability of these firms to maintain access to bank borrowing. Further, looking at the ratio of overdue bank credit and loans to sales after 1991, it appears that firms with declining sales consistently posted higher overdue credit to sales ratios. Indeed, overdue credit accounted for at least half of total credit in a subset of loss-making firms. Some caution should be exercised in interpreting these numbers, however, given the rather limited number of respondents; barely 15 percent of loss-makers reported overdue bank loans. Although an ambiguous indicator of soft finance, the scale of continuing access to the financial system is obviously an important factor in explaining why even chronic loss-makers have not been allowed to fail. [7]

A further source of financing has been the accumulation of interfirm credits, particularly in the early stages of transition. Looking at the evolution of net liabilities to sales, we see a switch across all categories to net borrowing in 1991, with declining sales firms reporting consistently higher ratios than the other categories. By 1994 the ratio of net liabilities to sales for these firms exceeded 20 percent of sales. Nevertheless, it should be observed that a far smaller share—roughly half—reported overdue liabilities, and that these were of small magnitudes, which should again caution against emphasizing the scale of this financing route.

Unfortunately, we have no reliable information on the use of tax arrears to government as a financing mechanism for poorly performing firms. As

6. Privatized firms are defined as those that are reported as private in the current period but were state in the previous period.

7. Given the limitations of our dataset, we are unable to distinguish effectively between the flow of new credits to loss-makers and capitalization of interest on overdue borrowing.

indicated above, other sources suggest that this has been an important channel for some of the chronic loss-makers. If so, it would supplement the clear ability of poorly performing firms not only to extract subsidies, but also to continue borrowing from banks and other firms. In conclusion, despite these continuing financing options, it is important to note that the bulk of Polish firms, indeed, the majority of the branches, were receiving small, if not negligible, soft finance in 1994. There is evidence of significant concentration in the distribution of such finance.

Employment and Wage Responses to Shocks

We now know that in our panel of firms, product-market shocks have generally been large and quite persistent. We have picked up some evidence of cost-side rigidity as the ratio of labor costs to sales has increased substantially across branches, ownership forms, and profitability groups. It will be helpful to take a closer look at the distribution of product-market shocks over employment and wages by Polish firms. As already indicated, earlier firm surveys picked out the presence of major employment reductions early in the transition. On the wage side, although they found some responsiveness of wages to firm-level financial performance, the dispersion across performance categories does not appear to have been large. These findings are consistent with the evidence coming from our dataset.

Table 4-6 has already indicated the differential response of firms, graded by changes in sales, to employment and wages. The numbers are revealing in several respects. First, even firms with increasing sales had declines in both mean and median employment. The decline, however, was not large—of the order of 10 percent—and the coefficient of variation is quite large. Indeed, a significant number of firms in this category actually experienced positive net hiring. Real product wage increases were very substantial and significantly in excess of the growth in real sales. For firms with declining sales the story is markedly different. Employment declines are large—in excess of 50 percent—and were marked by less variability. We also observe real wage increases in this category, despite the very substantial drop in sales. The gap between the mean and median values is large, and there is great variation in wage changes. Median wage growth was minimal, which points to broad real wage stability over the period.

Table 4-9 offers more information from both the short and the long panels on the evolution of real wages. What is most telling is the difference that emerges after 1990 between firms, conditional on their sales perfor-

Table 4-9. Real Wages, 1989–94
(zloty)

Mean wage rate	Short panels			Long panel	
	1989	*1992*	*1994*	*1990**	*1994*
Overall	3,917	2,833	4,417	2,417	3,500
Change in real sales >= 0	3,875	4,333	6,583	3,167	7,000
Change in real sales < 0	4,250	2,400	3,083	2,250	2,833
State		3,750	4,167		3,583
Private		2,158	4,583		3,417

Note: All classification is "end of period," except 1989 for short panels and 1990 for the long panel unit. "Privatized": private firms that were state-owned in the previous period.
Source: GUS.

mance. Firms experiencing sales growth have tended to pay real wages at twice the level of firms with decreasing sales. Indeed, in the long panel, the rough wage equivalence of 1990 had been supplanted by a large gap at the end of the period.

The evidence on the incidence of the *popiwek*, or excess wage tax, shows that firms with worse financial performance generally did not sanction larger than normal wage settlements. *Popiwek* per worker payments remained very small after 1991, and it was consistently the better performing firms that paid higher excess wage taxes. This seems to confirm the positive link between profitability and wages, rather than pointing to decapitalizing behavior.

From the above, it is clear that real wages have tended to drift upward, but not significantly in the bulk of firms in our sample. If we had used 1989 as the reference year, however, it is clear that for the whole sample, real wages in 1994 had barely recovered to their 1989 level.[8] It is also apparent that in firms experiencing sales expansion, real wage growth has been quite substantial. Labor costs relative to sales have also increased, although at the start of transition the labor cost to sales ratio was very low, in the range of 0.2. This suggests some cost rigidity. Looking at the path of the ratio of wages to gross value added—where the latter is defined as gross profits plus depreciation plus wage costs—table 4-10 shows that the ratio of wages to value added for firms experiencing sales decline did shift clearly upward through the period. By 1994, wages accounted for around 0.8 of gross value added. However, there was rela-

---

8. Of course, this does not correct for shortages and hence grossly overstates the 1989 wage.

Table 4-10. Wage Bill/Gross Value Added (Nominal)
(real wage rate/real gross value added per worker)

	1990, change in real sales from 1989		1992, change in real sales from 1991		1994, change in real sales from 1993	
	>= 0	< 0	>= 0	< 0	>= 0	< 0
Mean	0.67	0.65	0.57	0.72	0.68	0.80
Median	0.44	0.64	0.68	0.75	0.69	0.81
n	682	263	150	444	317	519
	Change in real sales over 1990–94				Change in real sales over 1990–94	
	>= 0	< 0			>= 0	< 0
Mean	0.45	0.43			0.60	0.76
Median	0.41	0.39			0.58	0.75
n	97	482			97	482

Note: Gross value added = gross profit + depreciation + wage bill.
Source: GUS.

tively little variation across firms with different changes to sales, either in the short or the long panels; those experiencing sales increases had ratios around 0.6–0.7.

Finally, a basic question needs to be addressed: given the emergence of large-order unemployment along with major regional disparities in unemployment rates, have local labor market conditions begun to exert some influence on the wage setting? Figure 4-3, which provides a simple scatter of the change in regional wages over 1990–94 against the unemployment level at the end of the period, suggests that they have not. It is readily apparent that real wages have tended to move within a very narrow band across regions, and that local unemployment has exerted a negligible effect, if any, on wage setting.[9] We return more systematically to this issue below.

---

9. More generally, using data from nine macroregions, Bentolila (1997) finds a more conventional Phillips curve with a percentage point increase in the macroregion's unemployment rate that is associated with a fall in real wage growth of between 0.2–0.3.

Figure 4-3. Regional Unemployment and Change in Real Wage

1990–94 change in product wage

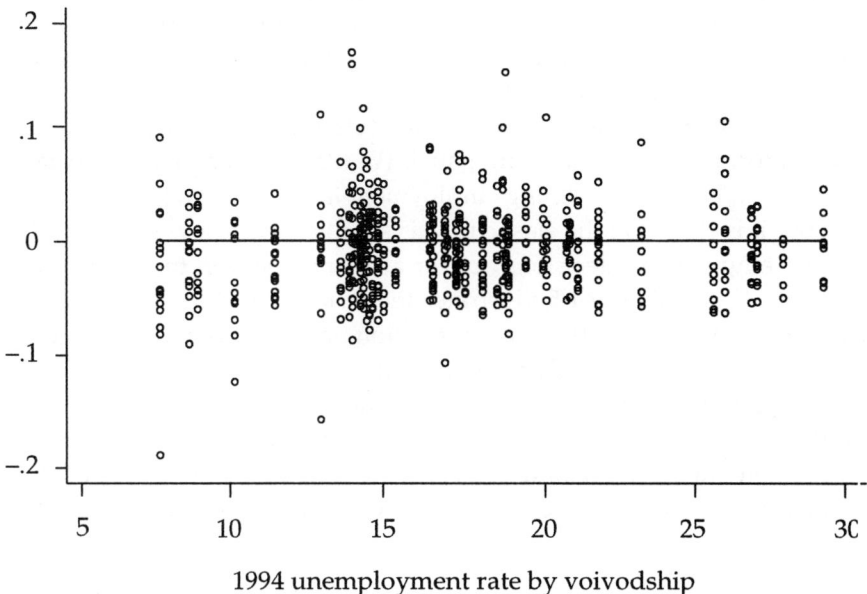

1994 unemployment rate by voivodship

Sensitivity to Financial Performance

We know that Polish firms entered the transition with very significant overmanning and wages that were largely determined outside the firm. Monetary compensation was fixed at low levels and wages comprised a fairly small proportion of GDP. Wage relativities were guided across sectors and skills by the planners' preferences. At that point, given the widespread presence of subsidies and other supports and the institutional hostility to any departure from full employment, we can think of these firms as having an employment-wage combination that would likely be to the right of even the average product curve. With the cumulative erosion in soft financing and the tolerance of open unemployment, firms would at the very least have been forced to get their wage-employment combinations back to the average product curve. Over time, we can think of several possible paths, depending on the structure of control and associated objectives of the firm.

In short, at the height of the central planning period, employment would have been largely independent of sales, and wages would have been roughly comparable across firms and branches. By 1989 this had already broken down. Employment moved more closely with sales, and there was greater scope for firms to adjust wages, a feature already manifest in the apparent wage inequality reported in table 4-3. A simple working assumption would be that over the course of the transition, firms would increasingly be forced to align employment and wage decisions to the evolution of sales and productivity.

Figure 4-4 relates the change in employment to that in value added using information from the long panel. We readily observe that virtually all firms experienced declining employment in response to the fall in output, but it is clear that the elasticity was significantly below unity. Nevertheless, employment decisions appear at first inspection to be related to the output path. Figure 4-5 illustrates the changes in wages and productivity. Here we see a fairly tight correlation between these two variables. Wages appear to be strongly responsive to changes in productivity; it can also be seen that firms experiencing productivity growth appear to have productivity changes that exceed wages. We now try and explore the association among wage and employment decisions, the financial status of the firm, and the local labor market environment more systematically.

Figure 4-4. Change in Value Added and Employment, 1990–94

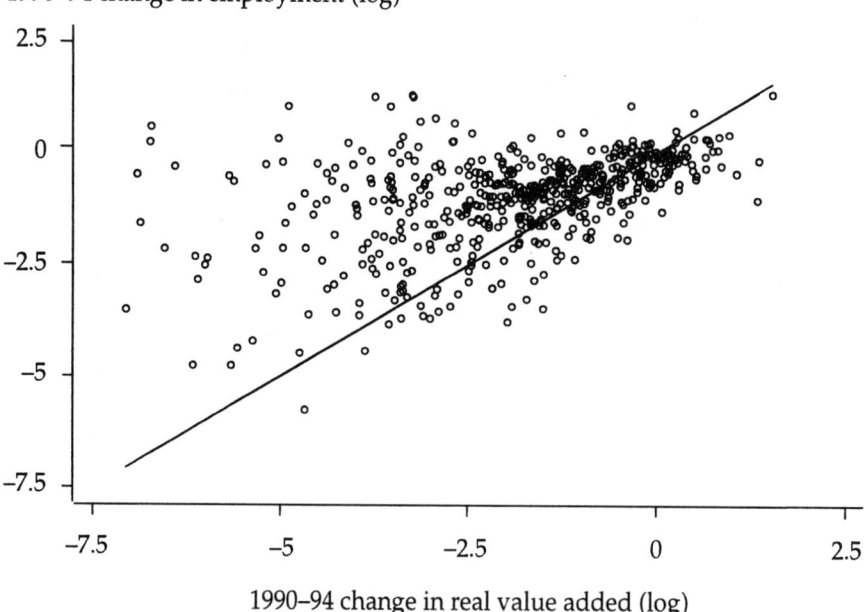

1990–94 change in employment (log)

1990–94 change in real value added (log)

Figure 4-5. Change in Average Product and Wage Rate, 1990–94

1990–94 change in real wage (log)

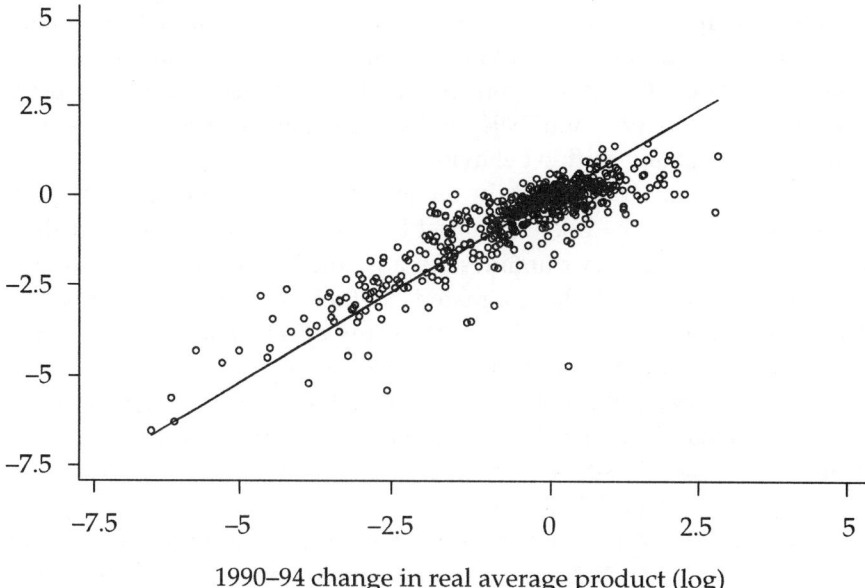

1990–94 change in real average product (log)

Our starting point is a set of simple estimations that relate the change in employment and wages to the change in sales; these regressions were run on our set of short panels as well as the longer panel for 1990–94. These base regressions take the form

$$\Delta \log N = \alpha_1 + \alpha_2 \Delta \log S + \varepsilon$$

$$\Delta \log W = \beta_1 + \beta_2 \Delta \log(S/N) + \varepsilon$$

where N= employment; S= sales and W= consumption wage.

Most generally, what we are trying to do is pick up how productivity and employment have moved with output, as proxied by sales. These estimations clearly do not have any structural interpretation. Further-more, the coefficients on the sales or productivity terms that we are inter-ested in cannot tell us where—relative to the outcome of an employment maximizing objective and an efficient outcome—we are at any given time. Rather, these estimations allow us, particularly given the size of our sample, to get a feel for the responsiveness of wages and employment to changes in output or sales and to pick up any changes in that responsiveness over time. To do this, we estimate over our short panels as well as on the long panel. We are also interested in observing whether there is any asymmetry in the response over kinds of shocks, positive or negative. This is difficult to do for obvious reasons. First, firms entered the transition with a significant degree of labor hoarding. Second, with few exceptions, the upturn that has begun to take root in Polish industry mostly manifests itself in 1993 and 1994, and the changes may be too recent to allow us pick up any shift in behavior.

Tables 4-11 and 4-12 present the results from these estimations. We ran the regressions for the pooled dataset both in univariate form and then with region and industry dummies. Because the inclusion of the latter did not significantly affect the estimated coefficients, we report only the former. We subsequently tried to capture any effects that ownership may have exerted by interacting an ownership dummy with the sales coefficient. In addition, we introduced a dummy for firms experiencing sales decreases. Finally, we implemented the same estimations for discrete groups of firms, classified by whether they experienced increasing or decreasing sales over the given period.

Turning to the univariate results, we see a significantly different set of coefficients and their time evolution for employment and wages. In the case of employment, the elasticity for the long panel is around 0.3, an elasticity roughly comparable to that for the panel of Hungarian firms discussed in Chapter 3 of this volume. With respect to the short panels, we find smaller point estimates—in no case exceeding 0.2—and with no evident trend over time. We certainly find no evidence of increasing responsiveness over time. Once we interact the sales term with an ownership dummy for state firms, as well as including a dummy for firms with decreasing sales, we find little change in the coefficient on the sales term; being a state sector firm yields a negatively signed coefficient that is generally significant, while the direction of change in sales variable indicates that firms with decreasing sales have a consistently lower employment to sales elasticity. In the case of the wage equations, we find that the sensitivity to changes in productivity is very large, both in the long and short panels.[10] The coefficient is generally around 0.7–0.8 and stable, indicating that wage changes are highly correlated with productivity. When interacting an ownership dummy for state firms with the sales term, we get a negative coefficient throughout, although one that is not always signifi-

---

10. Note that when the same regression was run with the change in sales (not productivity) on the right hand side, the coefficients were fairly comparable: 0.53 for the long panel; 0.2, 0.6, 0.7 and 0.8 for the short panels, respectively.

Table 4-11. Change in Employment: OLS Regression

Dependent variable: Change in employment (log)

| | Long panel | | Short panels | | | | | | | |
| | 1990–94 | | 1989–90 | | 1991–92 | | 1992–93 | | 1993–94 | |
Independent variables	Coefficient	Adj. R^2	Coefficient	Adj. R^2	Coefficient	Adj. R^2	Coefficient	Adj. R^2	Coefficient	Adj. R^2
All firms										
Change in sales (log)	0.323 ***	0.24	0.167 ***	0.10	0.182 ***	0.08	0.187 ***	0.08	0.034	0.00
All firms										
Change in sales (log)	0.313 ***	0.31	0.197 ***	0.24	0.185 ***	0.23	0.244 ***	0.25	0.090 **	0.18
State firm* change in sales	−0.199 ***		—		−0.412 ***		−0.549 ***		−0.395 ***	
Decreasing sales dummy	−0.405 ***		−0.057 *		−0.372 ***		−0.162 **		−0.188 ***	
n	579		945		594		533		836	
Firms with increasing sales										
Change in sales (log)	0.262	0.10	0.183 ***	0.14	0.548 ***	0.18	0.307 **	0.13	0.478 ***	0.25
n	97		682		150		194		317	
Firms with decreasing sales										
Change in sales (log)	0.281 ***	0.20	0.151 **	0.23	0.176 ***	0.18	0.238 ***	0.26	0.064 *	0.17
n	482		263		444		339		519	

Note: *** Significant at 1 percent. ** Significant at 5 percent. * Significant at 10 percent. Status of ownership is unavailable for 1989–90. All regressions include a constant. Last three regressions include dummy variables for industry and region, compared with "services" and "Warsaw," respectively. Last two regressions also include an interaction term between change in sales and state ownership for the short panels.

Source: GUS.

Table 4-12. Change in Wage Rate: OLS Regression

Dependent variable: Change in wage rate (log)

| | Long panel | | Short panels | | | | | | | |
| | 1990–94 | | 1989–90 | | 1991–92 | | 1992–93 | | 1993–94 | |
Independent variables	Coefficient	Adj. R^2	Coefficient	Adj. R^2	Coefficient	Adj. R^2	Coefficient	Adj. R^2	Coefficient	Adj. R^2
All firms										
Change in productivity (log)	0.769 ***	0.78	0.285 ***	0.20	0.774 ***	0.81	0.838 ***	0.82	0.826 ***	0.85
All firms										
Change in productivity (log)	0.786 ***	0.80	0.572 ***	0.47	0.826	0.83	0.866 **	0.82	0.859 ***	0.86
State firm * productivity change	−0.021		—		−0.028		−0.031		−0.078 ***	
decreasing sales dummy	0.048		0.120 **		0.185 ***		0.095 **		0.113 ***	
n	579		945		594		533		836	
Firms with increasing sales										
Change in productivity (log)	0.261 ***	0.36	0.326 ***	0.40	0.631 ***	0.63	0.569 ***	0.59	0.743 ***	0.60
n	97		682		150		194		317	
Firms with decreasing sales										
Change in productivity (log)	0.794 ***	0.79	0.738 ***	0.55	0.841 ***	0.84	0.938 ***	0.84	0.875 ***	0.87
n	482		263		444		339		519	

Note: *** Significant at 1 percent. ** Significant at 5 percent. * Significant at 10 percent. Status of ownership is unavailable for 1989–90. All regressions include a constant. Last three regressions include dummy variables for industry and region, compared with "services" and "Warsaw," respectively. Last two regressions also include an interaction term between change in sales and state ownership for the short panels.
Source: GUS.

cant. Firms with decreasing sales tend to be more responsive, as indicated by the positively signed coefficient in both the long and the short panels.

The picture is enriched by separating out the responses of firms explicitly differentiated by the direction of change in sales. These results are also reported in the lower panels of tables 4-11 and 4-12. We can see that with the employment equations in the long panels, the coefficients are very similar for both kinds of firms, and rather larger for firms with increasing sales in the short panels. There is little to differentiate behavior in employment matters. This is definitely not the case with the wage equations. Here, we find that in the long panel, the estimate of 0.8 for firms with decreasing sales is in sharp contrast to that of 0.26 for firms with increasing sales. Similarly, in the short panels, firms that face adversity in the product market tend to adjust wages more closely in line with changes in productivity. Both estimated coefficients are, of course, very large, at least compared with those in OECD economies, but the notably larger coefficient for firms doing relatively poorly again points to the ability of insiders to appropriate rents. Firms experiencing sales growth have generally been able to impose relative restraint on wage growth. This would be consistent with the strong investment story—indicated in table 4-7—that has characterized these firms. In short, the estimates point to the concentration of the greatest insider effects on wages in poorly performing firms.

Finally, we now simultaneously estimate a labor demand and wage equation in first differences using our short panels. We employ the two-stage least squares procedure. Table 4-13 provides the results. In the employment equation, the coefficients on the sales term are generally comparable to, or a little larger than, those in the previous estimations. Not only is the sales elasticity of employment quite high, but it also unequivocally increases after 1990/91. Firms' employment decisions are clearly responsive to changes in sales. We also find a strong and negative relationship between wage cost and employment for given sales. The size of the coefficient likewise climbs over time and suggests a clear tradeoff. Being in the state sector exerts a significant and positive effect, which implies that state firms cut employment more slowly than other firms, generally by substantial amounts. Similarly, introducing a dummy for firms that register positive net profits, we find that in all the short panels, the coefficient was negative and significant, again implying that profit-making firms adjusted employment more, holding other things equal. The size dummy, evaluated at the start of the period, was also negatively signed. For firms experiencing a positive shock to sales in the reference period, the coefficients switched signs and were generally not significant.

Table 4-13. Changes in Employment and Wage Rate
(Two-stage least squares)

	Short panels			
	1990–91	*1991–92*	*1992–93*	*1993–94*
Dependent variable: change in employment (log)				
Independent variables				
Change in real sales (log)	0.69***	0.88***	0.94***	0.09***
Change in real wage (log)	–0.96***	–1.12***	–1.09***	–1.11***
Unemployment rate	0.00	0.00	0.00	0.00
Size (small)	0.11**	-0.16***	0.61	0.05
Sector (state)	0.09***	0.30***	0.22***	0.12***
Change in revenue (increase)	0.06	0.01	–0.04	–0.07*
Profit maker	–0.10***	–0.21***	–0.11***	–0.06
constant	–0.15***	–0.24**	0.24***	–0.15**
R^2	0.45	0.55	0.53	0.49
Dependent variable: change in real wage (log)				
Independent variables				
Change in productivity (log)	0.74***	0.78***	0.85***	0.84***
Unemployment rate	0.00	0.00	0.01	0.00
Size (small)	0.13***	–0.19***	0.03	0.03
Sector (state)	0.13***	0.21***	0.19***	0.09***
Change in revenue (increase)	–0.03	–0.03	–0.04	–0.07***
Profit maker	–0.13***	–0.19***	–0.10***	–0.05
Constant	–0.11*	–0.12	–0.20***	–0.12*
R^2	0.87	0.83	0.83	0.86
n	1034	594	533	836

Note: *** Significant at 1 percent. ** Significant at 5 percent. * Significant at 10 percent. Unemployment rate: beginning of period. Size: beginning of period. Sector: end of period. Profit-maker: end of period.
    Source: GUS.

For such firms, given sales, employment tended to stay relatively high. We find that the local unemployment rate exerted no effect on employment decisions.

    Turning to the wage equation, we find that the size of the coefficient remained roughly stable and high, indicating that over three-quarters of any increase in productivity was carried through to wages. In the wage setting, it is clear that ownership and size generally matter. Firms that stayed in state ownership enjoyed a clear relative wage advantage over the panels. Being profitable actually generated a negative effect on wages, given sales, and this was significant across three of the four panels. Similarly, for firms experiencing sales increases, the sign on the coefficient was negative but, with the exception of 1993–94, not significant. Finally, confirming our earlier result, the local unemployment level appears to exert no predictable influence, and the coefficients in the wage equation are insignificant and perversely signed.

The absence of any identifiable playback from local unemployment is striking, given the very large and persistent disparities in regional unemployment rates. By way of illustration, at end-1994, unemployment in the major urban areas, such as Katowicke, Krakow, Poznan, and Warsaw, was in the range of 7–9 percent. By contrast, at least six *voivodships* had unemployment at over 25 percent, with the majority of regions reporting unemployment in the range of 10–20 percent. The absence of any robust playback from unemployment to wages at the regional level can likely be attributed to a variety of factors, including persistent constraints on mobility and the relative decline in previously high wage areas—mainly associated with heavy industry—that has prevented the top deciles of the wage distribution from increasing their distance from the bottom. It must also be related to the kinds of firms that comprise our panel and their control structures. Dominated by insiders, these larger state and privatized firms have been able to make their wage decisions largely independently of local labor market conditions. As such, wage rates in these firms have not only tended to move quite closely together (a point already established in table 4-9), but have also been significantly above the reservation values set by unemployment benefits. In short, the value of staying in these firms has considerably exceeded the fall-back outside option.

Implications for the Pace of Transition

The results reported above raise interesting and larger questions regarding their implications for the speed of transition. Given the continuing weight of the state and privatized sectors—at end-1995 the state sector still accounted for over half the number of firms in the Polish economy (see World Bank 1996, p. 53)—the manner in which these firms restructure has broad implications for the overall efficiency of the economy. To get some sense of what the responses reported in the previous section might mean, we now take a set of values estimated from this dataset and insert them in a model of endogenous restructuring that can be calibrated.

The full model is recorded in Chapter 6 of this volume. Briefly, the set-up involves two sectors—state and private—and three labor market states, including unemployment. State firms are governed by a zero profit constraint, and wages approximate average product. Output is generated by a Cobb-Douglas function, and the state sector's inefficiency relative to the private sector is imposed through the production function. The ratio of state to private productivity extracted from production functions estimated on the panel is set at 0.6. State firms face some probability of closure. They can also elect to restructure, after which they behave like private firms. These probabilities are subsequently endogenized. Their initial values can be calibrated. The values we use in this simulation are as follows: the initial probability of closure is set at 0.1, and that for restructuring at 0.2. While we lack precise information on the closure rate, the restructuring probability is consistent with the results from our panel. Because restructuring choices will depend on the outside, or reservation, wage, we set the initial value to be consistent with the Polish unemployment benefits system: about 36 percent of the average wage.[11] We also use the information from the panel to calibrate the share of workers who retain their jobs when a firm restructures; we set this parameter at 0.8.

Private firms in the model maximize profits and have capital accumulation. An investment function is specified. For this simulation, we use two values for the investment function, 0.05 and 0.08, remembering that the mean investment to sales ratio for firms in the panel was 0.05, and for firms experiencing increasing sales it was about 11 percent. Finally, we can calibrate the tax incidence for state and private firms. Taxation in this model is limited to payroll taxation and is effectively earmarked to finance the costs associated with unemployment. We set this parameter at 0.8; if this number were at unity, state and private firms would face equivalent tax burdens.[12]

Figure 4-6 reports two simulations where the only difference is in the investment function, as indicated above. In the first simulation, we can see—applying the rough closure and restructuring probabilities that we get from the panel—that unemployment rises quickly and peaks at just over 20 percent of the labor force, at $t = 160$. The subsequent decline is quite gradual. Output experiences a fairly shallow initial dip, but at the end of the period it comes to rest only a little above the value at the start

11. This implies a somewhat higher reservation wage than actually exists, given the significant number of unemployed who exhaust their entitlement and then have access only to social assistance.

12. Note also that for these simulations, the interest rate, r, is set at 0.1.

Figure 4-6. Simulations

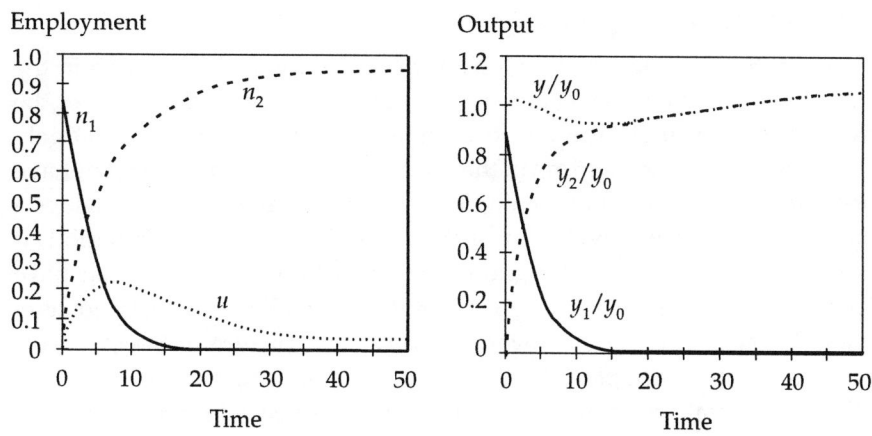

Low Investment Case

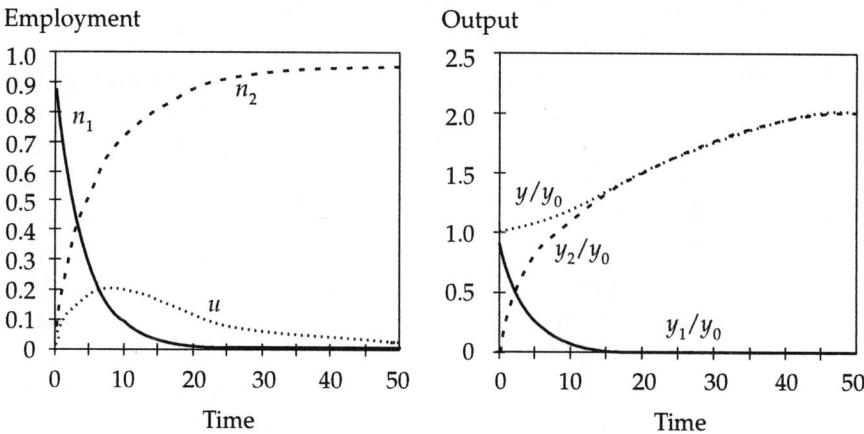

High Investment Case

of transition. Raising the value of the investment function to 0.08, we find little change in the peak and shape of the unemployment curve. Where the difference lies, predictably enough, is in output. There is only a small fall at the start of the transition, followed by a period of stable output, and then a sharp rise. At the end of transition, output has roughly doubled its initial value. In short, unemployment is not very sensitive to the investment function that characterizes the private sector; the main action is in the path of output.

Conclusions

This chapter has taken a close look at the behavior of Polish firms in the transition. The database included large firms and about 10 percent of the medium-size firms in the Polish economy. As such, it has been largely composed of industrial firms in the state sector, as well as some that have been privatized in the intervening period. This sample clearly provides a biased picture of the evolution of the Polish economy in this period. It does so because we largely ignore the smaller de novo firms that have emerged and have accounted for a significant share of aggregate job creation. What we do get, however, is a very clear picture of the extensive process of job destruction that has occurred since the start of transition. State and privatized firms have commonly experienced large and persistent adverse product market shocks. While there are signs of a clear turnaround in 1993/94, the bulk of firms in our sample have suffered nontrivial declines in output, as measured by sales, and a clear decline in soft financing options, whether through the budget or the banking system. We have shown that the ratio of gross profits to sales declined significantly between 1989/90 and 1994. Further, after 1991 a significant group of loss-making firms emerged. Such loss-makers were not concentrated in a few branches. Nevertheless, an important subsection of these loss-makers—those in the transport sector—continued to receive explicit subsidies, while others managed to maintain bank borrowing as well as borrowing from other firms. Thus, although the general financing environment for firms in our sample shifted markedly toward a hard budget constraint, a significant group of loss-makers continued to have access to soft finance and to avoid closure.

In response to these shocks, there appears to be clear heterogeneity of response and evidence of restructuring, if mostly of a defensive nature. Firms have cut employment severely. The declines that we report are of the order of 50 percent and more over the period 1990–1994. Such responses appear to be a common feature of state and privatized firms in Central Europe (see EBRD 1995: Chapter 8). The limited indicators on investment that we have for this universe of firms show that the investment/sales ratio has been around 3 percent since 1990 for the bulk of firms, but that firms experiencing sales increases have also been characterized by far larger investment ratios, in excess of 10 percent. The absence of any large increase over time can likely be related not only to continuing state ownership, but also to the way some of the privatization has been carried out, with insiders injecting little new capital.

While wages did indeed decline in all branches in the aftermath of the price shocks of 1990, what we subsequently observe is an unambiguous upward drift in real wages that appears to be common to virtually all branches. This points to some cost-side rigidity and is reflected in the upward shift in the ratio of labor costs to sales for all classes of firms. Wages to gross value added rose across all profitability categories, and at the end of the period they were roughly equivalent.

We looked at the sensitivity of wages and employment to changes in sales and productivity. For the long panel, we found an elasticity of employment to sales of around 0.3, with little differentiation over firms experiencing different sales paths. By contrast, for wages, insider effects have clearly been most strongly concentrated in firms doing relatively poorly. Finally, information extracted from the panel was used to calibrate a two-sector model of transition with endogenous restructuring. Applying Polish values for a range of key variables, including the reservation wage, the restructuring probability, and the separation rate contingent on restructuring, the unemployment and output paths under an array of assumptions on investment were demonstrated. Unemployment is shown to be only mildly sensitive to the investment rate; the difference is largely to be found in the respective paths of output.

References

Belka, Marek, Mark Schaffer, Saul Estrin, and Inderjit Singh. 1994. "Enterprise Adjustment in Poland: Evidence from a Survey of 200 Private, Privatized and State Owned Firms." Paper presented at a Workshop on Enterprise Adjustment in Eastern Europe, The World Bank, Washington, D.C.

Bentolila, S. 1997. "Polish Labor Market Institutions on the Road to the EU." CEMFI Working Paper 9712, Madrid.

Boeri, Tito. 1995. "Unemployment Dynamics in East and Central Europe." OECD, Paris. Photocopy.

Borensztein, E. R., D. Demekas, and J. Ostry. 1993. "Output Decline in the Aftermath of Reform: The Cases of Bulgaria, Czechoslovakia, and Romania." In M. Blejer, G. Calvo, F. Coricelli, and A. Gelb, eds., *Eastern Europe in Transition: From Recession to Growth*. Washington, D.C.: The World Bank.

Commander, Simon, and Fabrizio Coricelli. 1993. "Output Decline in Hungary and Poland in 1990 and 1991: Structural Change and Aggregate Shocks." In M. Blejer, G. Calvo, F. Corecelli, and A. Gelb, eds., *Eastern Europe in Transition: From Recession to Growth.* Washington, D. C.: World Bank.

Coricelli, Fabrizio, Krzysztof Hagemejer, and Krzysztof Rybinski. 1995. "Poland." In Simon Commander and Fabrizio Coricelli, eds., *Unemployment, Restructuring, and the Labor Market in Eastern Europe and Russia.* Washington, D.C.: World Bank.

de la Calle, Luis. 1990. "Macro- and Microeconomic Linkages of the Polish Reforms." World Bank Internal Discussion Paper, EMENA, Washington, D.C. October.

EBRD (European Bank for Reconstruction and Development). 1995. *Transition Report 1995: Investment and Enterprise Restructuring.* London.

Gora, Marek. 1995. "Workers' Transitions from Unemployment to Employment." Warsaw School of Economics. Photocopy.

Jackman, Richard, and Catalin Pauna. 1996. "How Have Labor Markets in Eastern Europe Performed?" London School of Economics, Center for Economic Performance.

Konings, Jozef, Hartmut Lehmann, and Mark Schaffer. 1995. "Employment Growth, Job Creation and Job Destruction in Polish Industry, 1988–1991." CEP Working Paper 707, London.

Pinto, Brian, Marek Belka, and Stefan Krajewski. 1993. "Transforming State Enterprises in Poland." World Bank Policy Research Paper, WPS 1101, Washington, D.C.

Rybinski, Krzysztof, and Piotr Mazurowski. 1995. "Wages and Employment during the Transition." Warsaw University. Mimeo.

Schaffer, Mark. 1993. "The Enterprise Sector and the Emergence of the Polish Fiscal Crisis, 1990–91." Policy Research Working Paper 1195, World Bank, Washington, D.C.

Schaffer, Mark. 1996. "Tax Arrears in Transition Economies." Heriot-Watt University. Mimeo.

Svejnar, Jan, 1986. "Bargaining Power, Fear of Disagreement, and Wage Settlements: Theory and Evidence from U.S. Industry." *Econometrica* 54 (5).

World Bank. 1996. *World Development Report 1996: From Plan to Market.* New York: Oxford University Press.

5

Labor Market Flows in the Midst of Structural Change

Tito Boeri

Despite the dramatic changes in the composition of output and in the ownership of firms that have occurred since the start of economic transition, and the strong recovery in most recent years, central and eastern European countries continue to display stagnant unemployment. The ongoing process of sectoral and ownership change seems to involve mainly direct job-to-job shifts, leaving aside unemployed jobseekers. Because reservation wages of employed jobseekers are typically higher than those of the unemployed, this hiring strategy is likely to negatively affect the pace of job creation in the private sector, while at the same time increasing the duration of unemployment.

The generosity of unemployment benefit systems in transitional economies is often blamed for this low turnover of the pool of the unemployed. The significant tightening of unemployment benefits that occurred in these countries at the beginning of 1992, however, has not resulted in an increase of outflows from unemployment—particularly in outflows to jobs—except in the Czech Republic, where unemployment is low.

The author wishes to thank Olivier Blanchard, Simon Commander, Hartmut Lehmann, Carmen Pages-Serra, and participants in a workshop in Washington for useful comments on an initial draft of this chapter.

Why do labor market flows continue to bypass the unemployed? Why did reductions in the generosity of unemployment benefits not result in an increase in exits from unemployment?

The theoretical literature on transitional economies has so far devoted little attention to the relation between structural change and the extent and nature of gross job flows. It has also considered workers as homogeneous, perfectly fungible across industries and occupations, and endowed with skills that are common knowledge. In this paper a model is developed that accounts for the stagnancy of the unemployment pools in these countries by drawing on a legacy of the previous regime, the poor signals that observables—such as past wages and educational attainment, as well as employment and occupational records—give regarding the actual productivity of workers. That workers' productivity is private information in economies undergoing radical transformation also contributes to the explanation of the ineffectiveness of reforms in unemployment benefits in boosting outflows to jobs. In high-unemployment transitional economies, reductions in the reservation wages of the unemployed need to be much larger to induce employers to modify their hiring strategies and start recruiting massively from the ranks of the unemployed.

Two empirical implications of the model are not contradicted by available evidence. In particular, patterns of labor turnover in state enterprises are consistent with the implications of the model, as are wage differentials across public and private firms for unskilled workers. Some support is also found for the hypothesis—embedded in the model—that stagnancy in the unemployment pool is consistent with large shifts of workers from state to private sector jobs.

The Evidence

Fast Structural Change

Table 5-1 displays some common measures of structural change in central and eastern Europe and for the group of OECD countries as a whole. In particular, the coefficient of variation of yearly employment growth rates across nine broad sectors[1] is reported, as well as two indexes increasing in

---

1. Agriculture; mining; manufacturing; electricity, gas, and water; construction, wholesale trade and hotels; transport and communications; finance and real estate; and community and personal services.

Table 5-1. Pace of Structural Change in Transitional Economies and OECD Countries

Country	Year	Standard deviation of employment growth[a]	Sectoral reallocation index (%)[b]	Privatization reallocation index (%)[c]
Czech Republic	1991–92	15.1	0.65	0.58
	1992–93	35.3	0.89	0.88
	1993–94	*10.1*	*0.77*	*1.00*
	1994–95	*3.3*	*0.10*	*0.92*
Hungary	1991–92	..	..	0.02
	1992–93	*9.3*	*0.25*	*0.66*
	1993–94	*7.0*	*0.55*	*0.87*
	1994–95	*6.9*	*0.51*	*0.72*
Poland	1990–91	6.5	0.08	0.62
	1991–92	20.2	0.90	0.83
	1992–93	*7.9*	*0.34*	*0.80*
	1993–94	*18.2*	*0.95*	*0.61*
	1994–95	*7.3*	*0.94*	*0.69*
Slovak Republic	1991–92	16.1	0.50	0.57
	1992–93	31.8	0.89	0.92
	1993–94	*4.8*	*0.15*	*0.92*
	1994–95	*9.1*	*0.60*	*0.79*
Bulgaria[d]	1991–92	12.4	0.06	0.41
	1992–93	14.5	0.65	0.95
	1993–94	10.4	0.90	0.85
	1994–95	..	..	*0.43*
OECD countries	1990–93[e]	*3.1*	*0.33*	*0.09*

Note: Italicized figures denote data from national Labour Force Surveys.

a. Standard deviation of employment growth rates across nine sectors.

b. Index calculated over gross employment variations in nine sectors (see text for details).

c. Index calculated over gross employment variations in the public and private sectors (see the text for details).

d. Seven sectors only.

e. Average of yearly measures of structural change.

Source: National Labour Force Surveys and Establishment Surveys.

the pace of job reallocation, respectively, across sectors (*SR*) and between the public and private sectors (*PR*). The two indexes are given by

$$SR = 1 - \frac{\Delta E}{\Delta E^+ + \left|\Delta E^-\right|} \quad \text{and} \quad SRPR = 1 - \frac{\left|\Delta E\right|}{\left|\Delta E^{PUB}\right| + \left|\Delta E^{PRIV}\right|}$$

where ΔE^+ denotes the sum of sectoral employment variations over expanding sectors, ΔE^- is the sum of employment variations across declining industries, and the superscripts *PUB* and *PRIV* stand, respectively, for public sector and private sector employment. Both indexes are bound between 0 and 1, and are increasing in the extent of job reallocation from declining to expanding industries and from public to private sector jobs. Unlike the standard deviation, which can take high values even when all sectors and firms of different ownership are experiencing employment declines, these two indexes isolate the extent of the job reallocation from *declining* to *expanding* units involved in the transition process.

The various measures of structural change proposed point to a much faster pace of structural change in Central and Eastern Europe compared with the group of OECD countries, and to significant *external* job reallocation of workers.

Low Turnover of the Unemployment Pool

Despite rapid structural change (as well as the steep employment declines previously documented; see OECD 1994), the turnover of the unemployment pool was very low in the initial years of transition and continues to be lower in central and eastern Europe than in most OECD countries. Figure 5-1 shows average monthly unemployment inflows and outflows as a proportion of the labor force in transitional economies and in selected OECD countries.[2] These data suggest that transitional economies continue to be characterized by unemployment turnover rates of the order *at most* of 2–2.5 percent of the labor force, compared with 4 to 5 per-

---

2. Data are drawn from administrative sources, which allow for continuous time measurement of unemployment inflows, but may be affected by differences in national unemployment benefit regulations, as argued below.

Figure 5-1. Turnover of the Unemployment Pool

Percentage of labor force

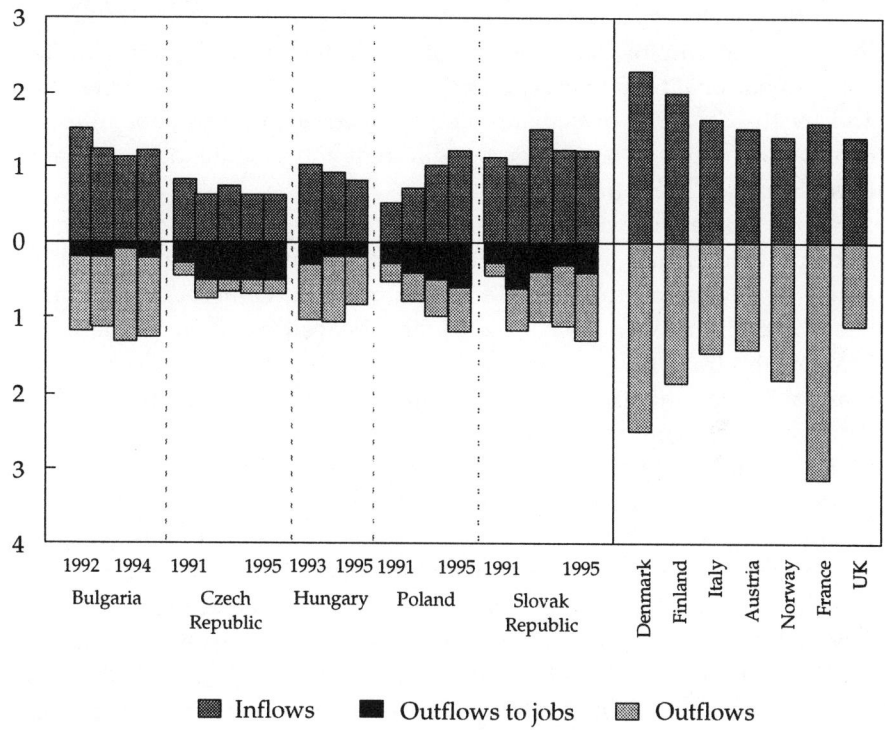

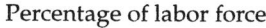

Note: For the OECD countries, the data refer to 1992, except for Denmark, Finland, and Italy, which refer to 1993.
Source: OECD-CCET Regional Database, OECD LFS Statistics.

cent in Nordic countries and more than 3 percent even in relatively low-unemployment countries such as Austria.

It is important to note that in 1992 a quite radical tightening of unemployment benefits occurred in most central and eastern European countries that entailed reductions in the duration of benefits, lower replacement rates, or both. Figure 5-1 does not point to a significant increase in outflow rates after these reforms.[3] In the two countries experi-

---

3. See OECD (1994) for details on reforms of the unemployment benefit systems enforced at the beginning of 1992 and OECD (1996) for an assessment of their effects.

encing some growth in outflows from unemployment in 1993–94 (Hungary and Poland), it appears that it is mainly outflows to destinations other than employment that have increased.

Additional information on the magnitude and characteristics of outflows from unemployment—and information that is unaffected by differences in national regulations on the duration of unemployment benefits[4] and by the scope of placement activities carried out by labor offices—comes from matched records across different waves of the national Labor Force Surveys (LFSs) (figure 5-2).[5]

Figure 5-2 reports yearly transition probabilities across employment, unemployment, and out-of-the-labor-force status by drawing on the panel component of national LFSs. Unfortunately, these surveys have been carried out only since 1992–93, and hence do not cover the initial years of the transition process. Moreover, for Bulgaria and Slovakia, the interval is nine months; therefore, yearly "mover coefficients" for these countries are larger than those displayed in the figure by, at most, a factor of 1.3.[6] With the above caveats kept in mind, figure 5-2 confirms that flows from unemployment to employment are still low in transitional economies. The probability that an unemployed person will find a job within twelve months (even in Poland, the fastest growing country in the region) is of the order of 0.35—that is, roughly one-half of the yearly transition probabilities for unemployment estimated (on the basis of matched records) for the United States (bottom panel, on the right-hand side of figure 5-2) and two-thirds of those of high-unemployment European countries such as Spain (OECD 1996).

---

4. This is especially true when no registration at labor offices is required for the jobless to draw social assistance payments after the exhaustion of unemployment benefits.

5. A general problem with this sort of data is that sample attrition (persons ceasing to respond to the questionnaire) may be particularly high among people changing their labor market status, which would tend to bias estimated outflow rates downward. Strategies for dealing with nonresponse are, however, becoming increasingly uniform across countries, which improves the cross-country comparability of the data displayed in figure 5-2.

6. Empirical literature on transition matrices suggests that predicting yearly flows from higher-frequency data by assuming that transition probabilities are constant over time leads to an overestimation of mobility. Put another way, by multiplying by four-quarterly transition probabilities, one obtains an upper bound for exit probabilities and a lower bound for the probability that individuals are still unemployed one year later.

Figure 5-2.   Labor Market Flows: Data from Matched LFS Records

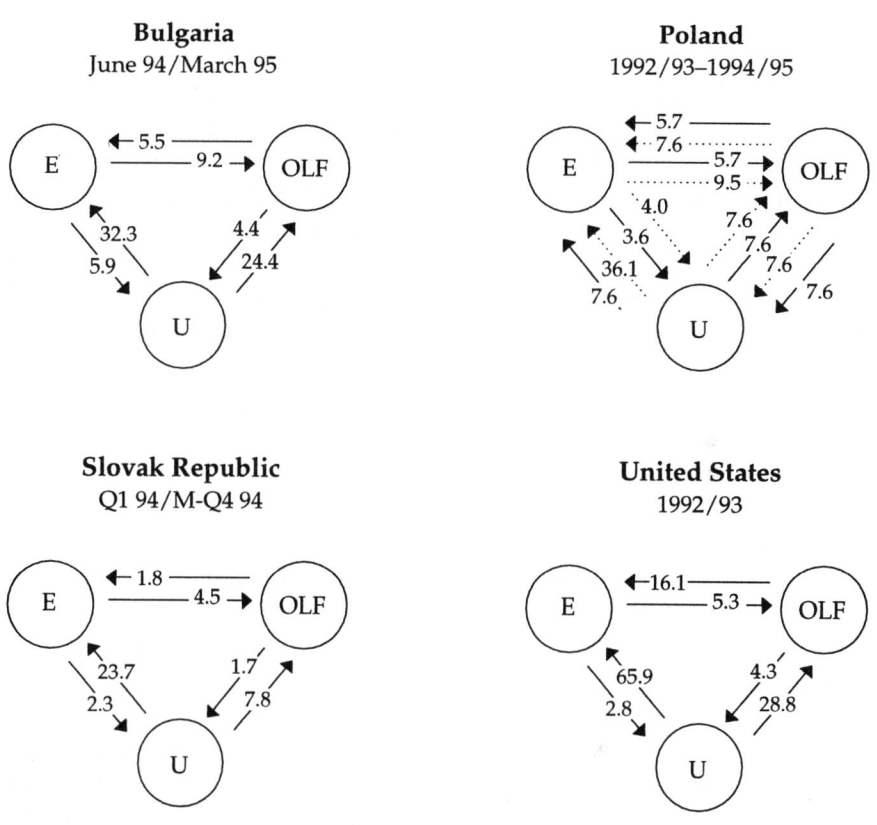

Source: National Statistical Offices.

In summary, unemployment turnover continues to be low, despite the scope of structural change and the significant tightening of unemployment benefits that occurred at early stages of the transition process.

Low reemployment probabilities and the low level and short duration of unemployment benefits would suggest that jobless people are likely to have rather low reservation wages. And the fast growth of employment in the private sector suggests that substantial hiring is occurring. Why, then, are private employers not hiring from the ranks of the unemployed? Why should they pay premiums on hirings—for example, by hiring state sector workers—rather than taking those who are ready to work at the lower end of the wage distribution? The model developed in the next section addresses this issue.

A Model

Formerly planned economies inherited a highly compressed wage distribution from the previous regime. Low wage differentials, if not quite paradoxical wage relativities, offered low returns to education (Boeri and Keese 1992; Orazem and Vodopivec 1996) and did not encourage the best-educated workers to develop their skills in the workplace. Moreover, the inherited education system did not promote "fungible" skills. Ongoing reviews of the education systems in transitional economies being carried out by the OECD point to narrowly based and rigid curriculums in the vocational education system. Specialized workers were also often trained in the workplace for very specific skills and occupations. Finally, managers of state enterprises were forced (and, at the same time, allowed by soft budget constraints) to provide jobs as benefits in kind, independently of the productivity of their workers. There was little, if any, monitoring of the productivity of individual workers, given that employees were all paid practically the same wage, and it was impossible to dismiss low-productivity workers.

Under these conditions, at early stages of transition, the educational attainment of individuals, as well as their employment and occupational records,[7] offered little guidance to employers screening for the most suitable job applicants or to managers wishing to keep the best workers attached to their firm. This created a fundamental informational asymmetry, not only between workers (who presumably had some clues about their own productivity) and employers (who did not), but also between employers at state enterprises, who faced a large and rather indistinguishable workforce, and new private entrepreneurs, who could at least assess the productivity of each new worker (or cohort of workers) being hired.

In the model below, the asymmetries between state and private enterprises are deliberately confined to the different information that employers in the two kinds of units could acquire regarding the productivity of their workers. Thus, there will be neither the predetermined technological asymmetries between state and private enterprises often posited by the literature nor the quality (and price) differences between the goods produced by firms of different ownership. Adding these features to the model would complicate its structure somewhat, without adding sub-

---

7. Occupational classifications used in these countries for statistical purposes (as well as in the registration of jobseekers) were extremely complex and based on fairly obsolete definitions of tasks.

stantially to the results. In the basic model, only the case in which there are high- and low-productivity workers will be considered. Extensions of this setup allowing for horizontal differentiation of skills and for decisions to drop from the labor force will be considered thereafter.

The Basic Model

At the beginning of the economic transition, everybody is employed in a state firm. By conveniently normalizing the total labor force to one and assuming that the firm produces under technologies allowing constant returns to scale,[8] total output is simply given by

(5-1) $$y = \bar{v}_0$$

where $\bar{v}_0 = v^+ s_0^+ + v^-(1 - s_0^+)$ is the average labor productivity; v^+ and v^- are, respectively, the productivity of high- and low-productivity workers (clearly, $v^+ > v^-$); and s_0^+ denotes the initial endowments of high-productivity workers.

The start of transition involves free entry of private firms producing under the same technologies as state firms.[9]

There is an exogenous layoff rate, q (for example, related to the obsolescence of the machines that workers use), affecting both private and public enterprises. As shown in the next section, separation rates in public and private enterprises are comparable, whereas significant asymmetries between the two kinds of firms are present on the hiring side. Those losing their jobs receive an unemployment benefit, b. Initially it is assumed that there is no utility of leisure (or, alternatively, that b is inclusive of the utility of leisure), so that b also equals the reservation wage of the unemployed.[10]

State sector managers cannot disentangle high- from low-productivity workers, and hence are forced to pay all workers the same wage $(\bar{w})$. Private employers can measure the productivity of each new worker being hired and, consequently, offer wages commensurate with productivity

---

8. The constant return to scale assumption allows the private sector to be treated as a monolith. Decreasing returns to scale technologies would yield the same results.

9. This is equivalent to assuming that subsidies to state enterprises are removed, imposing a hard budget constraint on enterprises, as in the models by Aghion and Blanchard (1994) and Blanchard and Keeling, in this volume.

10. Earnings-related benefits would not affect the result when all workers in the state firm receive the same wage.

(that is, w^+ and w^-, respectively, for high- and low-productivity workers). With state enterprises denoted by capital letters and private enterprises by lowercase letters, firms' net revenues in the two kinds of firms are therefore given by

(5-2) $$\Pi = \bar{v}L - \bar{w}L$$

and

(5-3) $$\pi = \bar{v}l - w^+l^+ - w^-l^-.$$

In the absence of subsidies to state enterprises, state sector workers are paid their average product.[11] Thus, the welfare of incumbents in the state firm can only be maximized by increasing $\bar{v}$. This means keeping (and recruiting) as many high-productivity workers as possible. State employers, however, can at best offer $\bar{v}$, which—as shown below—is too low to enable them to attract (and retain) high-productivity workers. Hence, no hiring takes place in state enterprises.

Private employers offer jobs at wages specified before hiring takes place.[12] If the value of a worker's output turns out to be lower than the wage specified in the contract, the worker is fired during the probationary period.[13] Otherwise, an employee continues to work with the firm at the contracted wage unless he or she quits the firm or the job is abolished. There is a fixed setup cost for creating new jobs and screening applicants. Because of these costs, there is a limited number (α) of jobs that can be offered during each period.[14] The choice of private employers of which

---

11. A simple extension of the model is to allow for just a fraction of the average product being distributed to workers.

12. Wage renegotiation is ruled out by the kind of job setup costs discussed below.

13. Probationary periods are allowed by labor codes in the various countries at the beginning of permanent contracts, and most of the jobs offered by new private enterprises are fixed-term appointments. Informal work relations in the small business sector and the weakness of trade unions in the emerging private sector are additional factors that allow employers to fire workers who are not found to have suitable skills. A simple extension of this model is to allow for firing to occur only after workers are paid a one-period wage, which implies that private sector firms, under the strategy given by equation 5-4, will preferentially offer jobs to state sector workers.

14. The case in which d is decreasing in the wage offered by firms is considered below.

wage-job combination to offer will depend on the expected surplus resulting from the new hires.

If private employers offer $w \geq \bar{v}$, they get

(5-4) $$a(v^+ - w).$$

All high-productivity workers (either in the state firm or unemployed) will accept any job in the private sector offering at least $\bar{v}$. Low-productivity workers will not apply for a private sector job offering more than v^-. If they do so, with a probability of one they would be fired.

If private employers offer any wage in the range $\bar{v} > w > v^-$, they get

(5-5) $$\min\left\{ s_u^+ U, \alpha \right\}(v^+ - w)$$

where s_u^+ is the proportion of high-productivity workers in the unemployment pool, U. Only high-productivity workers who have lost their jobs would be willing to take these job offers and be retained by private employers; those still employed in the state firm would be better off keeping their present positions.

Finally, the surplus associated with offering a wage in the interval is

(5-6) $$\alpha[(1 - s_u^+)v^- + s_u^+ v^+ - w] = \alpha(\bar{v}_u - w)$$

where $\bar{v}_u$ is the average productivity of workers in the unemployment pool. Only under a hiring strategy that offered a wage lower than v^- would low-productivity workers in the unemployed pool be hired by private employers.

A wage-job offer as in equation 5-4 will yield a higher (lower) surplus than under equation 5-5 in all cases where q times s_0^+ is sufficiently small (large). In other words, either a low layoff rate (for example, because of strict employment security schemes) or a low initial endowment of high-productivity workers may induce private employers to "poach" high-productivity workers from state firms, rather than selecting them only from the unemployment pool.

Similarly, private employers will rank strategy 5-4 above strategy 5-6 in all cases where the differential in productivity between high- and low-productivity workers is sufficiently marked. Moreover, if private employers initially offer $\bar{v}$, they will have no incentive to depart from this hiring strategy to the extent that there are high-productivity workers in the pool of jobseekers. This is because both $\bar{v}$ and s^+ are declining over time. It follows that a sufficient condition for 5-4 being larger than 5-6 throughout the transition is that

$$(5\text{-}7) \qquad\qquad v^+ > 2\bar{v}_0 - b$$

where $\bar{v}_0$ denotes, as usual, the pre-transition average productivity of state workers. Overall, the model suggests that the scope, speed, and unemployment outcomes of the transition process are crucially dependent on *initial conditions* such as the endowment of high-productivity workers, the degree of employment protection (embedded in the parameter q), and the generosity of unemployment benefits prevailing at the start of the transition process.

Figures 5-3a through 5-3c display numerical simulations of the model under the three different hiring rules of private employers outlined above.[15] This helps in understanding the kind of labor market adjustment entailed by the three different strategies of employers. In particular, total employment (bold line) and its distribution across state (L) and private (l) firms are plotted together with the associated levels of output (dotted line). Unemployment is represented in figures 5-3a through 5-3c by the area above the aggregate employment curve.

As shown by comparing figure 5-3a with figure 5-3b, the main difference between strategies outlined in equations 5-4 and 5-5 is in the speed of employment decline in the state firm and in the growth of the private sector. When private employers "poach" high-productivity workers from state firms, employment decline in the public sector is faster than in the other case, and the growth of the private sector is steeper. Because it is assumed that technological asymmetries between public and private firms do not exist, the path of output is the same under the two scenarios. And, since only the distribution (as opposed to the level) of employment

---

15. The chosen values of parameters are broadly in line with the experience of these countries. In particular, a layoff rate of 3.5 percent each period was chosen—an intermediate level between layoff rates observed in state enterprises in Hungary (about 1.5–2 percent) and Bulgaria (7–8 percent) at early stages of transition—and it was assumed that the skill distribution is not too unbalanced (the share of high-productivity workers is 30 percent). In the numerical simulations we kept the same values of the parameters in the three scenarios as if for exogenous reasons (such as a change in the level of unemployment benefits) employers had been induced to shift from one strategy to another.

Figure 5-3. Labor Market Adjustment under Three Hiring Strategies

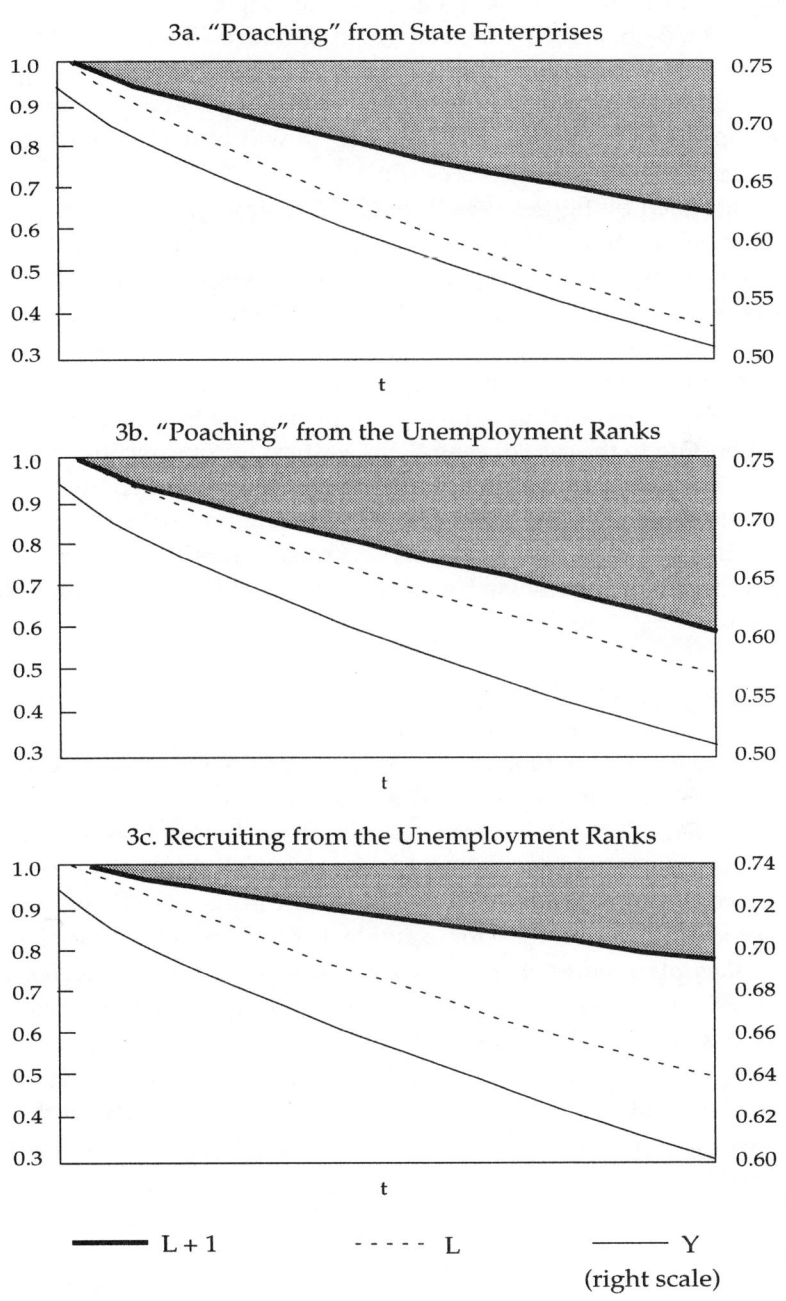

3a. "Poaching" from State Enterprises

3b. "Poaching" from the Unemployment Ranks

3c. Recruiting from the Unemployment Ranks

L + 1   L   Y
(right scale)

varies, the shift from strategy 5-4 to strategy 5-5 does not involve changes in the dynamics of unemployment.

Marked differences in the dynamics of unemployment emerge when figures 5-3a, 5-3b, and 5-3c are compared. Because all workers are hired from the ranks of the unemployed, strategy 5-6 generates less unemployment and higher output than the other two strategies at any phase of the transition process, although the speed of growth of the private sector is not faster than under the first scenario.

As suggested by figures 5-3a through 5-3c, strategy 5-4 can be ranked above or below strategy 5-5 only on distributional grounds. That private firms have a larger employment share under strategy 5-4 implies that the dispersion in earnings is greater in this scenario than under strategy 5-5. Strategy 5-6 is clearly Pareto-superior to the other two because it involves less unemployment and higher output throughout the transition process.

The scenario depicted in figure 5-3a appears to be the one most closely corresponding to the case of central and eastern European countries. This scenario involves a continuous reallocation of high-productivity workers from state to private firms, and hence increasing productivity and wage differentials between the two kinds of firms. Before the empirical relevance of the model is assessed, some extensions of the basic setup will be considered.

Extensions of the Model

In the simple model outlined above, wages play no role in the *pace* of new job creation in the private sector. The same number of posts, α, is created no matter which wage-job combination is offered by employers. A simple extension of the model is to allow for the fixed (job setup and screening) costs faced by employers to be higher when posts are offered only to high-productivity workers—for example, because the screening of applicants takes place only when posts are meant to be filled exclusively by high-productivity workers. This does not affect the ranking of strategy 5-4 over strategy 5-5, but it makes both of these strategies less appealing to employers than strategy 5-6. In particular, denoting respectively by α^+ and α^- the number of jobs being offered to high-productivity workers or to all workers (where, clearly, $\alpha > \alpha^+$), condition 5-7 should be rewritten as follows:

(5-8)
$$\frac{\alpha}{\alpha^+} > \frac{v^+ - \bar{v}_0}{\bar{v}_0 - b}$$

which makes it clear that the higher the screening cost (the larger α is with respect to α^+), the greater the productivity gap between the two kinds of workers that is necessary to induce employers to choose strategy 5-4 over 5-6. The asymmetries in labor market adjustment between, on the one hand, strategy 5-4 or 5-5 and, on the other hand, strategy 5-6 are also magnified by this extension of the model because strategy 5-6 now involves far more jobs (hence output) than the other two scenarios.

Several studies have pointed to significant flows of workers to nonparticipation in the labor force after the start of the transition process. Another possible extension of the model is thus to allow for the decision to drop out of the labor force. This can be done by introducing some costs of job search (say, c) and assuming that the utility of leisure (u) of some individuals (for example, those most productive in home production) can exceed the unemployment benefit net of the cost of job search[16] or the available wage offers (or both). In particular, define by $\bar{\lambda}$ and $\underline{\lambda}$, respectively, the highest and lowest support of the distribution of the utility of leisure across individuals and assume that either

$$(5\text{-}9) \qquad\qquad \bar{\lambda} > b - c$$

or

$$(5\text{-}10) \qquad\qquad \bar{\lambda} > \bar{v}\;,$$

or both.

When condition 5-9 holds and either strategy 5-4 or 5-5 is chosen by employers, some low-productivity individuals with a high utility of leisure would leave the labor force after losing their jobs. When condition 5-10 holds, flows to nonparticipation may originate directly from employment without involving job loss: some low-productivity workers may be induced by declining wages to quit the state firm. This new dimension of heterogeneity across individuals (varying utilities of leisure) somewhat complicates hiring strategies of private employers and their ranking, since the reservation wage can now be different for workers with the same level of productivity. However, a general implication of this exten-

---

16. This corresponds to the ILO-OECD definition of unemployment, involving some form of active job search on the part of the individual. In several countries, work tests are also enforced to check the eligibility of unemployment benefit claimants.

sion of the model is that a hiring strategy involving all workers implies lower declines in labor supply than strategies offering jobs only to high-productivity workers.

A third possible extension of the model is to allow not only for vertical, but also for horizontal, differentiation in productivity levels, at least in the case of low-productivity workers. As discussed above, the inherited workforce was trained in rather specific skills, and the transition process typically involves the creation of new production lines that do not necessarily require the same skills as those offered by the state firm's workforce. Suppose, for instance, that there are two kinds of private employers, A and B, and that some low-productivity workers have skills most suited for type-A jobs and others for type-B jobs. This is likely to make strategies 5-4 and 5-5 more appealing to employers than strategy 5-6, owing to the lower uncertainty associated with hiring high-productivity (and supposedly more fungible) workers. Furthermore, if low-productivity workers themselves do not know their own skill type, the reservation utility of low-productivity workers is higher because it should include a premium for the risk of being hired by the "wrong" employer.[17]

In summary, the basic model can be extended in several directions to improve its realism. These extensions are likely to modify the conditions under which a given hiring strategy is preferred to another, and they could magnify the asymmetries of labor market adjustment depicted in figures 5-3a through 5-3c without altering the ranking of the three scenarios from a normative standpoint.

Empirical Relevance and Policy Implications of the Model

"Churning," Job-to-Job Shifts, and Wage Differentials

Whatever the hiring strategy chosen by employers, the model points to significant asymmetries in labor turnover rates between state and private firms. Although managers of state firms do not hire new workers, at least until the average productivity is above v^-, some churning will occur in

---

17. The lower the minimum employment record required for eligibility for unemployment benefits, the higher will be the premium.

Table 5-2. Labor Turnover and the Extent of "Churning"

	H	POS	S	NEG	LT	JT	CHUR
Bulgaria, 1991							
State enterprises	12.9		31.5		44.3		3.5
Hungary, 1991							
State enterprises	20.6		30.5		51.1		15.7
Poland, 1991							
State enterprises	10.0	1.3	26.4	17.6	36.4	18.9	1.8
Private enterprises	39.5	17.9	41.8	21.3	81.3	39.2	38.4
All enterprises	13.0	3.0	28.0	18.0	41.0	21.0	5.5
United States, 1979–83	89.2	13.0	85.6	10.4	174.8	23.4	83.8
Germany, 1985–90	30.3	9.0	30.4	7.5	60.7	16.5	30.3
Denmark, 1984–91	29.0	16.0	29.0	13.8	58.0	29.8	29.0

Notes: H = hirings (as a percentage of employment); S = separations (as a percentage of employment); POS = gross job creation (as a percentage of employment); NEG = gross job destruction (as a percentage of employment); and CHUR as indicated in the text.

Source: Data on Poland are from Konings, Lehmann, and Schaffer (1996); data on Bulgaria are from Assenov (1995).

private firms because private employers will simultaneously hire and fire workers.

Unfortunately, little information is available on gross job and labor turnover rates in transitional economies. Table 5-2 reports data on gross job creation and destruction in Polish state and private manufacturing enterprises—drawn from a recent study by Konings, Lehmann, and Schaffer (1996)—as well as statistics on labor turnover in Bulgarian and Hungarian state enterprises with more than twenty-five employees. Labor turnover rates in a few OECD countries are also reported, although the international comparability of data is problematic, owing to differences in the coverage of the series. In particular, compared with the other countries, Polish data strongly undersample small units that typically display the highest job and labor turnover rates. Thus, labor and job turnover data for transition economies are likely to be biased downward.

With these caveats in mind, table 5-2 suggests that state enterprises at early stages of transition were—consistent with the predictions of the model—characterized by relatively low churning rates. Large gross separation and job destruction rates (third and fourth columns) in state enterprises were indeed associated with markedly low gross job creation (*POS*) and hiring (*H*) rates, suggesting that a "hiring freeze" occurred at early stages of transition.[18] Thus, Bulgarian, Polish, and (to a lesser extent), Hungarian state enterprises display separation rates significantly larger than hiring rates, and consequently low "churning" rates (last column on the right-hand side of table 5-2).[19] By contrast, data on Polish *private* enterprises, also reported in table 5-2, and evidence from enterprise panels in other countries point to large (by Western standards), hiring and separation rates in private enterprises of transitional economies, and hence suggest churning rates of the same order of magnitude (if not larger) as those observed in European OECD countries.

When private employers opt for strategy 5-4—the case, in our view, most closely corresponding to many transitional economies—a significant component of hiring in the emerging private sector is made of direct shifts of (high-productivity) workers from state to private sector jobs. As in most OECD countries, little information is available on job-to-job shifts. Table 5-3 shows flows from public to private sector jobs estimated on the basis of Bulgarian, Polish, Slovak, and Slovenian LFS and the Hungarian Household Panel Survey. In these surveys, households are not only asked about their current jobs, but also whether they have changed jobs since the last interview. Hence, it is possible, in principle, to disentangle genuine shifts across the two sectors from uninterrupted employment spells in firms undergoing privatization.

---

18. Konings, Lehmann, and Schaffer (1996) also report data on labor turnover in state enterprises in the years immediately preceding the start of transition (1988 and 1989). These data show that hirings have halved with respect to their pre-reform levels, but separation rates have only marginally increased. According to official labor turnover statistics, hirings also declined in Hungary from 1988 to 1991 (from about 23 to 21 percent), but in this case employment reductions seem mainly to have involved an increase in separation rates (from 22 to 30 percent). Köllo (in this volume) suggests that in Hungary, a different pattern of employment adjustment may have occurred that involved the use of "soft measures" (such a greater reliance on attrition as a way to reduce the workforce) only in later stages of the transition.

19. The measure of churning reported on the right-hand side of table 5-2 is computed as follows:

$$CHUR = 0.5 * (H + S) - |H - S|,$$

where H and S denote, respectively, total hirings and separations as a percentage of total employment in the base year.

Table 5-3. Public-Private Shifts of Workers

Country and year	Percentage of inflows into PR	Percentage of outflows from U to PR	Percentage of outflows from the PUB	Net flows between U and PR[a]
Bulgaria (6/94–10/94)	43	152	16	20
Bulgaria (6/95–10/95)	46	182	20	13
Hungary (91–92)	71	478	23	–431
Hungary (92–93)	52	150	22	–78
Poland (92–93)	33	127	43	37
Poland (93–94)	32	98	50	20
Poland (94–95)	26	65	48	50
Slovak Republic (94)[b]	41	86	50	50
Slovenia (92–93)	48	113	24	481

Note: PUB = employment in public sector; *PR* = employment in private sector; *U* = unemployment; *PR* includes self-employment and cooperatives in Poland; *PR* includes self-employment in Hungary.

a. As a proportion of flows from *U* to *PR*.

b. Q1 to Q4 1994

Source: For Poland, matched records from May to May LFS; for Hungary, Household Panel Survey; for Slovak Republic, Q1 to Q4 1994 matched.

Table 5-3 points to sizable direct flows from public to private sector jobs in these three countries.[20] A large component (up to 70 percent) of inflows into private employment originates from job-to-job shifts. In most countries these are larger than flows from unemployment to private sector employment (second column). Job-to-job shifts also appear to be a major vehicle for achieving employment reductions in state enterprises, since in some years and countries up to 50 percent of outflows from state sector employment was associated with shifts of workers to private sector jobs (third column). Put another way, private employers appear to have recruited at least as many workers from the ranks of state enterprises as from the unemployed. In Hungary, at early stages of transition, flows

---

20. Whereas in the Hungarian Household Panels Surveys individuals are asked whether they had experienced intervening spells of unemployment since the last interview, in the Polish LFS they are not. Hence, these flows may conceal short spells of unemployment that occur during the shift from one job to another.

from unemployment to private sector jobs were so low that the private sector, rather than absorbing unemployment, was a net contributor to its growth (fourth column of table 5-3).

The relevance of direct job-to-job shifts in flows from public to private enterprises is also confirmed by microeconomic evidence on the early stages of transition in the former Czechoslovakia (Vecernik 1992), Bulgaria (Beleva, Jackman, and Nenova-Amar 1995), and Hungary (Köllo 1993). An indirect indication of the importance of job-to-job shifts in transitional economies is also the relatively large share of employed jobseekers in these countries. Insofar as actual job-to-job shifts are increasing in the number of employed jobseekers, LFS data suggesting that no less than 6 percent of the employed in transition countries[21] (compared with 2 to 5 percent in most countries of the European Union) are actively seeking jobs provide indirect support for the relevance of job-to-job shifts in these countries (Boeri 1996).

A third implication of the model concerns wage differentials. The model suggests that wage differentials between public and private firms are increasing over time and that low-productivity workers are better off staying in the state firm. There is ample evidence of increasing pay differentials between private and state firms when controls are added for the sector and size of firms, and there are indications that unskilled workers are paid more in the public sector than in the private sector. Rutkowski (1996) has shown that in Poland wages of workers with lower skills are, on average, 11 percentage points higher in the public sector than in the private sector.

Unemployment Benefits and Active Labor Market Policies

It has been shown above that a hiring strategy that does not leave aside the low-productivity workers leads to the most efficient labor market outcome. The natural question, therefore, is how policies can induce private employers to adopt the hiring strategy that will minimize the rise of unemployment and output losses.

---

21. Unfortunately, no question about job search activities is asked of employed persons in the Hungarian LFS, and it was not yet possible to obtain similar information for the Slovak Republic. Thus, reference is made in Boeri (1996) only to data on employed jobseekers in Poland, the Czech Republic, and Slovenia. See also Lehmann and Wadsworth (1996) for an analysis of employed jobseekers in Poland vis-à-vis the United Kingdom.

Figure 5-4. Unemployment and the Critical Replacement Rate
(numerical simulations of the model)

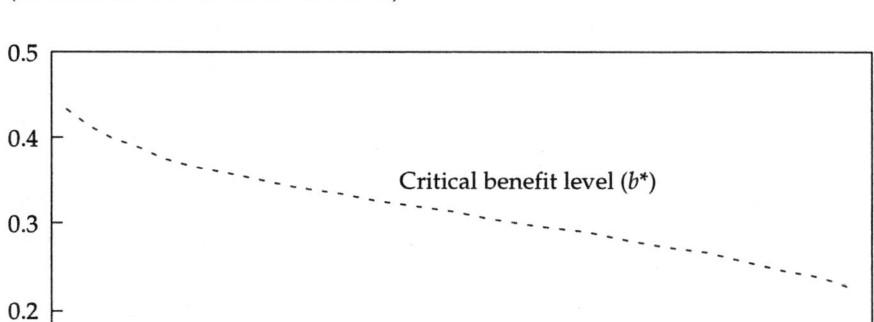

A crucial parameter in the choice among hiring strategies—and one that, in principle, can be altered at will by public authorities—is the level of unemployment benefits. Figure 5-4 displays the highest unemployment benefit levels (as a proportion of state sector wages) that—according to condition 5-7—are compatible with employers' ranking strategy 5-6 above the other two options.

As shown in the figure, this critical benefit level (b^*) is decreasing in the size of the unemployment pool. This is because higher unemployment involves a larger share of low-productivity workers in the unemployment pool. At early stages of transition, replacement rates of the order of 45 percent can significantly boost outflows from unemployment, but later a larger turnover of the pool can be achieved only by replacement rates lower than 25 percent—that is, below those typically offered by OECD countries and most transitional economies. In consideration of the low wages paid to state sector workers, the maximum replacement rate prevailing in high-unemployment economies may well fall in close proximity to (if not below) minimum subsistence levels, and hence be socially unsustainable in precisely those countries (economies with high rates of unemployment) where reductions in benefit generosity would be most required to avoid the marginalization of the unemployed.

This association between the level of unemployment and the effects of reductions in the generosity of unemployment benefit systems is consistent with the experience of the Czech Republic compared with the other countries of central Europe. In the Czech lands, unemployment benefits were reduced when unemployment was still below 5 percent. Elsewhere, reductions in the generosity of the system were not less radical than in the Czech Republic (Slovakia experienced the same reform of its unemployment benefit system as the Czech Republic), but they occurred only after two-digit unemployment rates had been reached. A boost in outflows to jobs occurred only in the Czech lands (Boeri 1996).

The model can also explain why labor market adjustment in Russia has so far differed markedly from the pattern in the other transitional economies. Owing to a combination of high inflation and a lack of indexation of unemployment benefits, replacement rates offered to registered jobseekers in Russia were extremely low from the very start. This may explain both why employment declines in state firms have been lower than in the other transitional economies (for example, because state sector workers were not "poached" by private employers) and why the turnover of the unemployed has been significantly larger than in central and eastern Europe (Commander and Yemtsov 1995).

As argued above, in high-unemployment countries, reductions in unemployment benefits are likely to be either ineffective or socially (and politically) unsustainable. What else, then, can be done in high-unemployment countries to promote outflows to jobs? Any policy that actually increases the "marketability" of the unemployed vis-à-vis employed jobseekers is likely to have some role in promoting outflows from unemployment. For instance, wage subsidies covering a portion of wages paid by private employers to persons recruited from the unemployment ranks may avoid the marginalization of the unemployed from labor market adjustment. Estimates of "augmented" (that is, including the effects of active labor market policies) matching functions in these countries (Boeri and Burda 1995; Boeri 1996; Burda and Lyubyova 1995) lend support to the positive effects that wage subsidies have on outflows from unemployment to jobs. The bottom line is that there is no guarantee that the employee will be retained after the interruption of the subsidy.

According to the model, the distortions of labor market adjustment in transitional economies ultimately arise from asymmetric information as regards the actual productivity of former state sector workers. Proper functioning of the public employment service, allowing private employers to obtain information about the previous employment record of unemployed jobseekers, can play an important role in stimulating larger unemployment outflows. In most countries, the public employment service is reluctant to provide employers with detailed information about job applicants because it fears that this information could be used by employers to discriminate against displaced workers. The model presented here suggests that failure to provide employers with information on unemployed jobseekers may indeed result in an even more radical form of discrimination—the ranking of employed above unemployed jobseekers.

Conclusions

In summary, the simple model developed in this chapter seems to account for several features of labor market adjustment in the transitional economies of central and eastern Europe. In particular, it explains why unemployment turnover is so low despite rapid structural change, and why major reforms of unemployment benefit systems have thus far had a minor impact on flows from unemployment to jobs.

Some implications for the scope of reforms of active and passive labor market policies can be drawn from this model that may have relevance not only for transitional economies but also for other countries undergoing rapid structural change. A main message of the model is that the *timing* of reforms of the unemployment benefit systems matters more than the *tightness* of reforms. Much lower reductions of statutory replacement rates are required to boost outflows to jobs when reforms are undertaken before a large pool of unemployed jobseekers has formed.

References

Aghion, P., and O. Blanchard. 1994. "On the Speed of Transition in Central Europe." In *NBER Macroeconomics Annual*. Cambridge, Mass.: MIT Press.

Assenov. 1995. "The Bulgarian Labor Market." Vienna Institute of Advanced Studies.

Beleva, I., Richard Jackman, and Mariela Nenova-Amar. 1995. "Bulgaria." In S. Commander and F. Coricelli, *Unemployment, Restructuring, and the Labor Market in Eastern Europe and Russia*. Washington, D.C.: World Bank.

Boeri, T. 1996. "Unemployment Outflows and the Scope of Labour Market Policies in Central and Eastern Europe." In T. Boeri, H. Lehmann, and A. Wörgötter, eds., *Labour Market Policies in the Transition Countries: Lessons from their Experience.* Paris: OECD.

Boeri, T., and M. Keese. 1992. *Labour Markets and the Transition in Central and Eastern Europe.* OECD Economic Studies, 18, Paris.

Boeri, T., and M. Burda. 1995. *Active Labour Market Policies, Job Matching and the Czech Miracle.* Centre for Economic Policy Research Discussion Paper 1302, London.

Burda, M., and M. Lubyova. 1995. "The Impact of Active Labor Market Policies: A Closer Look at the Czech and Slovak Republics." In D. Newbery, ed., *Tax and Benefit Reform in Central and Eastern Europe.* Cambridge, U.K.: Cambridge University Press.

Chadha, B., and F. Coricelli. 1994. *Fiscal Constraints and the Speed of Transition.* CEPR Discussion Paper 993, London.

Commander, S., and R. Yemtsov. 1995. "Russian Unemployment: Its Magnitude, Characteristics and Regional Dimension." In OECD, *The Regional Dimension of Unemployment in Transition Countries.* Paris.

Flanagan, R. J. 1993. "Were Communists Good Human Capitalists? The Case of the Czech Republic." Stanford University, Graduate School of Business, Stanford, California. Photocopy.

Köllö, J. 1993. "Unemployment and Unemployment-Related Expenditures." Report to the Blue Ribbon Commission, Budget and Social Policy Project, Budapest.

Konings, J., H. Lehmann, and M. Schaffer. 1996. "Job Creation and Job Destruction in a Transition Economy: Ownership, Firm Size, and Gross Job Flows in Polish Manufacturing, 1988–91." *Labour Economics* 3(3): 299–318.

Lehmann, H., and J. Wadsworth. 1996. "New Jobs, Worklessness and Households in Poland." Centre for Economic Performance, London. Photocopy.

OECD (Organization for Economic Cooperation and Development). 1996. "Lessons from Labor Market Policies in the Transition Countries." OECD Proceedings. Paris.

———. 1994. *Unemployment in Transition Countries: Transient or Persistent?* Paris.

Orazem, P., and M. Vodopivec. 1996. "The Value of Human Capital in Transition to Market: Evidence from Slovenia," Office of Development Economics and Chief Economist, World Bank, Washington, D.C. Photocopy.

Rutkowski, Jan J. 1996. *Changes in the Wage Structure During Economic Transition in Central and Eastern Europe.* World Bank Technical Paper 340, Social Challenges Transition Series. Washington, D.C.

Vecernik, J. 1992. "Changes in Income Distribution in 1988–92." *Sociologicky Casopsis* 5.

6

The Role of Unemployment and Restructuring in the Transition

Simon Commander and
Andrei Tolstopiatenko

Two apparently distinct paths can be identified in the transition from central planning. These are readily visible in table 6-1. In Central and Eastern Europe (CEE), unemployment rose high early in the transition and subsequently stabilized in the range of 10–15 percent of the labor force. Almost half of those without work are now among the long-term unemployed. Exit rates to jobs from unemployment remain low, of the order of 2–4 percent monthly. The Czech Republic remains the solitary exception. For those unemployed, benefits levels have been reasonably generous. Initially, the replacement rate was in the range of 40–50 percent, falling over time to 25–35 percent. Output declined sharply in the early stages of transition, but recovery has started, with official statistics now measuring output at no more than 15 percent below pre-transition levels. Labor costs, initially slashed by inflation and contained by incomes policies, have crept upward, but there have been few signs of sustained wage pressure and more evidence that wages have been traded down for employment.

The authors thank Olivier Blanchard, Tito Boeri, Fabrizio Coricelli, and Branko Milanovic for helpful comments on an earlier draft of this chapter.

Table 6-1. Central and Eastern Europe and the Former Soviet Union: Evolution of GDP, Employment, and Unemployment, 1990–95

| | Cumulative change 1995/90 | | Unemployment rate (1995) | | Share of long-term |
| | | | Labor Force | | unemployed |
Country	GDP	Employment	Survey	Registrations	(percent)
CEE					
Bulgaria	–32.5	–25.8	15.7	12.2	66.0
Czech Republic	–24.0	–8.3	3.7	3.0	31.5
Hungary	–15.2	–19.6	10.5	10.5	49.5
Poland	–1.7	–8.5	12.9	15.2	41.4
Romania	–10.7	–13.1	8.0	9.3	47.0
Slovakia	–14.0	–13.7	12.3	13.3	53.8
FSU					
Russia	–49.1	–10.2	7.9	3.1	23.1
Belarus	–45.5	—	—	2.5	—
Kazakhstan	–66.0	—	—	2.4	—
Ukraine	–55.5	–32.1	—	0.4	—
Uzbekistan	–20.0	—	—	0.5	—

Source: World Bank and EBRD.

A large private sector has emerged in CEE, in part through privatization but also through the rapid growth of a de novo private sector. In the Czech Republic, Hungary, and Poland, by 1996 the private sector accounted for over 60 percent of output and employment.

In the FSU, the paths of employment, output, and the private sector share have been quite different. Output has generally declined even more substantially than in CEE. The Russian GDP at end-1996 is estimated to be under half, and industrial output barely 40 percent, of pre-transition levels. Unemployment, in contrast, has remained very small relative to the size of shocks to output. For those in unemployment, benefits levels have been derisory, with replacement ratios barely touching 10 percent. Exit rates to jobs from unemployment have remained high, of the order of 8 percent monthly. A substantial share of the labor force, particularly in industry, has been subject to adjustment of their hours and arrears in wage payments. Large product-market shocks have consequently induced some decline in formal sector employment, wage flexibility, and a large fall in unit labor costs, but little unemployment. Although the state sector has declined everywhere, most of this decline has been brought about through insider-dominated privatizations. The share of the autonomous private sector, while rising, has remained small, at least in comparison with CEE figures. There has, however, been a large proliferation in the unofficial economy.

These striking differences might be partially attributed to lags, with regions at varying stages in the transition. This is not an adequate explanation. Several years after the start of their respective transitions, it is obvious that the FSU countries have explicitly chosen to limit unemployment. In contrast, policies to ensure employment smoothing have been far less prominent in CEE.

This chapter will address a number of basic questions that arise from these differences. We ask whether an explicit decision to smooth employment, coupled with a minimal benefits scheme, can achieve—with lower costs—the basic goals of transition: a reallocation of employment across sectors and ownership groups and a consequent rise in productivity. Expressed differently, does the FSU model offer a more efficient transition path, or, as CEE experience might suggest, has significant unemployment been a necessary condition for restructuring to get under way and for a private sector to emerge? Further, we look at the implications of different levels of benefits generosity and the financing base for the reallocation of employment and the pace of restructuring.

To address these questions, we develop a model of transition with endogenous restructuring. The setup has two sectors—private and state—and three labor market states, employment in either of these sectors or unemployment.[1] State firms, which were dominant at the start of transition, face probabilities of closure and restructuring. We endogenize these probabilities and look at the implications of the values of various states generated for the overall restructuring process. With this framework, we are able to explore the implications of changes in key variables—benefits generosity, the financing basis for benefits, and the incidence of taxation across sectors, for example—for outcomes, including the paths of employment and output and their sectoral compositions, as well as unemployment.

The next section of the chapter starts with an examination of motivation; some of the factors that might explain the differences across CEE and FSU economies are considered. We provide some key institutional

---

1. The model shares features with Aghion and Blanchard (1994) and Chadha, Coricelli, and Krajnyak (1993).

information, concentrating on the respective fall-back schemes operating in these two groups of countries. We then extend the information set by summarizing the information on the financing links between governments and firms. This is obviously important given the role of budget constraints in determining state firms' behavior. This section also signals the possible implications of differing compensation structures across these regions, particularly for attachment. The third section details our model of endogenous restructuring, which is followed by a match-up of the institutional information with the model and a simulation of a set of scenarios where benefits, taxation, and the probabilities of restructuring and closure are varied.

Accounting for the Variation in Unemployment

Institutional Factors: Benefits and Their Costs

What can explain the differences in unemployment across the CEE and FSU countries? An obvious starting place must be the relative incentives for being unemployed. These have varied quite significantly across regions. In CEE there was an initially high generosity in benefits, with open-ended access. Over time this has been transformed through cuts in entitlement durations and/or the replacement rate (see table 6-2). By 1995, most countries in CEE permitted twelve months of benefits receipt, and in both the Czech and Slovak Republics this had been cut to six months. Replacement rates that ranged between 0.4 and 0.7 at the start of transition had fallen to around 0.3 by 1995. On expiration of benefits, the unemployed have been entitled to social assistance at yet lower replacement values. By 1995, recipients of unemployment benefits accounted for less than 50 percent of registered unemployed in all CEE countries, except Romania.

Despite these changes, the benefits regime remains generous in CEE compared with the FSU. In Russia, unemployment benefits remain close to flat-rate benefits and fall below 10 percent of the average wage. On expiration, after one year, workers generally have no further entitlements to social assistance. Minimum wage and pension levels also remain very low.

Declining generosity and the increasing pass-through of claimants from unemployment insurance to social assistance has been one factor containing the direct fiscal cost of unemployment. Nevertheless, there is significant variation in expenditures for each unemployed individual across the CEE countries, as indicated in table 6-3. In Poland and Hungary, both passive and active labor market expenditure was in the range of 2/2.5 percent of GDP. In Slovakia and Bulgaria, it was below 1 percent, and in the Czech Republic, it was under 0.5 percent of GDP. These figures tend to be underestimates given the size of flows to nonparticipation and the importance of early retirement. In Poland, where early retirement offered a far higher replacement rate, factoring in these costs gives a truer estimate of the direct cost of unemployment of the order of 5–6 percent of GDP (Perraudin and Pujol 1994).

For the FSU countries, the direct fiscal burden of benefits has been small. In Russia, unemployment benefits in 1995 accounted for under 0.5 percent of GDP. Again, this may not be an appropriate measure of fiscal pressure, but for different reasons. Despite wage flexibility, a significant share of firms, whether state-owned or privatized, continue to receive subsidies and other financing supports for maintaining employment.

The Budget Constraint

While the divergence in benefit regimes will likely prove to have been an important factor affecting the rate of restructuring and unemployment, it is also important to consider the budget constraints facing firms. In CEE, explicit budgetary subsidies to firms have indeed declined significantly, but this is also true of FSU countries where information is available (table 6-3). By 1994/95, the mean subsidy to GDP rate in the FSU was clearly higher than in CEE, but not by a particularly large margin. The only major outlier was Ukraine. Yet these numbers do not adequately capture the range of financing options available to firms and the changing locus of subsidy provision over time. Aside from a host of implicit subsidies, including those embodied in energy prices and local government finance, FSU firms have continued to have access to soft bank borrowing, nonpayment of tax and social security payments, as well as borrowing from other firms, workers, and public utilities.[2]

The subsidy story, although important, is incomplete without considering it in tandem with the inherited structure of compensation. Firms in the FSU, particularly the larger industrial firms, have continued to provide a wide range of social benefits, including housing and child and health care, to their workers. Access to benefits has been explicitly linked

---

2. Commander, Fan, and Schaffer (1996). Schaffer (1996) puts the stock of tax arrears in the range of 3–9 percent of GDP in the CEE countries and 4 percent in Russia. Real flows fall in the range of 1–2 percent of GDP. In CEE, however, arrears tend to be very highly concentrated and not a widespread source of soft financing.

Table 6-2. Unemployment Insurance and Labor Taxation in Russia and CEE

	Bulgaria	Czech Republic	Hungary	Poland	Romania	Russia	Slovakia
Expenditure, active and passive programs (per centage of GDP, 1994)	0.7	0.4	2.0	2.4	1.6	0.4	0.9
Unemployment insurance system							
Duration	12 months	6 months	12 months	12 months	9 months	12 months	6 months
Eligibility Minimum employment	6 months	12 months	360 days	180 days	6 months	3 months	12 months
Quit penalty	5 months	Disqualified	180 days	90 days	n.a.	n.a.	Disqualified
Job refusal penalty	n.a.	n.a.	90 days	90 days	n.a.	n.a.	n.a.
Minimum/maximum	90%/140–155%	None/150–180%	96%/185% mw	None/none	75–85%/200% of mw	100%	None/150–180% mw
Registered unemployed receiving benefits (percent)	1995 = 31.2	1995 = 45.8	1995 = 36.0	1995 = 53.3	1995 = 33.5	1995 = 77.1	1992 = 23.6
Unemployment assistance system							
Duration	Indefinite	Indefinite	Indefinite	Indefinite	Indefinite	None	Indefinite
Replacement rate	45%	39%	27%	28%	26%		37%

Average unemployment benefit as percentage of the average wage							
Unemployment benefit							
1990	n.a.	n.a.	42.0	n.a.	73.0	26.9	n.a.
1991	60.6	46.3	41.0	36.0	62.6	23.6	43.8
1992	38.1	24.8	39.3	36.0	59.0	11.9	31.6
1993	35.5	28.3	36.6	36.0	37.2	8.4	29.2
1994	34.3	26.6	33.0	36.0	32.5	8.0	25.3
1995	34.9	25.1	33.5	36.0	28.5	8.8	27.5
Labor and personal tax rate (percent)							
Employer tax	42	46	51	46	41	39	38
Employee tax	20	13	12	None	1	1	12
Income tax rate							
Highest	52	47	40	40	45	30	47
Lowest	20	15	25	20	6	12	19
VAT (standard rate)	20	23	25	22	18	20	26
Effective marginal tax rate on labor income	57	69	73	62	57	63	68

n.a. Not available.
Note: mw represents minimum wage.

175

Table 6-3. Budgetary Subsidies to Firms, 1992 and 1994
(shares of GDP)

Country	1992	1994
CEE		
Bulgaria	3.2	2.4
Czech Republic	4.5	3.9
Hungary	2.1	4.4
Poland	1.4	2.2
Romania	3.0	3.2
Slovakia	4.1	4.9
FSU		
Belarus	n.a.	6.5
Kazakhstan	2.5	5.5
Russia	31.6	4.9
Ukraine	12.8	17.0
Uzbekhistan	n.a.	3.1

n.a. Not available.
Source: World Bank.

to the site of employment. This has continued to promote attachment. Since the start of transition, changes in both the scale and scope of benefits provision have been relatively limited.[3] This persistence can be traced, at least in part, to the control structure of these firms and the insider domination that privatization or nominal state control has conferred. Firms and governments have remained reluctant to sanction large-order employment losses, preferring to adjust hours and monetary compensation. Part of this response can be attributed to the fact that many firms—particularly the larger firms—have received major compensating finance for benefits provision from various levels of government. Regional and local governments in Russia have tended to subsidize or extend ad hoc tax exemptions to firms that maintain large stocks of social assets.[4] Aside from promoting attachment, the flow of financing to underpin this structure of compensation has effectively internalized fallbacks to

3. See Falkingham and others (1996) for Central Asia; Commander and Schankerman (1997) for Russia and Ukraine. The one exception appears to be child care; provision of this benefit has declined across the board.

4. A rough measure of the scale of support is that in Russia, subsidies for housing that had been divested from firms to municipalities exceeded 5 percent of GDP in 1995. See Le Houerou (1995).

the firm. The resulting incentive regime has not only been a strong incentive for workers to stay in those firms, but also to allocate their effort in part-time or moonlighting activity to the unofficial private sector. It also has implications for the growth of an autonomous private sector because it raises the reservation wage. Further, the choice of employment smoothing, while also allowing workers to participate in the unofficial economy, has created major fiscal implications because the unofficial economy remains largely outside of the tax net, certainly outside the reach of payroll taxes. We now turn to the implications of these institutional and other factors for the path of transition.

A Model of Restructuring and Transition

Our model is set around an economy composed of two sectors—state and private—and three basic labor market states—state employment, private employment, and unemployment. The labor force is given by $N_1 + N_2 + U = 1$, where N_1 designates employment in the state sector; N_2, employment in the private sector; and U, unemployment. At the start of transition, virtually all employment is in the state sector; there is negligible private employment and unemployment.[5]

State Sector

State firms are assumed to be governed by a zero profit constraint. The idea behind this is that state (and indeed, many privatized) firms are dominated by their insiders in the aftermath of central planning's collapse. With insiders in control of the firm, they can extract all surplus. With no capital accumulation, we can write the state firm's problem as

$$\max_{w_1, N_1} \left\{ \frac{N_1 - \bar{N}_1}{\bar{N}_1} V_u + \frac{N_1}{\bar{N}_1} V_1 \right\},$$

subject to $w_1 N_1 = p_1 Y_1$.

Output is generated through a Cobb-Douglas function, $Y_1 = C_1 L^{\beta_1} K^{1-\beta_1}$ where ($\beta_1 < 1$). We assume that the state sector is less efficient in production than the private sector. This efficiency difference is imposed through

---

5. Later, we set the initial values for our simulations as follows: state employment is equal to 0.96; private employment and unemployment are both equal to 0.02.

the production function, where the ratio of state to private productivity (C_2/C_1) is set equal to 0.6. Wages in the state sector are set equal to average product, which, incorporating taxes per worker, implies

$$w_1 = AP_{1L} - t_1 = \frac{C_1 K_1^{1-\beta_1}}{L_1^{1-\beta_1}} - t_1.$$

In our framework, insiders in state firms can choose to continue operating in this manner, subject to some probability of closure, or they can choose to restructure. If they restructure, this will result in a decline in employment, an increase in marginal product for remaining workers, and a change in wage setting, with wages now set as in the private sector. Thus, with restructuring, a certain proportion of workers $(1-\gamma)$ become unemployed, the rest, (γ), remain in the restructured firm. A restructured firm is equivalent to a private sector firm. The conditions under which restructuring decisions are made are indicated below ("Closure and Restructuring Probabilities").

Private Sector

The private sector is characterized by profit-maximizing firms that are constrained by their labor demand curves and pay competitive wages. Production is Cobb-Douglas. Wages in the private sector are set equal to marginal product, which, incorporating taxes per worker implies

$$w_2 = MP_{2L} - t_2 = \frac{\beta_2 \cdot C_2 K_2^{1-\beta_2}}{L_2^{1-\beta_2}} - t_2.$$

In our model, only the private sector hires. Hiring follows

$$H = \frac{\alpha U N_2}{U + N_2}.$$

This says that hiring (H/U) depends on the ratio of unemployment to private sector employment. The latter serves as a proxy for vacancies. The parameter, α, can be thought of as a pseudo-matching term. The private sector can thus grow through two channels. The first is, as above, by hiring from unemployment. The second is through state firm restructuring and transformation. In those cases, a share of the original workforce (γ) will become part of the private sector through restructuring.

Arbitrage Equations

We can now get the basic arbitrage equations for the respective values of
the three core labor market states:

$$rV_1 = w_1 + p_{1U}(V_u - V_1) + p_{12}(V_2 - V_1) + \dot{V}_1$$

(1) Value of being in the state sector

$$rV_2 = w_2 + \beta(V_u - V_2) + \dot{V}_2$$

(2) Value of being in the private sector

$$rV_u = b + (H/U)(V_2 - V_u) + \dot{V}_u$$

(3) Value of being unemployed

where β is the probability of job loss in the private sector; H/U = the hiring
rate from unemployment (probability of hiring); w_1 and w_2 are wages in
the state and private sectors, respectively; b = unemployment benefits;
$p_{1U} = (1 - p_R)p + p_R(1 - \gamma)$ is the complete probability of moving from
the state sector to unemployment; and $p_{12} = p_R\gamma$ is the probability of
moving from the state to the private sector through restructuring.

That state firms can stay as they are or restructure actually means that
there should be four possible states. For simplicity, we do not explicitly
include the value of being in a restructured firm. We can do this because
we make two assumptions. The first is that the time scale for restructuring is far longer than the other time scales. The second is that the value of
being in a restructured firm is a weighted average of the values of being
in the private sector (V_2) and being unemployed (V_u). With these assumptions, our setup is the limit case of the four-states model.[6]

From these arbitrage equations, we can derive the values $(V_2 - V_u)$ or
V_{2u} and $(V_1 - V_u)$ or V_{1u} as follows:

$$\dot{V}_{2U} = (r + \beta + H/U)V_{2U} - (w_2 - b)$$

$$\dot{V}_{1U} = (r + p_{1U} + p_{12})V_{1U} + (H/U - p_{12})V_{2U} - (w_1 - b).$$

---

6. Proof available from the authors.

Balance Equations for Labor

Collecting the dynamic equations written above, we get the following expressions:

$$\frac{dN_1}{dt} = -(p_{1U} + p_{12})N_1$$

$$\frac{dU}{dt} = p_{1U}N_1 - H(U) + \beta N_2$$

$$\frac{dN_2}{dt} = H(U) + p_{12}N_1 - \beta N_2 .$$

Summing up the balance equations, we get the consistency condition

$$\frac{dN_1}{dt} + \frac{dN_2}{dt} + \frac{dU}{dt} = \{-(p_{1U} + p_{12})N_1\} + \left\{\frac{H}{U}U + p_{12}N_1 - \beta N_2\right\}$$

$$+ \left\{p_{1U}N_1 - \frac{H}{U}U + \beta N_2\right\} = 0$$

since $N_1 + N_2 + U = 1$.

Balance Equations for Capital

Total capital in the economy is denoted by K, with the share in the state sector, $k1 = K_1/K$, and the share of capital in the private sector, $k_2 = K_2/K$. When a state firm closes, we assume that its capital also becomes redundant. When a state firm restructures, a part of its capital, γ_k, moves to the private sector and a part $(1 - \gamma_k)$ becomes idle, a process analogous to the redeployment of labor resources. The dynamics for the allocation of capital are

$$\frac{dk_1}{dt} = -(\bar{p}_{1U} + \bar{p}_{12})k_1 - \delta_1 k_1$$

$$\frac{dk_2}{dt} = \bar{p}_{12}k_1 + I(k) - \delta_2 k_2$$

where $\bar{p}_{1U} = (1 - p_R)p + p_R(1 - \gamma_k)$ and $\bar{p}_{12} = p_R \cdot \gamma_k$.

Here, δ_1, δ_2 are depreciation rates of state and private capital respectively. For simplicity we set $\delta_1 = \delta_2 = \delta$. If depreciation rates are the same for all forms of capital, then in the absence of private investment, the total stock of capital in the economy decreases with the rate δ during the transition. It is clearly more realistic to assume that the private sector will invest. To capture this, we have incorporated a private investment function [$I(k)$]:

$$I(k) = \alpha_k(MP_K^{(2)} - r) \cdot k_2$$

where $MP_K^{(2)} = \dfrac{\partial y_2}{\partial K_2}$ is the marginal productivity of capital in the private sector and r is the appropriate interest rate.

Taxation and the Financing of Benefits

Unemployment and its direct cost—benefits—has to be financed. As table 6-2 indicated, the tax burden, as measured by payroll taxes, has indeed been quite substantial in the transition economies. In the context of our model, while we assume that there is no taxation of capital, firms do pay payroll taxes. The incidence of these payroll taxes across state and private firms can vary. The different values for payroll taxes for the state (t_1) and private sector (t_2) are introduced through the parameter $\varepsilon = t_2/t_1$, where $t_1 = t$ and $t_2 = \varepsilon t$. We also assume that almost all of the costs of unemployment benefits— $(U - U^0)$ —are financed through these payroll taxes.

With these assumptions, we have

$$t = \frac{b(U - U^0)}{N_1 + \varepsilon N_2} = \frac{b(U - U^0)}{N_1(1 - \varepsilon) + \varepsilon(1 - U)}.$$

The effect of the benefits regime in this context will be complex and will depend on the way financing is distributed across sectors. With tax equivalence, generous benefits will tend to lower the value of staying in state firms, and hence to promote an outflow from state firms. But higher benefits will also tend to lower the rate of hiring from unemployment by the private sector, and this will duly raise the value of staying put. With inequality in incidence ($\varepsilon < 1$), and benefits financed primarily by taxation of state firms, this will result in lowering the available surplus to be distributed, and hence the wage. Aside from tending to raise unemployment, this will also raise the attraction of restructuring (see below) for insiders.

A rapid collapse of the state sector induced by taxation, however, will also lower the probability of being hired from unemployment, and hence act in a contrary direction.

Closure and Restructuring Probabilities

A salient characteristic of transition is that firms face changing institutional regimes and constraints. State firms confront a probability that their firm will close because of the implementation of a bankruptcy law or associated changes in the legal and other relevant environments. As soft budgets are withdrawn or reduced, some firms simply cannot survive and have to close. These considerations need to be incorporated into our framework. Decisions by insiders to restructure will depend on a variety of forces: for example, faced with these probabilities of closure, insiders may elect to restructure the firm, and hence possibly improve its survival options, albeit with job losses. This decision will be sensitive to the share of workers that retain their jobs after restructuring. It will also depend on the labor market; the level of unemployment; and, most important, the exit rate to private sector jobs. And it will further depend, of course, on the reservation wage or unemployment benefits. We do not make any strong assumptions regarding ownership and control behind the restructuring choice. Indeed, we assume that the choice is made by insiders conditional on these factors. Once the firm has restructured, however, its behavior conforms to that of the private sector, with standard profit-maximizing attributes. As such, crossing over into the private sector raises the productivity of the restructured firm.

While the initial values for these probabilities are predetermined in our model, and thus can be calibrated, the probabilities of closure and restructuring are subsequently endogenized by assuming that they depend on the difference between the values of various states. In addition, we impose a constraint on each probability and consider the probability of restructuring to be equal to some exogenous value determined by institutional and other factors when there are no benefits to be derived from restructuring ($V_R < V_1$). The probability of closure will be equal to some exogenous value determined by the same factors when ($V_1 < V_U$). With these constraints, we have

$$p = \begin{cases} p^0 e^{-d_1 V_{1U}}, V_1 \geq V_U \\ p^0, V_1 < V_U \end{cases}$$

$$p_R = \begin{cases} p_R^0 + (1 - p_R^0) \cdot (1 - e^{-d_2 V_{R1}}), \ V_R \geq V_1 \\ p_R^0, \ V_R < V_1 \end{cases} =$$

$$\begin{cases} p_R^0 + (1 - p_R^0) \cdot (1 - e^{-d_2(\gamma V_{2U} - V_{1U})}), \ \gamma V_{2U} \geq V_{1U} \\ p_R^0, \ \gamma V_{2U} < V_{1U} \end{cases}$$

where p = probability of closure of the state firm and p_R = the probability of restructuring. As before, we denote $(V_1 - V_U)$ through V_{1U}, $(V_2 - V_U)$ through V_{2U}, and $(V_R - V_1)$ through V_{R1} and use the following expression for the *a posteriori* probability of restructuring: $V_R = \gamma V_2 + (1 - \gamma) V_U$.

Implications for Transition

We now match up our model with the institutional and other information that we have already presented. We are particularly interested in capturing the implications of these institutional differences for the path and pace of transition. Our model permits calibration, and the implications of the varied institutional and financing regimes with endogenous restructuring are now discussed. We concentrate on the paths of employment, unemployment, and output. To do this, there are several critical values.

The first, (b), represents the generosity of the unemployment benefits regime and the reservation value. Unemployment benefits act through a variety of channels in our model. For instance, while higher benefits will raise the value of being unemployed and lower the incentive for workers to stay in state firms, it will also affect the rate at which the private sector can absorb labor from unemployment by influencing the reservation price. In addition, high benefits require financing.

The second, (ε), or the payroll tax ratio for state and private sectors, relates to the financing of unemployment. As already indicated, it is assumed that unemployment benefits are almost entirely financed through payroll taxes. When (ε) is small, the private sector's tax incidence will be negligible, and benefits will have to be financed primarily by taxing the state sector. A low tax incidence in the private sector, while fiscally damaging, will accelerate the outflow of labor from the state sector. Although this may lead to an increase in unemployment, through the playback from unemployment to wages and the private sector's profitability, offsetting job creation in the private sector will be stimulated. Conversely, an equivalent tax incidence ($\varepsilon = 1$) will lower the tax pressure on the state sector, thereby reducing the outflow and leading to lower unemployment. But it will also affect the hiring rate of the private sector.

The third, (p_0 and p_{0r}), concerns the institutional values attached to the probabilities of closure and restructuring, respectively. While these values are subsequently endogenized and affect the relative values of the labor market states, the initial values can be thought of as summarizing the policy and institutional setting. For example, low closure probabilities could testify to a combination of policy and legal constraints, such as the absence of a bankruptcy rule.

The simulations we report below involve experimenting with a range of plausible values. These values are drawn from the institutional information presented above. We also need to make explicit choices about the share of workers who retain their employment in a firm that restructures (γ) and the interest rate (r). In the results reported below, the following values are fixed throughout: $\gamma = 0.8$ and $r = 0.1$. We let p_0, p_{0r}, b, and ε vary.

Figures 6-1 and 6-2 provide a first pass at characterizing two systems differentiated only by the generosity of the unemployment benefits regime. There is tax equivalence ($\varepsilon = 1$), and the probabilities of closure and restructuring are set at the same intermediate value, 0.1. In figure 6-1, benefits are set at 1.2, or a reservation ratio of around 0.45. This is roughly the starting ratio adopted in CEE. In figure 6-2, benefits are set at 0.3, or around 12.5 percent of the wage. This is roughly the ratio now holding in Russia and other FSU countries.

The effects on both unemployment and output are significant. In the case of a generous benefits regime, unemployment rises rapidly and peaks at around 30 percent of the labor force at $t = 10$. The subsequent decline in unemployment is quite protracted. In figure 6-1, at the end of the simulation period ($t = 50$), unemployment stands at around 6 percent. Although the state sector effectively disappears by $t = 20$, or when unemployment still tops 20 percent, the private sector's ability to generate jobs is affected by the tax burden it faces through the benefits level. In this simulation, output declines to 0.8 of the pre-transition level before rising thereafter. Output recovers its pre-transition level only at $t = 22$, and at the end it is nearly 40 percent larger than at the start of transition.

A low benefits generosity—as given in figure 6-2—produces a far flatter unemployment curve. The peak is below 0.2 and there is a steady decline afterward. The state sector declines more gently. Output experiences little fall, even at the start, and it attains roughly the same level as in figure 6-1 at the end of the period. Evidently, with equivalence in the tax incidence and the same initial closure and restructuring probabilities, lower benefits generate significantly lower transitional costs.

Figure 6-1. High Unemployment Benefits

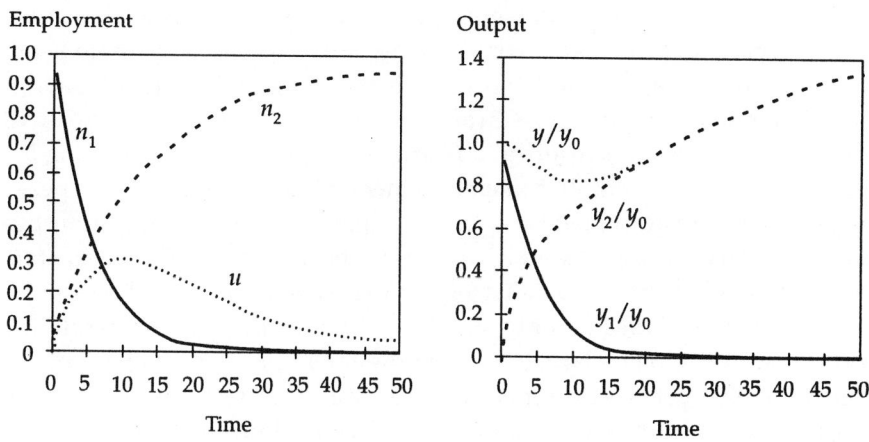

This simple conclusion needs be tempered by a number of important qualifications. In the first instance, neither in CEE nor in FSU has tax equivalence held. In both settings, the private sector has managed to skirt part of the tax net, particularly in the FSU. Nevertheless, making ($\varepsilon = 0.2$) has little impact on either the unemployment peak or the output trough, because the financing required to cover such benefits remains low. With generous benefits and ($\varepsilon = 0.2$), unemployment peaks slightly higher and earlier, as greater tax pressure on the state sector leads to a more rapid decline.

Figure 6-2. Low Unemployment Benefits

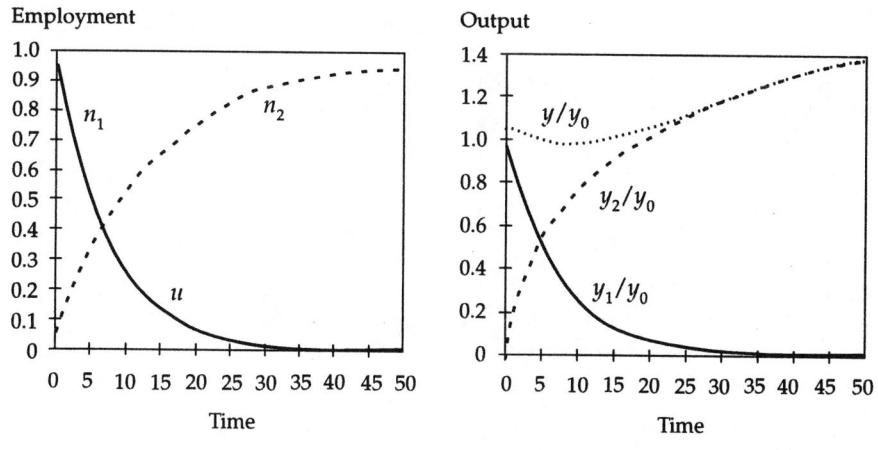

We are likely to arrive at a more realistic outcome if we consider not only the different effects of benefits levels and tax incidence, but also the closure and restructuring probabilities. Accordingly, we adjust the institutional probabilities so that $p_0 = 0.03$ and $p_{0r} = 0.05$. In the case where benefits have been set low and the private sector is able to avoid payroll taxation, one clear outcome—through the effect on relative values—will be a reduction in both closure and restructuring probabilities. Holding $b = 0.3$ and $\varepsilon = 0.2$, we find that unemployment climbs very gradually, peaking at around 10 percent at $t = 20$, and declines very slowly thereafter (figure 6-3). This process is largely driven by the very slow decline in state employment, because the value of staying in state firms remains high, and this value is affected only slightly by the tax burden. For while the private sector remains largely outside the tax net in this simulation, the small benefits generosity limits the pressure on state firms. The consequences for output, however, are very powerful indeed. Aggregate output declines sharply to a trough of around half its pre-transition level. Further, the recovery remains slight. At the end of the simulation period, output is no more than 60 percent of its starting level. In short, relative to the base case, with small closure and restructuring values, unemployment remains lower but is rather more protracted. The main effect is to cause a very large and persistent decline in output as the private sector's growth is restrained.

Figure 6-4, by contrast, looks at the effect of raising the closure and restructuring probabilities so that $p_0 = 0.2$ and $p_{0r} = 0.2$. We retain the values, $b = 1.2$ and $\varepsilon = 0.8$, that correspond more closely to the CEE case.

Figure 6-3. Low Closure and Restructuring Probabilities

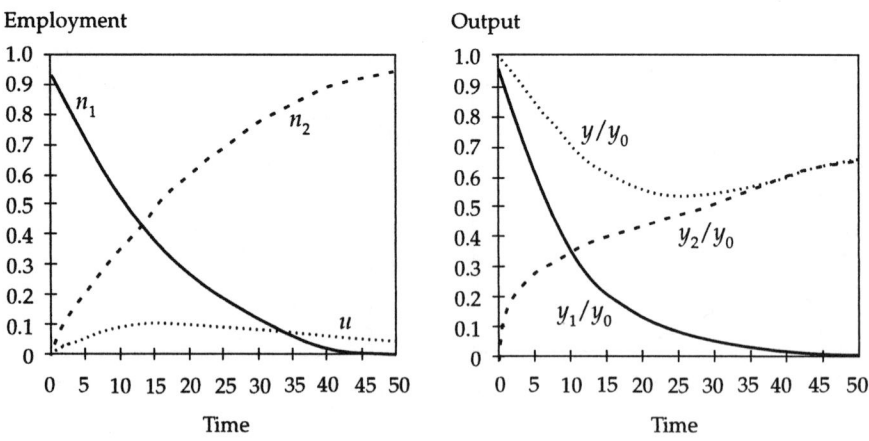

Employment

Output

Time

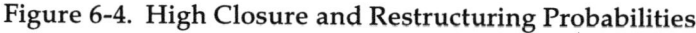

Figure 6-4. High Closure and Restructuring Probabilities

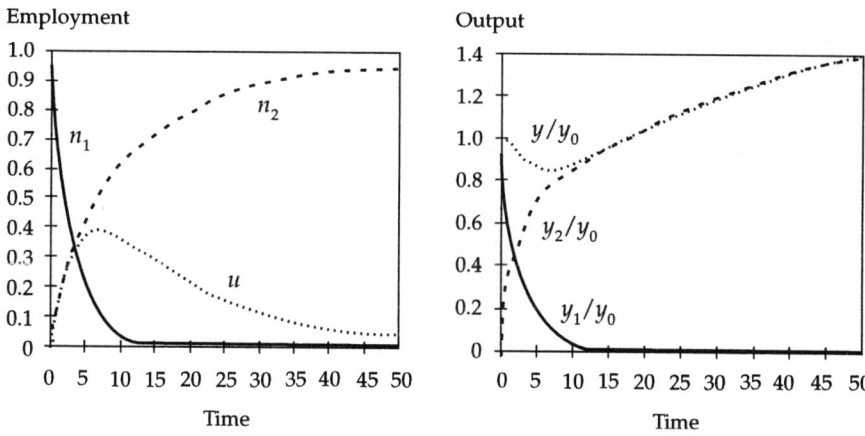

Again, the motive behind raising the institutional probabilities is that a generous outside opportunity will obviously have a direct effect on the value of staying in state firms. Further, we know that in some CEE countries, such as Hungary or Poland, closure—through bankruptcy and other mechanisms—has been far more widespread than in CEE. In this regard, we can think of the simulation in figure 6-4 as indicating the likely consequences of the more rapid closure and restructuring rate that is consistent with explicit policies to promote restructuring. It may thus offer a more realistic appraisal of the process under way in parts of CEE, as compared with the base case (figure 6-1). We can see that unemployment rises very steeply and reaches nearly 40 percent of the labor force by $t = 8$; it declines quite sharply thereafter. State sector employment collapses through the combination of closure, restructuring, and the high value of benefits acting to reduce the value for workers of staying, including the imposition of a significant tax burden. The offset from private employment initially remains limited. We can think of this, in part, as the effect of congestion in the labor market, as well as the autonomous effect of the benefits-financing constraint, given near equivalence in taxation on private firms ($\varepsilon = 0.8$). Note that for this level of benefits, but with lower tax compliance by the private sector—for example, $\varepsilon = 0.5$—the system becomes unstable. With regard to output, higher closure and restructuring probabilities lead to a rapid decline of over 20 percent relative to pre-transition levels. This is of comparable depth to the base case, although the subsequent recovery is more rapid. At the end of the simulation period, output is over 40 percent higher than at the start. In sum, relative to the base case, the unemployment peak is roughly one-third higher, but the rate of decay is more rapid, although not by a very significant margin. State sector employment collapses particularly quickly in this case, leading to a steeper initial fall in output, but a quicker recovery. Output regains its pre-transition level at $t = 18$ rather than at $t = 22$ in the base case. Pursuit of a more rapid transition by raising closure and restructuring probabilities but maintaining relatively generous benefits runs the risk of a very large initial jump in unemployment.

A measure of the benefits effect can be picked up from figure 6-5, which retains the same probabilities and tax incidence but sets $b = 0.6$, a replacement ratio of roughly 25 percent. We can see that this radically lowers the peak unemployment rate by around 15 percentage points and leads to a more rapid pace of transition, primarily through the more accelerated growth in private sector employment. Output experiences little initial decline, and a reasonably protracted period of stagnation follows.

Finally, we can note that the pace and efficiency of the transition will obviously also depend on the efficiency with which workers are matched to jobs. This will depend, of course, on the relative values of the labor market states, which in turn depend on wage setting and productivity. We know, however, that a particularly striking characteristic of the CEE countries has been the emergence of large regional disparities in unemployment (Boeri and Scarpetta 1995). The disparities can be partially attributed to labor immobility and failures in other markets, such as housing. To capture this feature, we can adjust the parameter, α, in the private sector's hiring function. We can think of this parameter as a

Figure 6-5. High Closure and Restructuring Probabilities with Low Unemployment Benefits

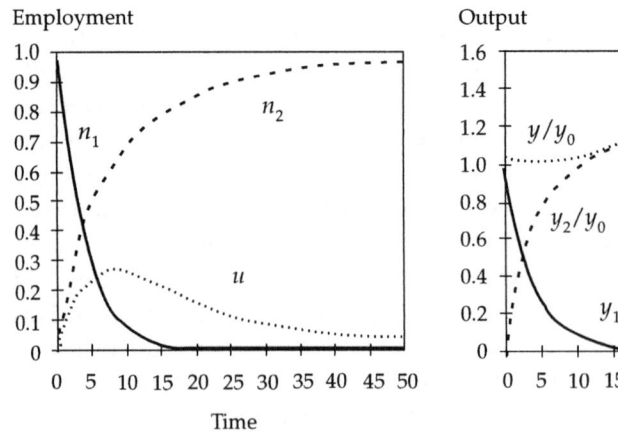
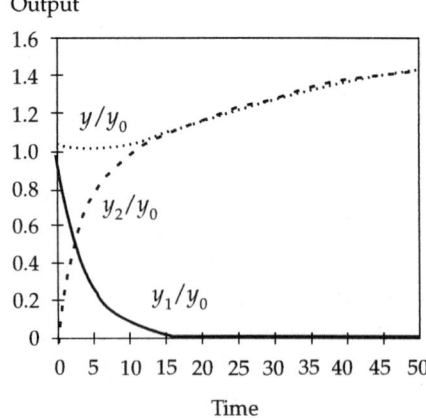

Figure 6-6. High Closure and Restructuring Probabilities with Low Unemployment Benefits and Low Matching

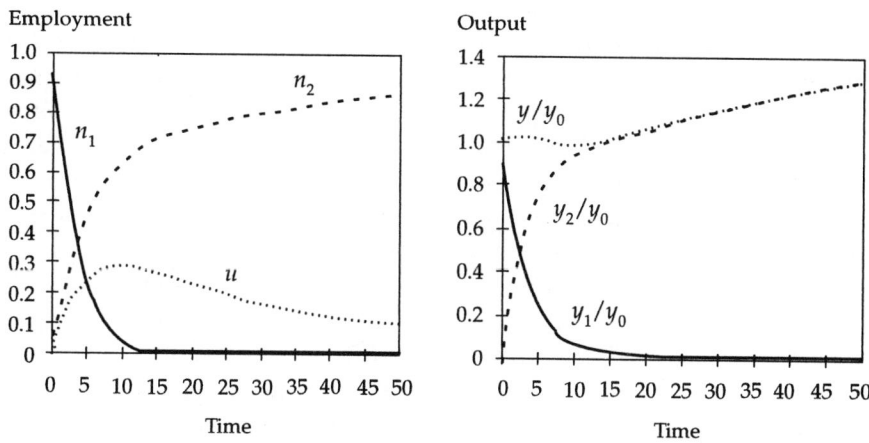

pseudo-matching term. Figure 6-6 retains all the same values present in figure 6-5, save for α, which is reduced from 0.1 to 0.05. The result is to push up the peak level of unemployment by around 5 percentage points and, more significant, for that unemployment to persist at high levels. At $t = 20$, unemployment still stands at around 16 percent. While the state sector declines, the lower matching efficiency—for example, across regions—impedes the ability of the private sector to offset unemployment through new job creation.

Conclusions

This chapter has been concerned with the different labor market evolutions that have occurred in CEE and the FSU since the start of transition. In CEE, large-scale unemployment has emerged; in FSU, despite large adverse shocks, unemployment has remained small. In CEE, systems of unemployment support of relative generosity have been created. By contrast, in the FSU, public fallbacks have remained derisory. The incentives for workers to stay in firms have been raised, and their ability to do so has been sustained by continuing soft budgets, the dominance of insiders in decisionmaking in state or privatized firms, and a structure of compensation that has promoted attachment and informalization. As a consequence, most of the private sector in the FSU has remained outside the tax net. With state or privatized firms extracting soft finance and running arrears with government and public utilities, as well as defaulting on taxes, the implications for the revenue side of the budget have been serious and adverse.

These differences were calibrated using the model of restructuring and transition that was laid out earlier in the chapter. These exercises indicated that benefits generosity exerts a powerful influence on the unemployment peak generated, its persistence, and the overall pace of the transition. In the base case, where only benefits were modified, a higher fallback option—a replacement ratio of around 0.45— led to a much higher unemployment peak and a more gradual decline. Output similarly experienced a large decline and took a long time to recover its pre-transition level. A less generous benefits regime—a replacement ratio of around 0.12—yielded an unemployment peak 10 percentage points lower, followed by a more rapid decline, as well as little output loss.

But while these contrasting paths are interesting and predictable, they are based on equivalence in the tax burden across sectors. Drastically reducing the tax rate facing the private sector and lowering the initial probabilities of closure and restructuring—a situation akin to that in the FSU—we found that while the unemployment level that was generated was indeed small, it was persistent, and the associated output path implied not only a very large initial fall, but one that was also persistent. The main costs of a gradualistic approach are on the output side, because the incentives to restructure are limited.

By contrast, faster restructuring and closure with a high replacement ratio—a scenario seen in parts of CEE—leads to a large and rapid increase in unemployment, but with less persistence and less output loss than in the base case. The least attractive feature of this choice, of course, remains the cost in unemployment and that the rise in unemployment is not only large, but quick in the coming. This has obvious political economy implications, and it is likely to have been a major factor behind the dismissal of most of the first reforming governments in the region.

Appendix

Parameters, Definitions, and Values in the Benchmark Case

p (probability of closure of state firm): 0.1

P_r (probability to start restructuring): 0.2

$1 - \gamma$ (probability of losing job as a result of restructuring): 0.2

$p_{1U} = (1 - p_R)\, p = p_R\, (1 - \gamma)$ (the complete probability of moving from the state sector to unemployment)

$p_{12} = p_R\gamma$ (the probability of moving from the state to the private sector)

β (the probability of job loss in the private sector): 0.003

$\varepsilon = t2/t1$ (tax ratio): 1

$t1 \equiv t$ (taxes per worker in the state sector)

$t_2 \equiv \varepsilon t$ (taxes per worker in the private sector)

α (matching term relating the sensitivity of the hiring rate to the private sector's performance): 0.1

b (unemployment benefits): 1.2

α_k (sensitivity of investment rate to the private sector's performance): 0.05

$\delta 1, \delta 2$ (depreciation rates of state and private capital, respectively): 0.12

$d1, d2$ (parameters giving sensitivity of the probabilities of closure and restructuring to the values of being in different sectors): 0.2

r (interest rate): 0.1

T (time scale of the simulation): 50

dT (step in time in numerical simulations): 0.01

Main Variables

u (unemployment rate)

n_1 (state sector employment rate)

n_2 (private sector employment rate)

V_1 (value of being in the state sector)

V_2 (value of being in the private sector)

V_U (value of being unemployed)

$V_{1u} = V_1 - V_U$

$V_{2u} = V_2 - V_U$

w_1 (wage in the state sector)

w_2 (wage in the private sector)

$k_1 = K_1 \mid K$ (the share of capital in the state sector)

$k_2 = K_2 \mid K$ (the share of capital in the private sector)

References

Aghion, Philippe, and Olivier Blanchard. 1994. "On the Speed of Restructuring." In *NBER Macroeconomics Annual*. Cambridge. Mass.: MIT Press.

Boeri, Tito, and Stefano Scarpetta. 1995. "Emerging Regional Labour Market Dynamics in Central and Eastern Europe." In OECD, *The Regional Dimension of Unemployment in Transition Countries*. Paris.

Boeri, Tito. 1995. "Unemployment Dynamics and Labor Market Policies." In S. Commander and F. Coricelli, eds., *Unemployment and Restructuring in Eastern Europe and Russia*. Washington, D.C.: The World Bank.

Chadha, Bankim, Fabrizio Coricelli, and Kornelia Krajnyak. 1993. "Economic Restructuring, Unemployment and Growth in a Transition Economy." *IMF Staff Papers* 40 (4): 744–80.

Commander, Simon, and Fabrizio Coricelli, editors. 1995. *Unemployment and Restructuring in Eastern Europe and Russia*. Washington, D.C.: World Bank.

Commander, Simon, and Mark Schankerman. 1997. "Enterprise Restructuring and Social Benefits." *Economies in Transition* 5:1–24.

Commander, Simon, and Andrei Tolstopiatenko. 1996. "Restructuring and Taxation in Transition Economies." Policy Research Working Paper 1625, World Bank, Washington, D.C.

Commander, Simon, Qimiao Fan, and Mark Schaffer, editors. 1996. *Enterprise Restructuring and Economic Policy in Russia*. Washington, D.C.: World Bank.

EBRD (European Bank for Reconstruction and Development). 1995. "Transition Report 1995: Investment and Enterprise Restructuring." London.

Falkingham, Jane, Jeni Klugman, Sheila Marnie, and John Micklewright. 1996. *Household Welfare in Central Asia*. London: Macmillan.

Le Houerou, Philippe. 1995. *Fiscal Management in the Russian Federation*. Washington, D.C.: World Bank.

Perraudin, William, and Thierry Pujol. 1994. "Unemployment Benefits and Pensions in Poland." *IMF Staff Papers* 41: 643–74.

Schaffer, Mark. 1996. "Tax Arrears in Transition Economies." Edinburgh: Heriot-Watt University. Photocopy.

7

A Numerical Model of Transition

O. Blanchard and J. Keeling

Figure 7-1 outlines the behavior of output and unemployment for five central European countries—Poland, Hungary, the Czech and the Slovak Republics, and Bulgaria—since 1989 (output, measured by official GDP, is normalized to 1 in 1989 for each country). This figure raises the basic questions confronting economists working on the transition in central Europe: Can we explain the U-shaped behavior of output, the initial decline followed by a strong recovery? Can we explain why unemployment has increased so much, and is declining so slowly, despite strong output growth?

Behind these questions are a number of more specific issues. What have been the interactions between state firms and new private firms? Has the collapse of output in the state sector helped or hindered private sector growth? What have been the effects of unemployment on the growth of new private firms and on restructuring in existing firms? What have been the effects of the safety net on the path of transition? What have been the effects of alternative privatization rules?

We thank Todd Leih for research assistance. We also thank Tito Boeri, Simon Commander, and Alan Gelb for their comments. The Gauss programs used for simulations are available on request.

Figure 7-1. The Evolution of Unemployment and GDP

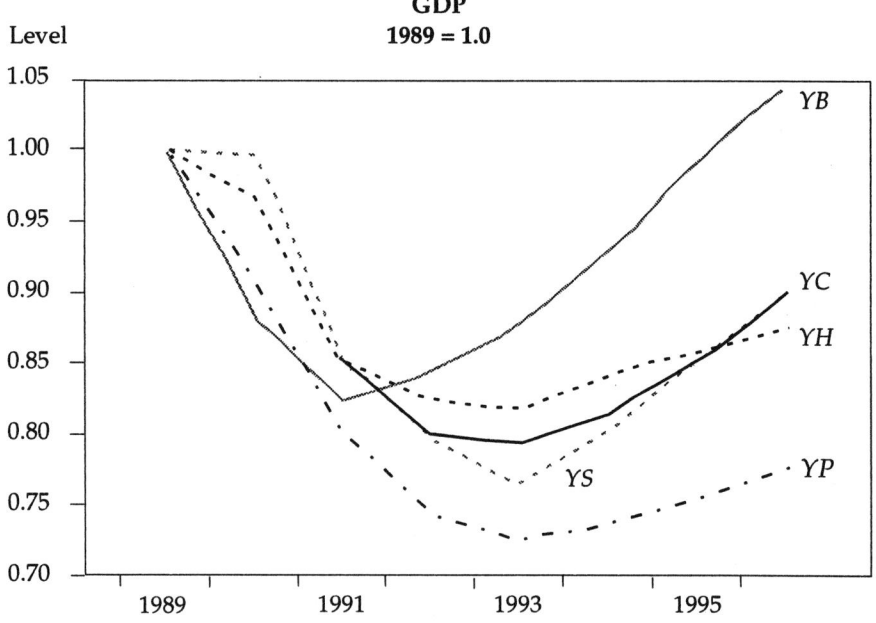

And finally, there are the questions raised by the differences across countries. Within central Europe, why has Bulgaria done so much worse than, say, Poland? Can we link differences in privatization strategies to differences in performance? Going beyond central Europe, can we explain why the former republics of the Soviet Union appear to have done so badly in output, and why China is doing so much better than central and eastern Europe?

Economists have made great progress in thinking about these issues in the last five years. A general framework has emerged, based on two basic mechanisms: reallocation (from existing firms to new firms; from existing activities to new ones) and restructuring (of state firms).[1] These two mechanisms have been embodied in a number of analytical general equilibrium models.[2] To remain tractable, each of these models has made a number of simplifying assumptions, not all of them innocuous, even for the issues at hand. The thinking was that analytical tractability was too constraining, which has led us to explore an alternative strategy in this chapter, that of developing a slightly larger simulation model, too large to be solved analytically, yet simple enough that the mechanisms at work can be easily understood.

This chapter is a progress report. We feel that the model we have developed yields a number of insights about the shape of transition, the effects of policies, and differences across countries. Yet we believe the model can—and should—be improved. We will point out areas that would benefit from additional work as we go along.

The Pre-Transition Economy

Think of the pre-transition economy as composed of two sectors: a large state sector with inefficient firms and a more efficient, but small, private sector. Think of the state firms as surviving, despite their inefficiency, with the help of subsidies from the state. In the next section, we will think of transition as triggered by the removal of these subsidies.[3]

Assume that the pre-transition economy has two sectors, a state sector (indexed by s) and a private sector (indexed by p). In each of the two sec-

---

1. This proposition is the theme of Blanchard (1997).

2. Among them are Aghion and Blanchard (1994), Alexeev and Kaganovich (1995), Brandt and Zhu (1995), Chandha, Coricelli, and Krajnyak (1993), Coricelli (1995), and, for this project, Commander and Tolstopiantenko (Chapter 6 of this volume and 1996).

tors, output is produced using capital and labor, according to the constant returns to scale production function:

$$Y_i = F_i(K_i, N_i) \; ; i = s, p.$$

We want to capture the notion that the state sector is less efficient than the private sector. This can be done either by assuming that the state sector is less efficient in production, or that it produces inferior goods. The second route is more convenient. Thus, assume that state goods and private goods are produced using the same production function (so that $F_i(\,.\,,\,.\,) = F(\,.\,,\,.\,))$, and are perfect substitutes up to a quality difference, y. That is, a private good is worth $(1 + y)$ state goods.

Choose private goods as the numeraire, so that $P_p = 1$. Under the assumption that people are willing to buy both state and private goods, the price consumers will pay for state goods must be lower than that for private goods. More precisely, P_s must be equal to $P_p / (1 + y) = 1 / (1 + y)$.

To explain why state firms are able to survive pre-transition, despite their production of inferior goods, assume that state firms receive subsidies. It follows from our assumption of identical production functions and perfect substitutability up to a factor y, that the subsidy rate must be equal to y. In that case, the after-subsidy price received by state firms for each good is equal to $P_s(1 + y) = 1$, the same as the price received by private firms.

Assume that the pre-transition stocks of capital and labor in the economy as a whole are both equal to 1 (a normalization), and both are fully employed. Let W^* be the equilibrium wage, equal to both the after-subsidy marginal product of labor in state firms and the marginal product of labor in private firms. And let R^* be the interest rate such that the user cost $(R^* + \delta)$ (where δ is the depreciation rate) is equal to both the (after-subsidy) marginal product of capital in state firms and the marginal product of capital in private firms.

Under the assumption that both sectors face the same (after-subsidy) price for goods, are governed by the same production function, and face the same factor prices, they have the same capital-labor ratio. Let ε be the

---

3. Obviously, this characterization does not do justice to the way pre-transition economies actually functioned, to the difference between the private sector pre-transition and the incipient post-transition private sector, or to the nature of the changes triggered by transition. But it captures the basic aspects that we want to focus on here—that existing firms were inefficient, and that transition implies the emergence of activities and firms that did not exist under the previous system.

proportion of capital and labor used in the private sector. As the mnemonic indicates, we think of this share as being small. We will think of transition as a process where this share—if nothing goes wrong—moves from ε to 1.

We have thus characterized the pre-transition economy as an economy in which both labor and capital are fully employed, but the allocation of production is inefficient. It is easy to characterize the inefficiency created by subsidies and the scope for improvement after transition. Define $X \equiv P_p F(1, 1) \equiv F(1, 1)$: X is the level of output (in the private good, which is the numeraire) that would be produced if capital and labor were used only in private, efficient firms.

Pre-transition, however, aggregate output is given by:

$$Y = Y_p + P_s Y_s = X\left[\varepsilon + \frac{1}{(1+y)}(1-\varepsilon)\right] = X\frac{1+\varepsilon y}{1+y}.$$

If, for example, $y = 1$ (the goods produced by private firms are twice as valuable as state goods) and $\varepsilon = 0.2$, then $Y = 0.6 X$: initial output is equal to 60 percent of the efficient level; this gives the scope for improvements in efficiency during transition.[4]

In what follows, we shall assume that $y = 1$ and $\varepsilon = 0.2$ (the appendix to the chapter gives a listing of the definition and the benchmark values for all the parameters in the model). The value of ε is roughly equal to the average share of the private sector in central Europe pre-transition, excluding agriculture. And a value for y of 1—which implies, as we have just seen, an efficiency loss of 40 percent—is roughly consistent with what we know about relative GDP (gross domestic product) per capita at purchasing price parity (PPP) in the relatively advanced countries in central Europe and the middle-income countries in Western Europe. For example, using Heston-Summers, PPP GDP per capita in Czechoslovakia in 1990 was 70 percent that of Spain and 51 percent that of the United Kingdom. PPP GDP per capita in Poland was 55 percent that of Spain and 41 percent that of the United Kingdom.

---

4. This computation implicitly assumes that after transition, the capital stock returns to 1—the same as its pre-transition value—in the long run. Under the assumptions made above, and the assumption we make in the next section that the interest rate remains constant, this is indeed the case. If transition succeeds, the total capital stock converges to a value of 1 in the long run.

Transition Through Reallocation and Factor Prices

Think of transition as being triggered by the elimination of subsidies in the state sector. Leave aside restructuring for the time being. It is clear that transition requires the decline of inefficient state firms and the growth of efficient private firms. The essential question is whether—or when—this transition will be characterized by a U-shaped response of total output and a long period of unemployment.

In this section, we take up the question under thoroughly neoclassical assumptions. We take the wage to be equal to the reservation wage; state and private firms to be profit maximizing, both in their choice of employment and in the adjustment of capital over time; and we ignore tax distortions. As we shall see, even this standard model delivers interesting results; it will serve as a benchmark in what follows.

The General Shape of Transition

Suppose that the pre-transition economy is represented in figure 7-2. Employment in the private sector is measured from the left, employment in the state sector from the right. *PP* represents the marginal product curve in the private sector, given private sector capital (which is given at a point in time). *SS* represents the (after-subsidy) value marginal product curve in the state sector, given state sector capital. The initial equilibrium is at point *A*, with wage W^*, and with employment equal to ε in the private sector and $1 - \varepsilon$ in the state sector.

Now consider the effects of eliminating subsidies. In the short run (that is, given the capital stock in each sector), the demand for labor in the state sector will shift proportionally down by a factor $(1 + y)$ from *SS* to *S'S'*. The demand for labor in the private sector, *PP*, will not shift.[5] Thus, unless the wage decreases sufficiently, unemployment will initially increase.

Over time, lower profit (because of a higher product wage) in the state sector will lead to capital decumulation in the state sector and a steady shift of *SS* to the right. Conversely, higher profit (because of a lower product wage) in the private sector will lead to a steady shift of *PP* to the right. What will happen to output and unemployment will thus depend on the

---

5. If the two goods were imperfect substitutes, there would be a shift in the relative price of the two goods, and *PP* would shift *inward* as well. The elimination of subsidies would increase the relative price of state goods, leading to an increase in the private sector product wage for a given consumption wage. For further discussion, see Blanchard (1997), Chapter 2.

Figure 7-2. The Labor Market

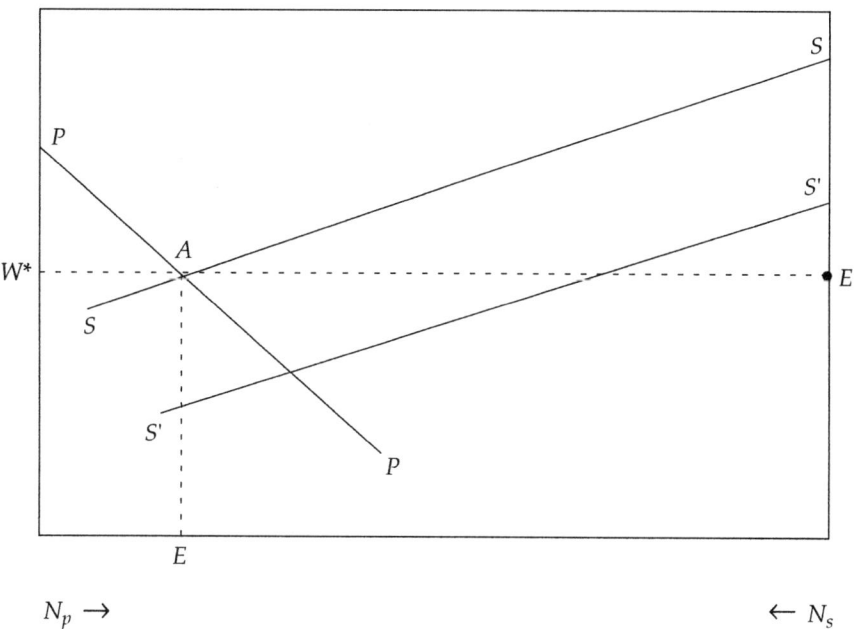

$N_p \rightarrow$ $\leftarrow N_s$

relative speeds of the two shifts; this, in turn, depends on adjustment of factor prices and on the dynamics of capital accumulation or decumulation in each sector.

In the long run, the elimination of subsidies will lead to the disappearance of the state sector. The long-run equilibrium (if it is ever reached) will be at point E, with all capital and labor in private firms. Note that the values of the equilibrium factor prices in the long run will be the same as those pre-transition: W^* and R^*. The difference is that, while wages were sustained by subsidies to state firms pre-transition (and thus financed by taxes), they will now be sustained by the higher efficiency of the economy.

The Adjustment of Factor Prices and Capital Accumulation

The first crucial assumption is thus how factor prices, W and R, respond to the elimination of subsidies. We shall assume that $R = R^*$ throughout the transition. This is not very appealing, but we do not know how to improve on this assumption in a simple way.[6] Thus, the burden of adjustment will fall on the wage. In this section, we will make the simple assumption that whenever there is unemployment, the wage in both sectors falls to the level of the reservation wage, which renders workers indifferent to either working or not working. How should we choose this reservation wage? The structure of the model suggests a natural range of values.

Suppose that, at the start of transition, the real wage fell to $W^*/(1 + y)$ (thus, for a value of y equal to 1, it fell to half of its pre-transition level). The product wage facing state firms would remain constant (with both the after-subsidy price and the wage falling by the same proportion), and the product wage facing private firms would decrease. In the short run (given the capital stock), total employment would increase; at worst, it would remain the same (if short-run labor demand in the private sector were fully inelastic). If the wage fell to $W^*/(1 + y)$, there would be no unemployment in the short run. Because profit was unchanged in the state sector, and higher in the private sector, capital would increase over time, and so would employment. There would be no unemployment in the medium or long run. Transition would take place with (more than) full employment.

Suppose instead that the real wage remained constant at W^*, its pre-transition level. In this case, the product wage would be unchanged for private firms, and it would be lower for state firms. Employment would unambiguously decrease in the short run. Because the profit rate remained the same in the private sector, and dropped in the state sector, capital in the state sector would decline over time, as would employment. Both capital and employment would remain constant in the private sector. The transition would eventually fail—the state sector would disappear, but the private sector would not grow, and those employed in the state sector would remain unemployed.

This discussion motivates our assumption. We assume that the reservation wage, B, is a weighted average of these two extreme values:

$$B \equiv \theta W^* + (1 - \theta)W^* / (1 + y)$$

---

6. Given the nature of credit markets and the importance of retained earnings, closing the model by deriving consumption from utility maximization and determining the interest rate from the equality of saving and investment under perfect competition in financial markets does not strike us as more appealing in this context. A pretentious way of "deriving" our assumption of a constant R^* is to assume that utility is linear in consumption, so that the interest rate is equal to the discount rate.

where θ is a parameter between 0 and 1, which can be thought of as an index of wage rigidity. A value of θ equal to 1 corresponds to full wage rigidity, and implies the derailment of transition. A value of θ guarantees full employment along the transition path.

This equation implies:

$$\frac{B}{W^*} \equiv \frac{1 + \theta y}{1 + y}.$$

We choose a benchmark value for θ equal to 0.2. Together with a value of y of 1, this implies that whenever there is unemployment, the post-transition wage drops to 60 percent of its pre-transition level.

The second crucial set of assumptions concerns capital accumulation. We assume that net investment is proportional to net earnings (profit minus user cost) if positive, and equal to minus depreciation otherwise. Along the transition path, the marginal product of capital is less than the user cost in the state sector, and larger than the user cost in the private sector. Net capital accumulation is thus given by:

$$dK_s/dt = -\delta K_s$$

$$dK_p/dt = m^* \, (F_{Kp} - R^* - \delta) \, K_p.$$

These two equations can be interpreted as coming from adjustment costs (infinite on the downside so that the capital stock can only decrease at the rate of depreciation) and static expectations. We prefer to think of the equation for private capital accumulation as capturing, in a crude way, the notion that the private sector is credit constrained, so that capital accumulation is constrained by earnings. A value of m of 1, the value we will use as a benchmark, simply states that private firms reinvest all earnings net of imputed interest payments.[7] A value of m greater than 1 can be interpreted as allowing retained earnings to be used as collateral, so that net borrowing by firms is a multiple of earnings. A value of m of less than 1 can be interpreted as coming from profit extraction by government offi-

---

7. The assumption that firms reinvest earnings net of imputed interest payments, rather than simply earnings, is made for convenience. It implies that net investment falls to zero as the economy reaches its new steady state, and the marginal product of capital is equal to the user cost. If we assumed that firms reinvested all earnings, we would have to add the additional condition that they did so until the marginal product of capital was equal to the user cost; this would lead to a slightly more complex specification.

cials or the Mafia, along the lines of Shleifer and Vishny (1993). We will not take a stand on what determines the value of m, but we will look at the effects of different values of m, using it to reflect the strength of the private sector.

Simulations

All that remains to be done is to specify the values for the remaining parameters. In all the simulations, we think of the time unit as a *quarter*. In addition to the values of $y = 1$, $\varepsilon = 0.2$, $\theta = 0.2$, and $m = 1$ discussed earlier, we assume:

- A constant elasticity of substitution σ between capital and labor in production equal to 0.2 (We will discuss implications of higher values below.)
- A share of labor in production in the pre-transition steady state of 60 percent
- A depreciation rate of 2.5 percent (per quarter)
- A capital-output ratio in the pre-transition steady state of 8 (this is the ratio of capital to quarterly output; equivalently, the ratio of capital to annual output is equal to 2), so that X, which can be interpreted as the ratio of output to capital at full employment, is equal to 0.125. These assumptions imply a quarterly interest rate R^* equal to 2.5 percent (and thus a quarterly user cost of 5 percent).

Unemployment and output dynamics under this benchmark, as well as under two alternative values for m (0.8 and 1.2), are presented in figure 7-3. Figure 7-3a shows the path of unemployment, U, during transition; figure 7-3b shows the path of aggregate output (divided by X, to make it easier to read the scale; with this normalization, output pre-transition is equal to 0.6 and tends to 1.0 in the long run).

Look at the benchmark case (represented by the thick line in the figure) first. When subsidies are removed, the unemployment rate jumps from 0 percent to 3 percent. It then increases to about 10 percent after three years, and reaches 0 after about seven years. The reason that unemployment increases for some time was first identified by Chadha, Coricelli, and Krajnayk (1993): profitability is high in the private sector from the start. But at the beginning, the private sector is small and, because it cannot invest more than its net earnings, it can only grow so fast. Thus, for some time, the decline in the state sector dominates the increase in the private sector, leading to an increase in unemployment. Eventually, the private sector is large enough that unemployment starts declining. This happens after roughly three years.

Figure 7-3. The Evolution of Unemployment and Output: Different Values of *m*

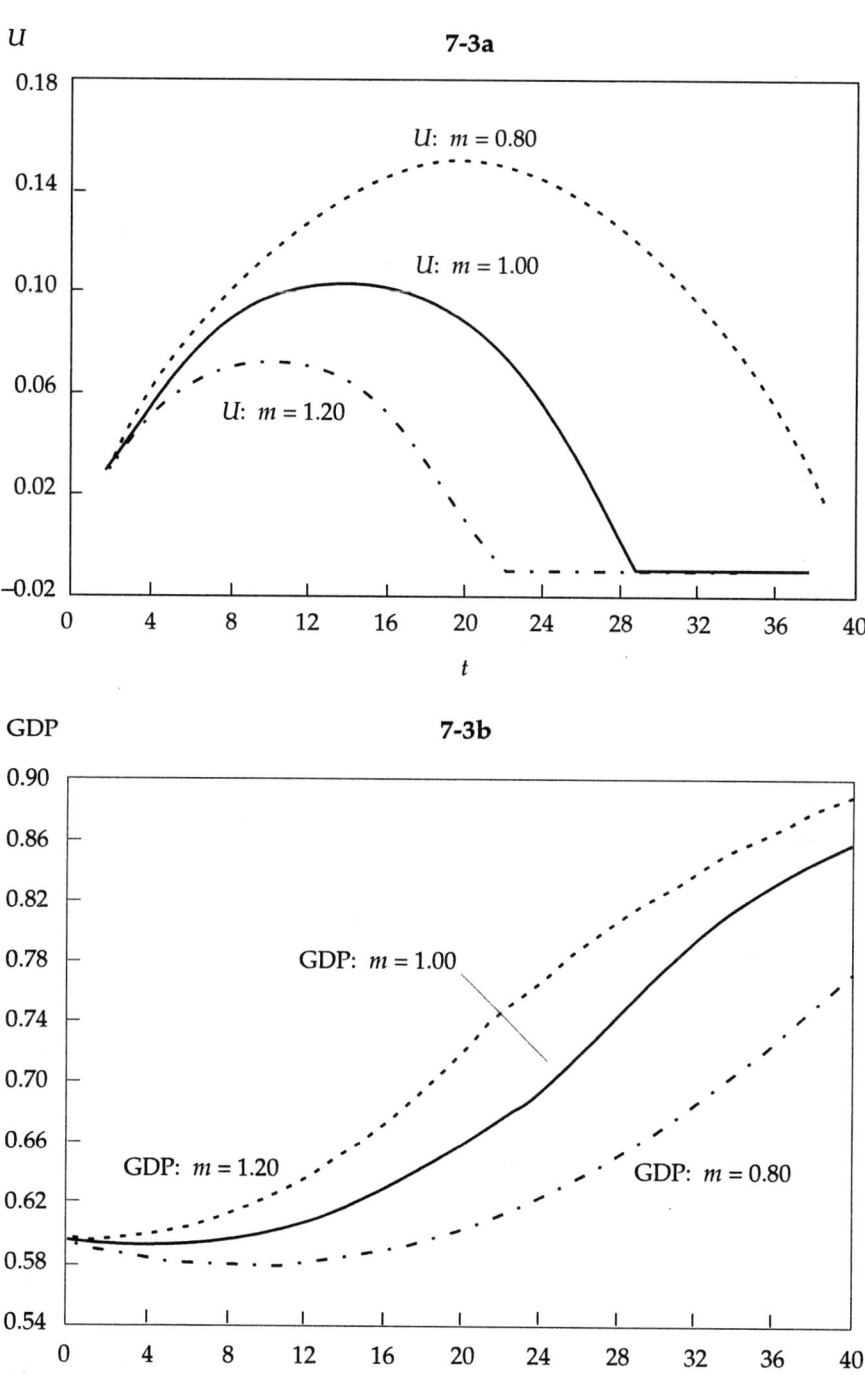

Similarly, the evolution of output is U-shaped. Output initially drops from its pre-transition level of 0.6. But while unemployment increases to 10 percent, the decrease in output is much more limited: this reflects the gains in efficiency (productivity) as activity is reallocated from state to private firms. Output remains (slightly) lower for two-and-a-half years, before increasing steadily thereafter. Ten years out, it is 45 percent higher than its pre-transition level.

The basic conclusion from the benchmark simulation is that realloca-tion can explain the qualitative features of figure 7-1, the U-shaped behavior of output, and the sustained increase in unemployment. The two other paths show the effects of private sector strength, as measured by m on the transition. A value of m of 1.2 (instead of 1.0, as in the bench-mark) leads to almost no decrease in output and an unemployment rate that peaks at only 7 percent. In contrast, a value of m of only 0.8 leads to a larger increase in unemployment, and a larger and longer decline in out-put: the unemployment rate increases to more than 14 percent, and it takes the economy more than five years to reach its pre-transition level of output.

The effects of alternative values for other parameters on transition are, for the most part, straightforward. The depth of the initial recession and the increase in unemployment are highly sensitive to the reservation wage. A value of θ of 0.1 (in which case, $B/W^* = 55$ percent, in contrast to the benchmark case, where θ is equal to 0.2 and $B/W^* = 60$ percent) leads to a peak unemployment rate of only 3 percent and an increase in output from the start. A value of θ of 0.3 (so that $B/W^* = .65$) leads to a peak unemployment rate of 17 percent and a decrease in output for more than five years.

Changes in the elasticity of substitution between capital and labor have two opposite effects on employment. The lower the elasticity of substitu-tion, the steeper the two labor demand curves in figure 7-2, and the smaller the initial impact of the removal of subsidies on unemployment. But the lower the elasticity, the smaller the effect of the removal of subsi-dies on the marginal product of capital in the private sector, and thus the slower the accumulation of capital in the private sector, and the slower the increase in private sector employment over time. When σ is lowered from its benchmark value of 0.2 to a value of 0.1, the initial increase in unemployment is smaller, but unemployment eventually peaks at 13 per-cent and lasts for nine years; output declines for four years. When $\sigma = 0.3$, initial unemployment is 4 percent, but unemployment disappears in six years, and output increases from the start.

Fiscal Interactions

Our first model ignored fiscal policy. Put another way, it implicitly assumed that government expenditures were financed through lump-sum taxes. Governments do not, however, have lump-sum taxes at their disposal. And fiscal issues have played a central role in transition (for a discussion of the evidence and the various mechanisms at work, see Blanchard 1997). Some have argued that high unemployment may increase the tax burden and derail the transition (see, for example, Aghion and Blanchard 1994; Coricelli 1995). Others have argued that for precisely that reason, it might be preferable not to tax private firms until later in transition. We now extend the initial model to take a first pass at these issues. We assume that the government must finance current spending—in our model, unemployment benefits—by current taxes, but that it has the choice of taxing the two factors of production and the two sectors at different rates.[8]

The Budget Constraint

We write the budget constraint of the government as:

$$\psi \, U \, B = t_{Np} \, F_{Np} \, N_p + t_{Ns} \, F_{Ns} \, N_s + t_{Kp} \, F_{Kp} \, K_p + t_{Ks} \, F_{Ks} \, K_s \,.$$

Take the term on the left-hand side. The parameter ψ, which is between 0 and 1, can be interpreted in two ways. Under the assumption that the utility of leisure is zero, B is the unemployment benefit for each unemployed individual, and UB is total unemployment benefits. Then, ψ gives the proportion of unemployment benefits that must be financed through distortionary taxation. The case where ψ is equal to zero (the government has access to lump-sum finance) is, in effect, the case we considered in the previous section. The alternative interpretation is that the utility of leisure is actually positive, and that ψ represents the fraction of the reservation

---

8. Thus, one issue we do not take up here is whether it may be desirable for the government to finance spending through deficits, and increase taxes only later, when the tax base has become larger. The issue is examined in an extension of this model by Keeling (1997), who concludes that deficit finance may sometimes be appropriate. Indeed, the model shows that deficit finance may be necessary. Some transition paths that are not feasible under budget balance become feasible under intertemporal budget balance.

wage that corresponds to unemployment benefits. Under that interpretation, $\psi = 0$ corresponds to the case where the utility of leisure is equal to
B, and the government does not pay unemployment benefits. In either
case, we can think of ψ as measuring the strength of fiscal feedbacks—the
degree to which higher expenditures require higher taxation.

The right-hand side of the equation gives the four sources of tax revenue. There are four tax rates: t_{Np} and t_{Ns} are the tax rates on labor in the
private and state sectors, and t_{Kp} and t_{Ks} are the tax rates on profit in the
private and the state sectors.

Simulations

The first question we ask is the following. Suppose that all four tax rates
are the same (think, for example, of a VAT). Can the need to finance the
transition through distortionary taxation kill the expansion of the new
private sector and derail the transition? To answer that question, we
present in figure 7-4 the evolution of unemployment and output for three
different values of ψ: 0.4 as the benchmark value of ψ, and 0.0 and 0.8 for
the other two (the value of 0.0 replicates the benchmark path in figure 7-3).[9]

Figure 7-4 yields two conclusions. The first is that fiscal feedbacks
indeed slow down transition. An increase in ψ from 0.0 to 0.4 increases
peak unemployment from 10 percent to 14 percent and leads to a longer
and deeper recession. The second is that the effect is highly nonlinear: an
increase in ψ from 0.4 to 0.8 leads to an increase in peak unemployment
from 14 percent to 32 percent, and it now takes more than fourteen years
for output to reach its pre-transition level. Indeed, in our model, for values of ψ above 0.8, the transition fails—high taxes lead to a decrease in
after-tax profits and a slowdown in capital accumulation in the private
sector. Unemployment increases and, at some point, the economy is
above the maximum of the Laffer curve. There is no tax rate that will

---

9. By assuming that the economy starts from the same pre-transition equilibrium
as in the previous section, we implicitly assume that pre-transition subsidies to
state firms were financed by lump-sum taxes. This is a convenient assumption, but
one that ignores an important and relevant issue. To the extent that pre-transition
subsidies were financed by taxes on labor income, and to the extent that workers
care about the after-tax wage, a decline in subsidies, which leads to a decrease in
labor income taxes, will lead workers to accept a reduction in the pre-tax wage. Put
another way, the elimination of subsidies may lead workers to lower their reservation wage. By taking B as exogenous, our model does not take this dependence explicitly into account.

Figure 7-4. The Evolution of Unemployment and Output: Different Values of ψ

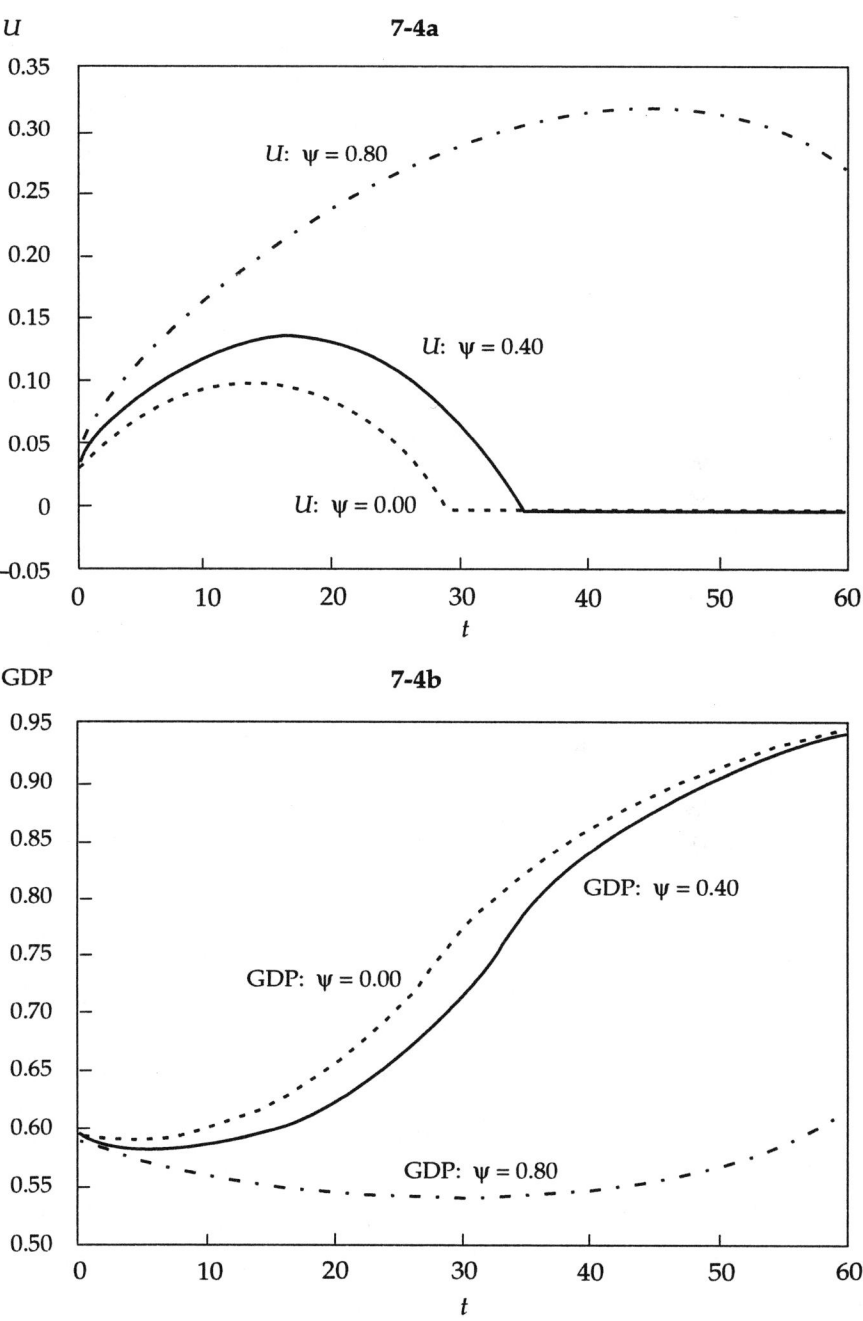

allow unemployment benefits to be financed (in the last period during which the government can balance the budget, the tax rate is 29 percent).

This simulation serves as a warning of the potential strength of adverse fiscal feedbacks on transition, a warning that has been heeded to different degrees across countries in transition. In general, governments have decreased the generosity of unemployment benefits as unemployment increased, and spending on unemployment benefits has been limited. But part of the decrease in employment has taken the form of early retirement, which has led to a large increase in pension benefits. Investment in public infrastructure has often been drastically cut, with adverse effects on foreign direct investment and private sector growth similar to those captured above. Thanks to low initial unemployment and a tough fiscal stance, the Czech Republic has succeeded in keeping its budget in balance without large increases in taxation and without large reductions in public investment. Under pressure from high unemployment and a large decrease in output, the Bulgarian government has been much less successful (for numbers and further discussion, see Blanchard 1997).

The second question we ask is: subject to the budget constraint, what taxes should the government select as its primary base? The tradeoffs a government faces are clear:

- Higher taxes on capital relative to labor lead to smaller employment effects in the short run, but larger employment effects in the long run, because capital accumulation responds to lower after-tax profits.
- Taxes on the state and the private sector have very different effects. For example, profit taxes on the state sector have no adverse effect on the transition; under our assumptions, the state sector is not investing in the first place. Profit taxes on the private sector, however, directly affect capital accumulation, and thus employment creation.

Figure 7-5 shows some of these tradeoffs in play by focusing on three alternative tax treatments of the private sector. The three paths are derived under the assumption that $\psi = 0.6$. The benchmark simulation assumes that all four tax rates are the same. The second simulation assumes that the tax rate on capital income in the private sector is equal to zero, and the three remaining tax rates are equal. The third simulation assumes that neither private capital nor private labor income are taxed. The effects are clear: not taxing the private sector implies higher taxes on the state sector and a slightly higher rate of unemployment at the beginning. But after three to four years, it produces lower unemployment and higher output. Eight years out, output is 25 percent higher if the private

Figure 7-5. The Evolution of Unemployment and Output: Different Tax Treatments of the Private Sector

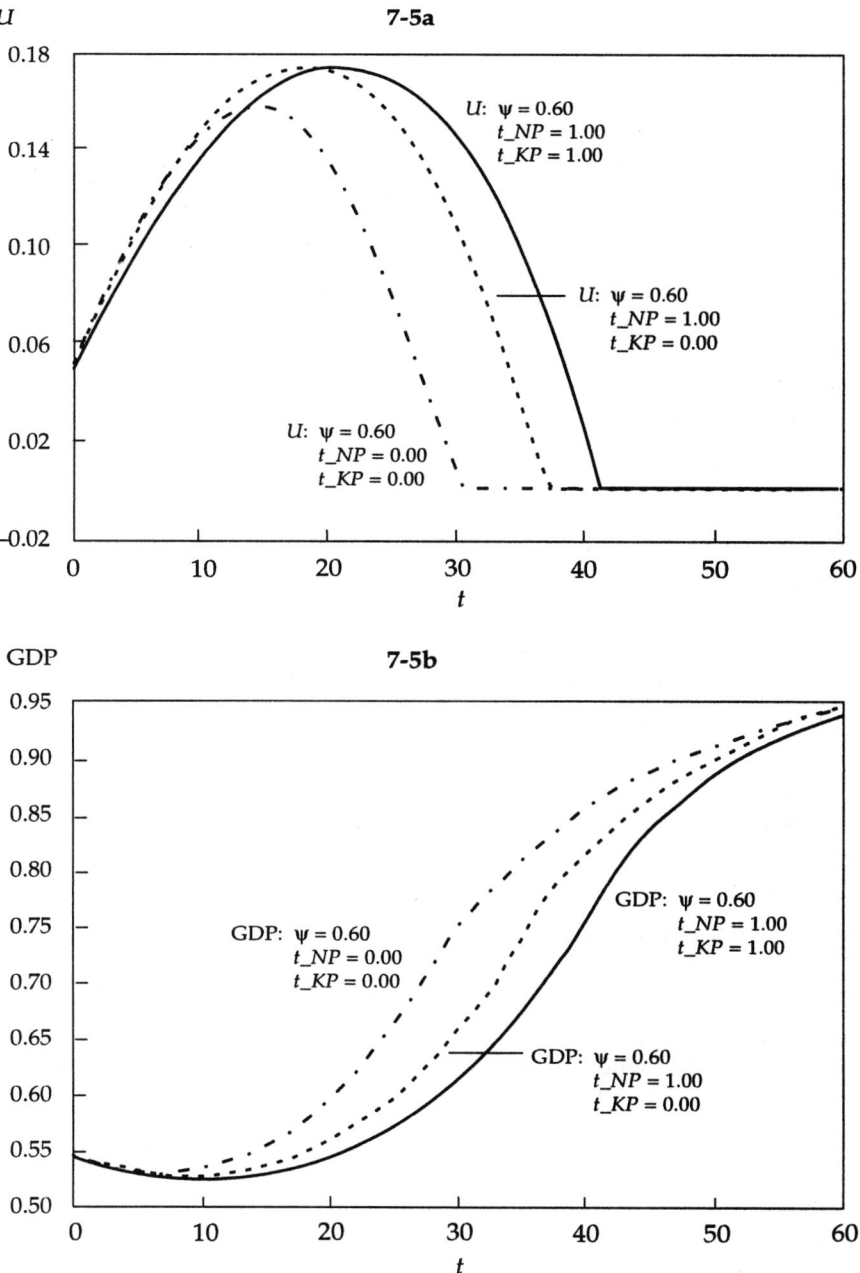

sector is not taxed than under uniform taxation. This suggests the desirability of taxing the private sector more lightly early in transition.[10]

Finally, the simulation in figure 7-6 focuses on the interactions between the strength of the private sector and fiscal feedbacks. Earlier, figure 7-3 showed the effects of three different values of m, the parameter determining the relationship between profit and capital accumulation in the private sector in transition, under the assumption of no fiscal feedback ($\psi = 0.0$). Figure 7-6 does the same, but allows for a value of $\psi = 0.6$ and uniform taxation. A comparison of figures 7-3 and 7-6 yields a clear conclusion: the adverse effects of weak private sector growth (a low value of m) are magnified in the presence of distortionary taxation. A weak private sector means lower private employment growth, more unemployment, more distortionary taxation, lower after-tax profit, and thus lower capital accumulation. In figure 7-6, this feedback comes close to derailing the transition: for $m = 0.8$, unemployment reaches nearly 30 percent, and only starts decreasing ten years into transition.

Wage Setting Revisited

Our first model assumed that wages in both private and state firms were equal to the reservation wage, so that the workers were indifferent to being employed or unemployed. But in transition economies, as elsewhere in the world, most unemployed workers would surely rather work. Certainly labor market conditions affect the wage paid by private firms, and wage setting in state firms reflects the strong role of workers in those firms. This section represents our attempt to introduce more realistic descriptions of wage determination and to draw the implications for the shape of transition.

Wage Setting in Private Firms

Building on the formalization in Aghion and Blanchard (1994), we assume that private firms pay wages such that the value of being employed in a private firm exceeds the value of being unemployed by a constant equal to c. It is well known (see, for example, Shapiro and Stiglitz 1984) that this leads to a relationship between the wage, unem-

10. The argument will be reinforced when we allow for restructuring, below. Lower tax rates on private firms imply higher tax rates on state firms, and thus, from the point of view of workers in state firms, increase the desirability of privatization and restructuring.

Figure 7-6. The Evolution of Unemployment and Output: ψ = 0.06; Different Values of *m*

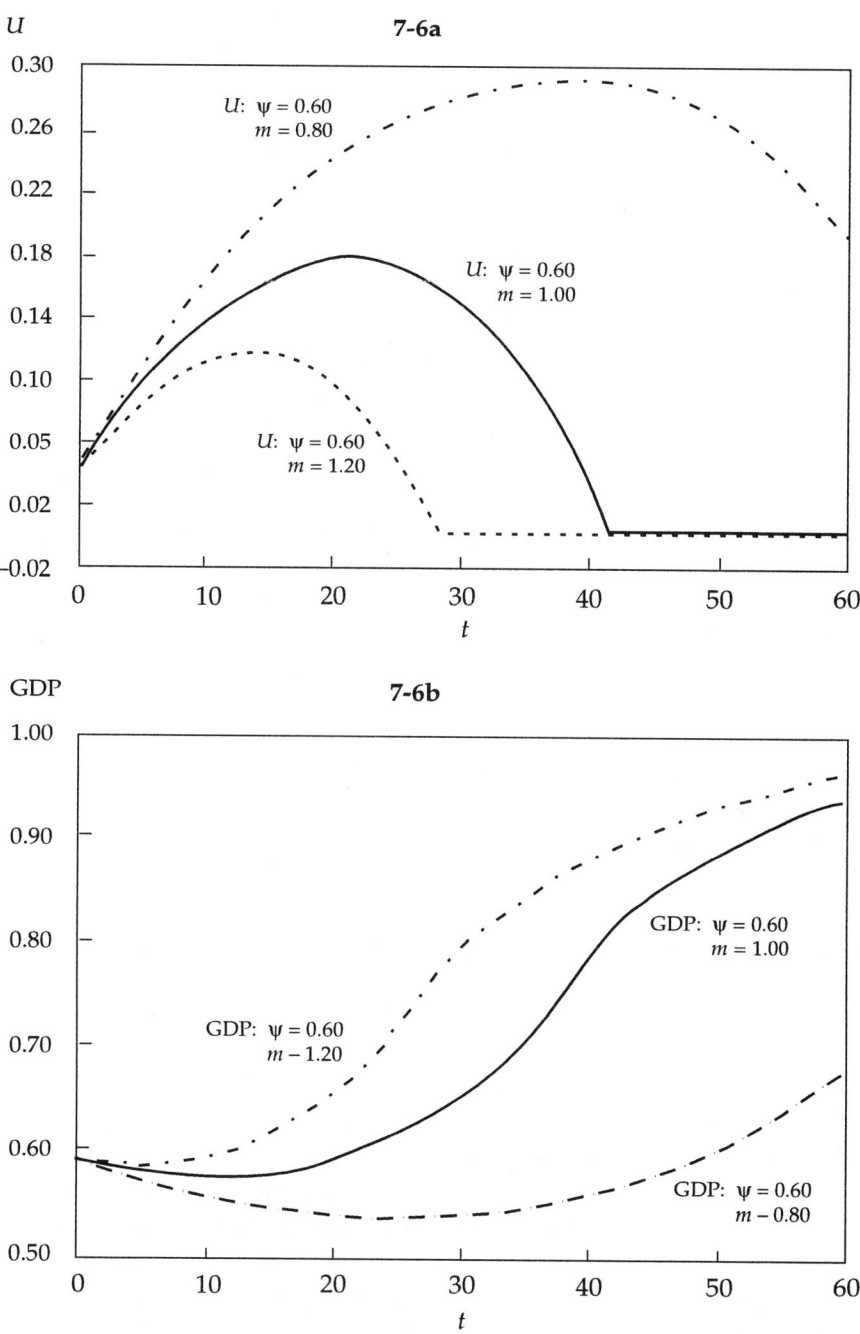

ployment benefits, and the exit rate from unemployment (see Aghion and Blanchard 1994 for more discussion and a derivation). This assumption implies that the wage in the private sector, W_p, is given by:

$$W_p = B + c\,(R + H/U).$$

And the reservation wage, the wage equivalent of being unemployed, is given by:

$$W_r = B + c\,H/U$$

where B is unemployment benefits (under the assumption that the utility of leisure is zero), c is a parameter measuring the difference between the value of being employed and that of being unemployed, R is the interest rate, and H is the flow of hires in the economy. Both the wage paid by firms and the reservation wage exceed unemployment benefits.[11] Both depend on labor market conditions, as summarized by (H/U), the probability of getting a job when unemployed. The wage paid by firms exceeds the reservation wage by cR.

In general, H is likely to reflect both net hires by private firms and turnover in state and private firms. We ignore turnover and assume that hires are equal to the increase in private sector employment, so that:[12]

$$W_p = B + c\left(R + \frac{dN_p/dt}{U}\right).$$

This specification has three characteristics. The higher the unemployment benefits, the higher the wage. The higher the growth of private employment, the higher the wage. The higher the unemployment rate, the lower the wage.

---

11. The reservation wage exceeds unemployment benefits because of the probability of getting a job when unemployed.

12. The assumption that turnover is equal to zero is clearly counterfactual, as is the implicit assumption that all hires are from unemployment. The evidence is of both substantial turnover and a high proportion of job-to-job movements (see Blanchard 1997). In Chapter 5 of this volume, Boeri explores the macroeconomic implications and the reasons behind these two findings.

Wage Setting in State Firms

The determination of wages and employment in state firms is still poorly understood. To the extent that they controlled firms, insiders have often appropriated profits, allowing them to sustain higher wages at a given level of employment, or higher employment at given wages. How they have chosen between wages and employment is less clear. What is clear is that factors such as the structure of bargaining among insiders and the existence of national wage limits or guidelines have played a role. But economists are still a long way from having a good understanding of their relative importance, let alone a reliable formalization. Indeed, one of the main objectives of the research reported in this volume has been to learn more about wage and employment in state firms.[13] At this stage, we have adopted something of a black box representation, which captures what we see as the main dimensions of wage setting in state firms.

- The state wage, W_s is set according to:

$$W_s = \lambda W_p + (1 - \lambda) W^*$$

  where λ is between 0 and 1, and W^* is, as before, the wage both pre-transition and post-transition, in the long run. We will think of λ as measuring relative state wage flexibility.[14]
- Workers appropriate profits, so that they choose a point on the average product curve. In other words, employment is such that the wage is equal to the average, rather than the marginal, product of capital:

$$W_s = P_s \, F(K_s, N_s)/N_s \, .$$

  Because workers appropriate all profits, measured profit is equal to zero, there is no investment, and the capital stock decreases at the rate of depreciation.

---

13. For a review of the evidence and further discussion, see the introduction to this volume, as well as Blanchard 1997, Chapter 3; Commander and Coricelli 1995 for evidence on central Europe; Commander, Dhar, and Yemtsov 1996 for evidence on Russia.

14. Allowing for λ to be less than 1 is not central here, but it will play an important role when we introduce restructuring in the next section. A value of λ of less than 1 will imply that, when labor market conditions are worse, state workers will be more opposed to any measure that increases their probability of either becoming unemployed or having to work at the private wage.

This specification is crude, but it captures two relevant features of reality. The first is that wages in state firms are likely to react less than the private wage to labor market conditions: for given conditions within state firms, workers have no particular incentives to cut wages in response to labor market conditions. The second is that, in most countries, the profits of state firms have indeed been appropriated in the form of wages, allowing workers to limit the decline in employment triggered by the removal of subsidies.

Simulations

Our description of wage determination in the private and state sectors leads to the introduction of two new parameters: c, which determines the effects of labor market conditions on the private and the reservation wage, and λ, which determines how much state wages move with private wages. Without much justification, we choose as benchmark values $c = 0.05$ (this implies that the wage paid by private firms exceeds the reservation wage by about 25 percent) and $\lambda = 0.6$. The features of the simulations we want to focus on here are invariant to reasonable variations in these two parameters. The values of the other parameters are the same as in our earlier benchmark, and we ignore fiscal feedbacks ($\psi = 0$).

The simulation in figure 7-7 presents the behavior of unemployment and output for both the benchmark case and for two alternative values of λ: 0.4 and 0.8. The simulations in figure 7-7 can be compared with the benchmark simulation in figure 7-3; they differ only in their assumptions about wage determination.

Start with the benchmark simulation. Compared with figure 7-3, the dependence of wages on labor market conditions leads to a smoother shape for the adjustment of unemployment. In particular, unemployment reaches zero only asymptotically.[15]

---

15. If unemployment reached zero in finite time, as in figure 7-3, this would lead to an infinite exit rate, and thus infinite wages as well. That the unemployment rate is equal to zero asymptotically—rather than to some positive value—comes from our assumption that there is no turnover in steady state. If there were, the long-run unemployment rate would be positive (and equal to the long-run natural rate). Technically, that both H and U converge asymptotically to zero implies that their behavior in the limit is given by l'Hopital's rule. Asymptotically, (H/U) must be such that the private sector wage converges to W^*, the wage consistent with zero excess profit in the steady state.

Figure 7-7. The Evolution of Unemployment and Output: Different Values of Lambda

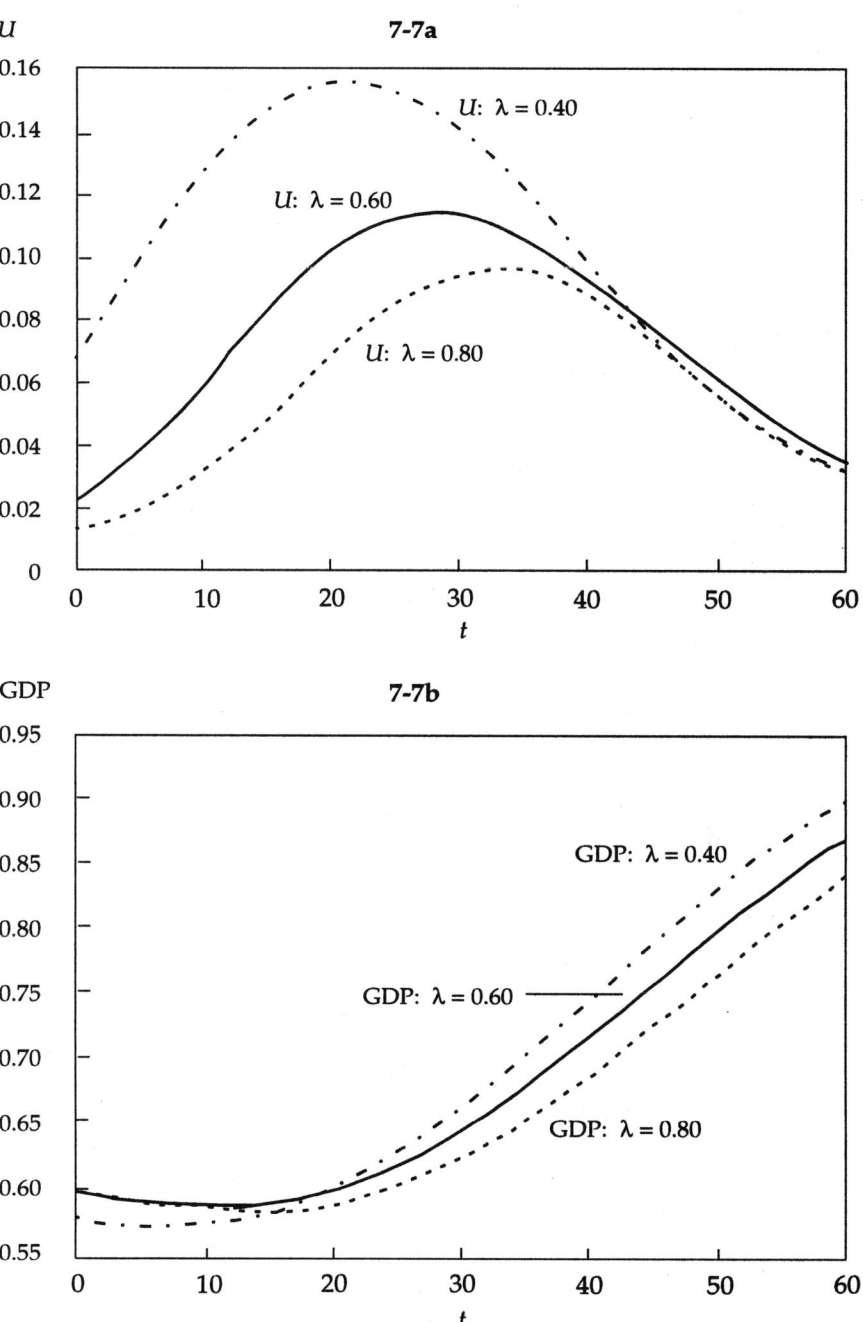

The other two simulations show the interactions between the state sector and the private sector that arise from our assumptions about wage determination. Lower state wage flexibility (a lower value of λ) leads to a relatively higher state wage, and thus to more unemployment and less output at the beginning of transition. But while unemployment remains higher than under the benchmark, and does so for a long time, output quickly becomes higher. In short, lower state wage flexibility leads to a worse performance in unemployment, but a better one in terms of output. The reason for these results is not hard to find: higher unemployment leads to lower private wages and faster growth of the private sector. This captures one theme of the transition literature: that higher unemployment may lead, through lower wages, to faster transition. As we have seen in the section on fiscal interactions, however, there is another effect, which works in the other direction: higher unemployment implies a larger tax burden, and this may slow down private sector growth.

Reallocation versus Restructuring

We have assumed, so far, that transition happened only through reallocation: the eventual disappearance of state firms, and their replacement by new private firms. We now introduce the possibility of restructuring by state firms.

Implications and Determinants of Restructuring

Our formalization of restructuring relies heavily on the conclusions reached in Aghion and Blanchard (1996) on the relationship between privatization and restructuring (see also Blanchard 1997). These conclusions are essentially threefold:

- Restructuring generally implies substantial labor shedding, some plant closings, layoffs of a number of managers, and the replacement of much of the existing capital equipment (see, for example, the surveys by Carlin, Van Reenen, and Wolfe 1994; Grosfeld and Roland 1994; EBRD 1995, Chapter 8).
- Mainly because of the need for outside finance, such *deep* restructuring can only be done by outsiders, and thus requires outside owners.
- Insiders in the firm will accept such outsider ownership only if they can be made better-off in the process—for example, through receiving shares in the restructured firm.

To capture these three features, we make the following assumptions:

- A state firm can be restructured. Only a proportion π of employees in the firm can be kept on, and the remaining workers are laid off. Once restructured, the firm produces goods of the same quality as a private firm, and thus is indistinguishable from new private firms. Note that if $\pi(1 + y) > 1$, then, at the same capital-labor ratio, the new firm produces more output, but with fewer workers than before restructuring.[16]
- Restructuring requires outside ownership. Thus, the wage of workers in the restructured firm is given by the private wage W_p. Workers who do not get a job in the restructured firm become unemployed, and thus implicitly receive W_r, the reservation wage associated with being unemployed.
- Workers may also receive part ownership in the new private firm. Rather than compute the value of the restructured firm and the implied value of the shares within the model, we treat this simply as a privatization bribe A. Privatization rules that are more generous to insiders than to others lead to a higher value of A.

We then assume that restructuring takes place if—and only if—workers will be no worse-off in expected value under restructuring. Thus, the following condition holds:

$$W_s \leq \pi \, W_p + (1 - \pi) \, W_r + A.$$

Or, using the equations for W_s, W_p, and W_r from above, and rearranging:

$$c\frac{H}{U} \geq (W^* - B) - \frac{(\pi - \lambda)cR + A}{(1 - \lambda)}.$$

Note that all the terms on the right-hand side are constant during the transition. The equation has a simple implication. Restructuring will not take place if labor market conditions are bad, when workers have too much to lose from restructuring. In general, the better the labor market conditions (higher (H/U)), the smaller the probability of being laid off (the higher π), and the more generous the terms of privatization are to insiders (the higher A), the more likely it becomes that restructuring will occur.

---

16. For simplicity, we assume that when a firm is restructured, enough capital is maintained to give the new firm the same capital-labor ratio as other private firms. The remaining capital stock is scrapped.

Simulations

This formalization of restructuring introduces two new parameters: π, the proportion of employment kept under restructuring, and A, the bribe to insiders. We use as benchmark values $\pi = 0.6$ (60 percent of the workers are kept under restructuring) and $A = 0.01$ (to get a sense of magnitudes for A, recall that the steady-state wage is 0.075, so that, expressed as a flow, the privatization bribe represents roughly 15 percent of wage income). The values of the other parameters are the same as before; we ignore fiscal feedbacks here, so that $\psi = 0.0$.

Figure 7-8 shows the path of transition under the benchmark, as well as under two alternative values for m (the parameter reflecting private sector strength): $m = 1.2$ and $m = 0.8$.[17]

Look at the benchmark simulation first. Until about ten years into the transition, adverse labor market conditions block restructuring. The evolution of unemployment and output reflect the process of reallocation, with the gradual decline of the state sector and the increase in the private sector. In year ten, however, the improvement in labor market conditions makes restructuring attractive, and within a year and a half, all state firms have restructured. The result is both a large increase in output, by about 13 percent within a year and a half, and a large increase in unemployment, from 9.5 percent to about 13.5 percent, as restructuring leads to labor shedding. From then on, all firms are either new private enterprises or restructured firms, and output increases until all workers are again employed. The simulation shows both the adverse effect of labor market conditions on restructuring and how restructuring is associated with both higher unemployment and higher growth for some time.

The other two simulations show the direct and indirect effects of private sector strength. A value of m of 1.2, for example, leads, as before, to faster reallocation and lower unemployment. And, because it leads to both lower unemployment and increased hires, it triggers faster restruc-

---

17. We impose the condition that restructuring does not take place in the first ten quarters of transition. Otherwise, there would be a burst of restructuring at the very beginning of transition, when unemployment is still low and labor market conditions are still quite good. For reasons not captured in the model (the time needed to design privatization, constraints on the supply of outsiders, the anticipation of worse labor market conditions), we think that restructuring is unlikely to happen at the beginning, and thus rule it out in the simulations. This restriction is not essential, and we could obviously follow the logic of the model as written, in which case there would be restructuring for a few quarters at the beginning, which would then stop until starting again later in the transition.

Figure 7-8. The Evolution of Unemployment and Output: Different Values of *m*

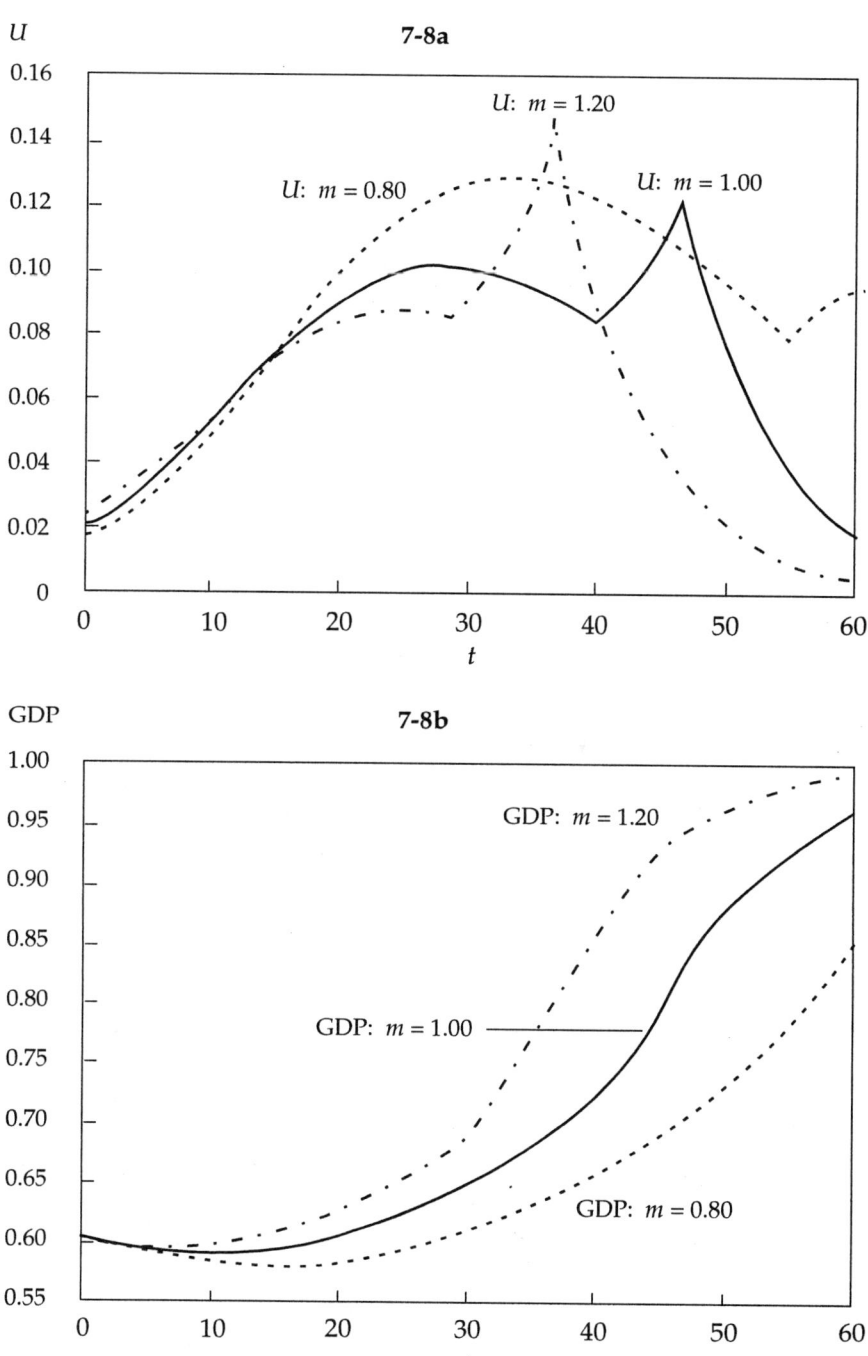

turing in the state sector. Thus, a stronger private sector leads, both directly and indirectly, to faster transition.

Putting Things Together

To offer a sense of the implications of the full model, in this final section we look at the effects of two dimensions of policy: the design of privatization rules and the generosity of the safety net.

How generous privatization should be to insiders in state firms has been the subject of a long-running debate in transition economies. The initial strategy, based on considerations of fairness to the population as a whole and the desire to achieve outsider ownership quickly, was based on outsider privatization. In most cases, however, the result was strong opposition from insiders, both at the firm and the national level, and little progress on privatization. For that reason, privatization rules have often become more generous to insiders. Russian privatization, for example, has largely given the firms to insiders; the assumption has been that, if they do not have the skills or the ability to restructure themselves, insiders will have adequate incentives to resell to outsiders, who will then restructure (see Boycko, Shleifer, and Vishny 1995; for a discussion of whether and when outsiders will have the proper incentives to resell, see Blanchard 1997).

We cannot do justice here to the complexity of privatization issues. But we can look at the effects of alternative degrees of generosity to insiders, as measured by the parameter A, on the transition. Figure 7-9 shows the effects of three values of A on the transition. The benchmark simulation assumes a value of A of 0.01, or equivalently, a value of A/W^* of 0.12. The other two simulations assume values of A such that $A/W^* = 0.13$ and $A/W^* = 0.11$, respectively. Other parameters are equal to their benchmark values; we also ignore fiscal feedbacks here, so that $\psi = 0.0$.

The simulations make a simple point: more generous terms to insiders lead to earlier restructuring. This, in turn, leads to a burst of unemployment, but also to higher growth from then on. Output is higher the greater the stake of insiders in restructuring. Governments thus face a clear tradeoff—insider privatization may be less fair to the population as a whole, but it is likely to lead to faster transition.[18]

---

18. The model leaves out at least one important factor, the time it may take for insiders to resell the firm and for restructuring actually to start. Similar lags are relevant even in the case of outside privatization. Despite the rapid implementation of outsider privatization in the Czech Republic, restructuring has lagged behind. One of the main reasons has been the time it has taken for large shareholders to emerge and take effective control of the firms.

Figure 7-9. The Evolution of Unemployment and Output: Different
Values of *A/W**

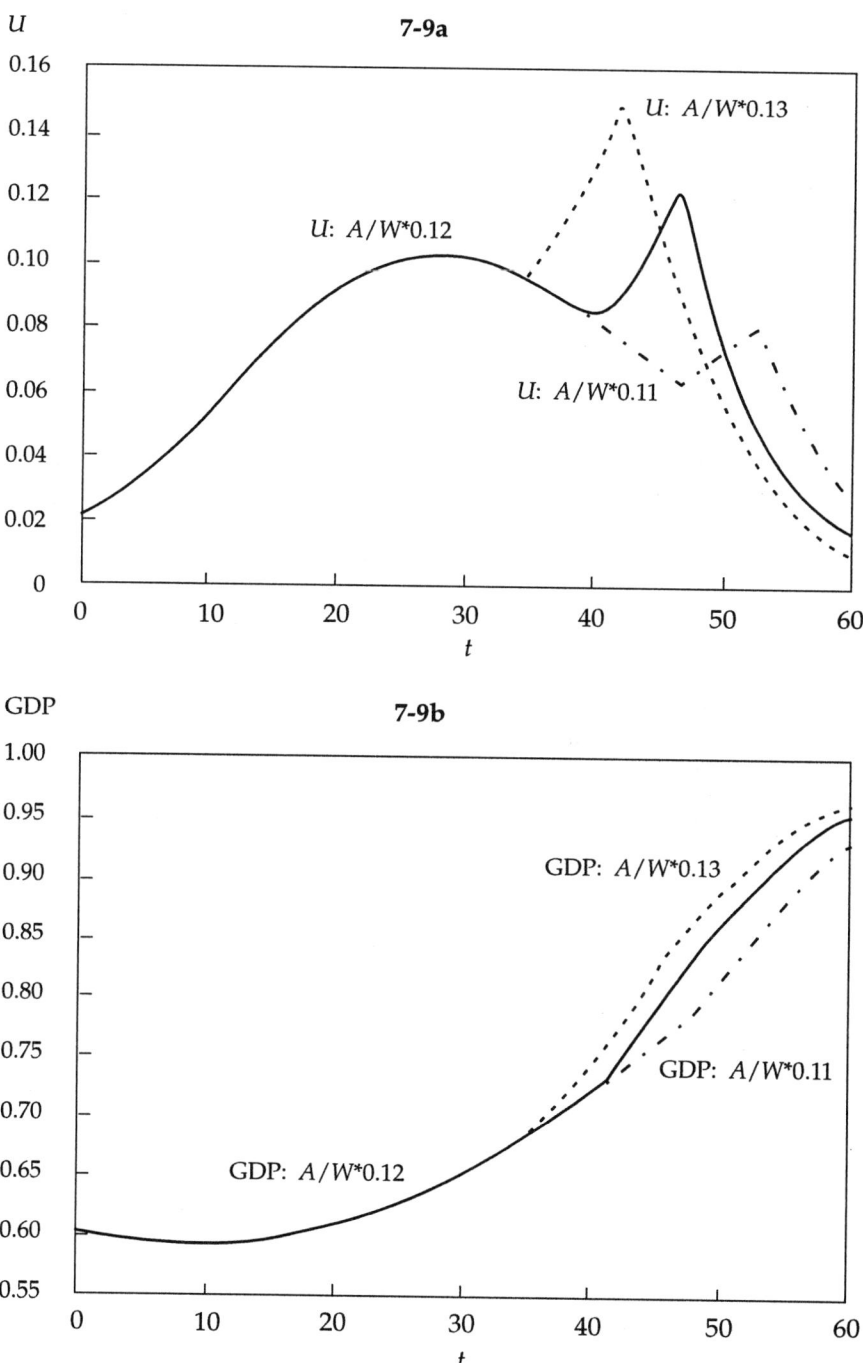

Another dimension of policy has been the generosity of the safety net, and more specifically, the generosity of unemployment benefits. Faced with tight budget conditions, governments have typically reduced the generosity of unemployment benefits. While the main justification for such benefits is clearly distributional, some have argued that there may be an efficiency argument as well: by making unemployment less unattractive, the argument goes, unemployment benefits may decrease opposition to restructuring and accelerate transition.

With this in mind, we show in figure 7-10 the path of unemployment and output for three different values of θ; recall that θ determines the level of B, which, in the absence of utility from leisure, represents the level of unemployment benefits. The thick line corresponds to an θ of 0.3; this corresponds to a ratio of unemployment benefits to the pre-transition wage (B/W^*) of 0.65. The other two lines correspond to values of θ of 0.2 $(B/W^* = 0.6)$ and 0.4 $(B/W^* = 0.70)$, respectively. The simulations show three effects at work.

First, leaving restructuring aside, higher unemployment benefits lead to higher unemployment and slow down the transition (although unemployment is higher and the exit rate from unemployment lower, the unemployed are relatively better-off; more formally, the value of being unemployed is higher, the higher the unemployment benefits). Eight years into transition, unemployment is equal to 16 percent for $\theta = 0.4$, versus only 10 percent for $\theta = 0.2$; output is equal to 0.62 versus 0.65.

Second, by making unemployment less unattractive for workers in state firms, higher unemployment benefits lead restructuring to start at a higher level of unemployment: restructuring starts when unemployment is equal to 15 percent when $\theta = 0.4$, versus 10 percent when $\theta = 0.2$. This is the sense in which the efficiency argument for unemployment benefits is correct: higher unemployment benefits lead restructuring to start at higher rates of unemployment.[19] Nevertheless, even taking this effect on restructuring into account, output is lower and unemployment higher, the higher are unemployment benefits. Thus, the case for higher benefits on efficiency grounds is, at best, a weak one.

---

19. In the simulations reported in figure 7-10, while higher unemployment benefits lead restructuring to start earlier, the effect is generally ambiguous. Although higher unemployment benefits lead restructuring to start at higher unemployment, they also lead to higher unemployment in the first place.

Figure 7-10. The Evolution of Unemployment and Output: Different Values of θ

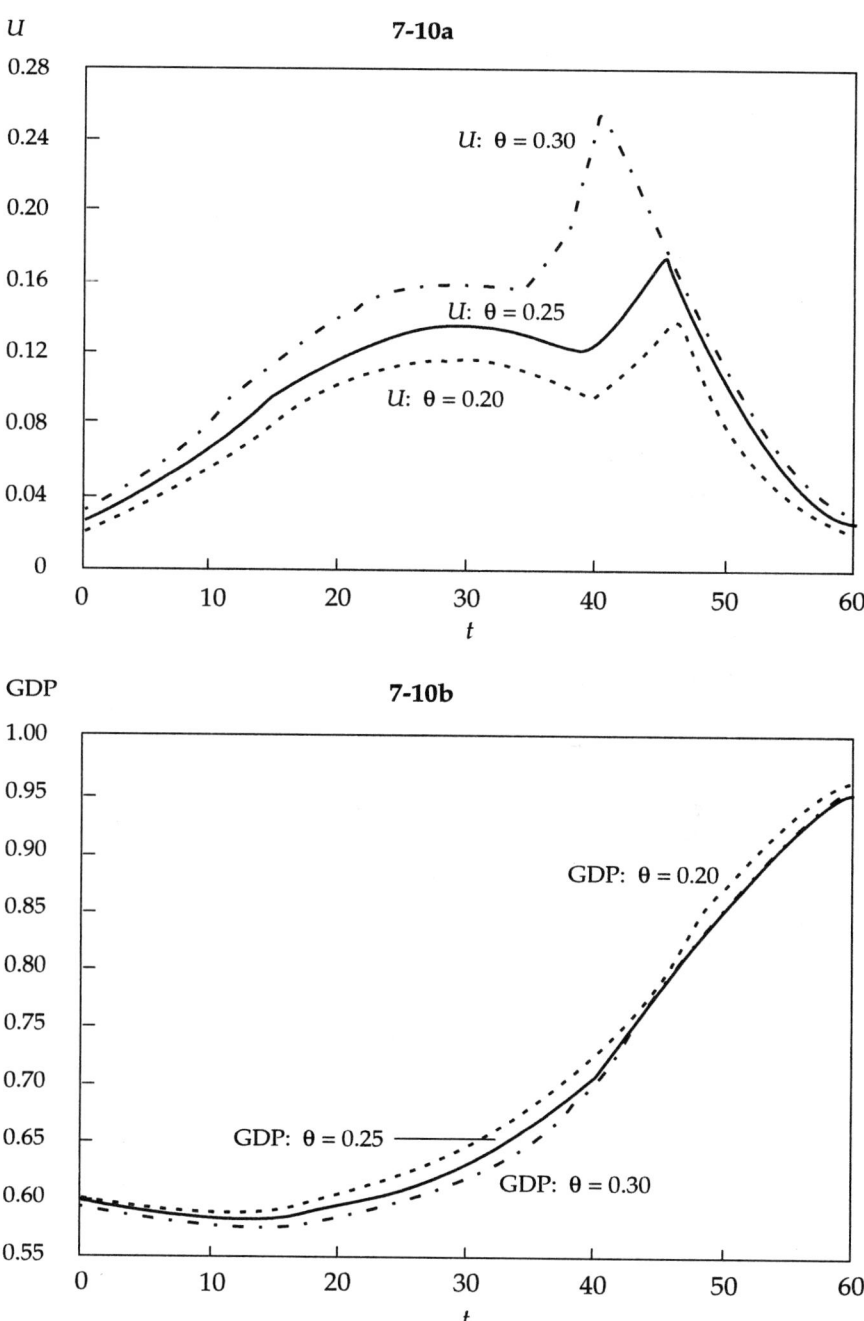

Conclusions

Our purpose in this chapter has been to build a numerical model of transition that incorporates the main mechanisms that are shaping the transition process. We have built a model based on two basic mechanisms: reallocation from state to private firms and restructuring of state firms. We have explored both fiscal and labor market interactions among private sector growth, state sector decline, and state sector restructuring. And we have explored the implications of alternative policies, from various degrees of generosity in the safety net to the form of privatization.

This chapter is in the nature of a progress report. We think that the model needs refining. We are not satisfied with the formalization of wage and employment setting in state firms. We believe that insiders may be more willing to accept wage cuts in the face of a decrease in adverse shifts in the marginal product of labor than we have allowed. A more explicit formalization of the nature of restructuring, and of specific privatization rules, also strikes us as an important extension. But we think that, even in its current shape, this model is a useful vehicle for organizing thoughts and discussing the effects of alternative policies. It can also serve to explain differences across countries. We have discussed some of them along the way, showing, for example, how both larger initial adverse shocks and a weaker private sector may explain the poor performance of Bulgaria compared with Poland or the Czech Republic, but a more systematic analysis clearly remains to be done.

Appendix

Parameters, Definitions, and Values in the Benchmark Case

- y (1 private good is worth $(1 + y)$ state goods) : 1.
- ε (share of output in private sector pre-transition): 0.2.
- δ (depreciation rate of capital per quarter) : 0.025.
- θ (determines the level of the reservation wage) : 0.2.
- m (effect of earnings on private sector investment) : 1.0.
- σ (elasticity of substitution between capital and labor) : 0.2.
- a (share of labor in production pre-transition) : 0.6.
- t_{Np}, t_{Kp} (tax rates on labor and capital in the private sector) : 0.0.

- t_{Ns}, t_{Ks} (tax rates on labor and capital in the state sector) : 0.0.

- ψ (proportion of spending financed by distortionary taxation) : 0.0.

- c (difference between the value of being employed and the value of being unemployed) : 0.05.

- λ (relative weight of the private wage on the state wage) : 0.6.

- A (privatization bribe) : 0.01.

- π (proportion of workers kept under restructuring) : 0.6.

Variables (in Pre- and Post-Transition Steady States)

- R (real interest rate, per quarter) : 0.025.

- W^* (real wage) : 0.075.

References

Aghion, P., and O. Blanchard. 1994. "On the Speed of Transition in Central Europe." *NBER Macroeconomics Annual*: 283–320.

———. 1996. "On Privatization Methods in Eastern Europe and their Implications." MIT and EBRD, Cambridge, Mass., and London. Photocopy.

Alexeev, M., and M. Kaganovich. 1995. "Dynamics of Privatization under a Subsistence Constraint." Department of Economics, Indiana University. Photocopy.

Blanchard, O. 1997. *The Economics of Post-Communist Transition. Clarendon Lectures*. Oxford, U.K.: Oxford University Press.

Boycko, M., A. Shleifer, and R. Vishny. 1995. *Privatizing Russia*. Cambridge, Mass.: MIT Press.

Brandt, L., and X. Zhu. 1995. "Soft Budget Constraints and Inflation Cycles: A Positive Model of the Post-Reform Chinese Economy." University of Toronto. Photocopy.

Carlin, W., J. Van Reenen, and T. Wolfe. 1994. *Enterprise Restructuring in the Transition: An Analytical Survey of the Case Study Evidence from Central and Eastern Europe*. Working Paper 14, EBRD, London.

Chadha, B., F. Coricelli, and K. Krajnyak. 1993. "Enterprise Restructuring, Unemployment, and Growth in a Transition Economy." *IMF Staff Papers* 40(4): 744–80.

Commander, S., and F. Coricelli. 1995. *Unemployment, Restructuring, and the Labor Market in Eastern Europe and Russia*. Washington, D.C.: World Bank.

Commander, S., S. Dhar, and R. Yemtsov. 1996. "How Russian Firms Make Their Wage and Employment Decisions." In S. Commander, Q. Fan, and Mark Schaffer, eds., *Enterprise Restructuring and Economic Policy in Russia*. Washington, D.C.: World Bank.

Commander, S., and A. Tolstopiatenko. 1996. "Restructuring and Taxation in Transition Economies." World Bank, Washington, D.C. Photocopy.

Coricelli, F. 1995. "Fiscal Issues in Economies in Transition: The Case of Central-Eastern Europe." CEPR, London. Photocopy.

EBRD (European Bank for Reconstruction and Development). 1995. *Transition Report: Investment and Enterprise Development*. London.

Grosfeld, I., and G. Roland. 1994. "Defensive and Strategic Restructuring in Central European Enterprises." DELTA, Paris. Photocopy.

Keeling, J. 1997. "Transition and Government Borrowing in Central Europe." M.A. thesis, MIT, Cambridge, Mass.

Shapiro, C., and J. Stiglitz. 1984. "Equilibrium Unemployment as a Discipline Device." *American Economic Review* 74: 433–44.

Shleifer, A., and R. Vishny. 1993. "Corruption." *Quarterly Journal of Economics* 108(3): 599–618.

Index

Other EDI Development Studies
(In order of publication)

Poverty in Russia: Public Policy and Private Responses
Edited by Jeni Klugman

Enterprise Restructuring and Economic Policy in Russia
Edited by Simon Commander, Qimiao Fan, and Mark E. Schaffer

Infrastructure Delivery: Private Initiative and the Public Good
Edited by Ashoka Mody

Trade, Technology, and International Competitiveness
Irfan ul Haque

*Corporate Governance in Transitional Economies:
Insider Control and the Role of Banks*
Edited by Masahiko Aoki and Hyung-Ki Kim

*Unemployment, Restructuring, and the Labor Market
in Eastern Europe and Russia*
Edited by Simon Commander and Fabrizio Coricelli

*Monitoring and Evaluating Social Programs in Developing Countries:
A Handbook for Policymakers, Managers, and Researchers*
Edited by Joseph Valadez and Michael Bamberger

Agroindustrial Investment and Operations
James G. Brown with Deloitte & Touche

Labor Markets in an Era of Adjustment
Edited by Susan Horton, Ravi Kanbur, and Dipak Mazumdar
Vol. 1—Issues Papers; Vol. 2—Case Studies

Does Privatization Deliver? Highlights from a World Bank Conference
Edited by Ahmed Galal and Mary Shirley

*The Adaptive Economy: Adjustment Policies
in Small, Low-Income Countries*
Tony Killick

Financial Regulation: Changing the Rules of the Game
Edited by Dimitri Vittas

The Distribution of Income and Wealth in Korea
D. M. Leipziger and others

Public Enterprise Reform: The Lessons of Experience
Mary Shirley and John Nellis

(Also available in French and Spanish)

Privatization and Control of State-Owned Enterprises
Edited by Ravi Ramamurti and Raymond Vernon

*Finance at the Frontier: Debt Capacity and the Role of Credit
in the Private Economy*
J. D. Von Pischke